The GENESIS CREATION ACCOUNT in the DEAD SEA SCROLLS

The GENESIS CREATION ACCOUNT *in the* DEAD SEA SCROLLS

JEREMY D. LYON

PICKWICK *Publications* · Eugene, Oregon

THE GENESIS CREATION ACCOUNT IN THE DEAD SEA SCROLLS

Pickwick Publications
An Imprint of Wipf and Stock Publishers
199 W. 8th Ave., Suite 3
Eugene, OR 97401

www.wipfandstock.com

PAPERBACK ISBN: 978-1-5326-0776-9
HARDCOVER ISBN: 978-1-5326-0778-3
EBOOK ISBN: 978-1-5326-0777-6

Cataloguing-in-Publication data:

Names: Lyon, Jeremy D., author.

Title: The Genesis creation account in the Dead Sea Scrolls / by Jeremy D. Lyon.

Description: Eugene, OR: Pickwick Publications, 2019 | Includes bibliographical references and index.

Identifiers: ISBN 978-1-5326-0776-9 (paperback) | ISBN 978-1-5326-0778-3 (hardcover) | ISBN 978-1-5326-0777-6 (ebook)

Subjects: LCSH: Dead Sea scrolls. | Bible. Genesis—Criticism, interpretation,etc. | Creation. | Biblical cosmology.

Classification: BS651 L9 2019 (print) | BS651 (ebook)

Manufactured in the U.S.A. 04/22/19

CONTENTS

ACKNOWLEDGMENTS

THIS BOOK HAS ITS genesis in the classroom, where I was lecturing on the Dead Sea Scrolls to university students. As we examined an image of an ancient fragmentary copy of Genesis, a seed was planted, which grew into this research on the Genesis creation account in the Dead Sea Scrolls. A number of people have been instrumental in helping me bring this research to fruition. I want to thank my colleagues at Truett-McConnell University, who encouraged and supported me in various ways during the writing of this work. I am also grateful to our librarians—Teresa Haymore, Vonda Henderson, and Judy Gillentine—who tracked down numerous books and articles that I requested.

In addition, I would like to thank several people who helped improve the quality of this work by providing thoughtful feedback: Andrew Perrin, Robert Cole, Maël Disseau, John Baumgardner, Tom Lewis, and Ashley Lyon. Regarding some of the images provided for this publication, I would like to thank Maryilyn Lundberg and Bruce Zuckerman at West Semitic Research (University of Southern California) and Yael Barschak at the Israel Antiquities Authority. Also, I would like to extend my gratitude to the team at Pickwick, especially Chelsea Lobey, Calvin Jaffarian, and Chris Spinks, for investing their time and expertise in publishing this work.

My loving family has been supportive, as always, during the research and writing process. I would like to thank my wife Ashley and our precious children, Isaiah and Hadassah, for the many ways they have helped.

Above all, I thank the Lord Jesus Christ, who blessed me with this opportunity and enabled me to complete this work. May He get the glory.

ABBREVIATIONS

1Q27	*Book of Mysteries*
1QGen	1QGenesis
1QH[a]	*Hodayot (Thanksgiving Hymn Scroll)*
1QpHab	*Habakkuk Pesher*
1QM	*War Scroll*
1QS	*Community Rule*
2QGen	2QGenesis
3 Apoc Bar	*3 Baruch (or Apocalypse of Baruch)*
4Q159	*4QOrdinances*
4Q164	*Isaiah Pesher* (4QpIsa[d])
4Q166	*Hosea Pesher* (4QpHos[a])
4Q216	4QJubilees[a] (4QJub[a])
4Q219	4QJubilees[d] (4QJub[d])
4Q265	*Miscellaneous Rules*
4Q287	*4QBerakhot[b]*
4Q303–305	*Meditation on Creation A–C*
4Q381	Non-canonical Psalms
4Q416–17, 23	*Musar le-Mebin* (4QInstruction)
4Q422	*Paraphrase of Genesis and Exodus*
4Q436	*4QBarkiNafshi[c]*

4Q504	*Words of the Luminaries*
4QGen^{b-n}	4QGenesis^{b-n}
4QGen-Exod^{a}	4QGenesis-Exodus^{a}
6QpaleoGen	6QpaleoGenesis
8QGen	8QGenesis
11QPs^{a}	11QPsalms^{a}
b. Hag.	Hagigah (Babylonian Talmud)
BDB	*The Brown-Driver-Briggs Hebrew and English Lexicon*
DJD	*Discoveries in the Judaean Desert*
Gen. Rab.	*Genesis Rabbah*
HALOT	*The Hebrew and Aramaic Lexicon of the Old Testament*
Jub	*Jubilees*
LXX	Septuagint
MT	Masoretic Text
NT	New Testament
OT	Old Testament
PAM	Palestine Archaeological Museum
Sir	*Wisdom of Ben Sirach*
SP	Samaritan Pentateuch
Test Levi	*Testament of Levi*
Tg. Neof.	*Targum Neofiti*
Wis	*Wisdom of Solomon*

CHAPTER ONE

INTRODUCTION

IN 1947, SOME BEDOUIN were shepherding their flocks of sheep and goats when one of them tossed a rock into a cave opening and heard pottery shatter. Inside the cave, one of the Bedouin found some cylindrical earthenware jars and ancient scrolls.[1] This discovery would turn out to be one of the greatest archaeological finds in history, leading to the search for more scrolls. Between 1947 and 1956 some nine hundred manuscripts, dated 250 BC–AD 68, were discovered in eleven caves around Qumran, along the northwestern shore of the Dead Sea. Among these manuscripts were Jewish sectarian writings, pseudepigraphal and apocryphal writings, and biblical books. These largely fragmentary manuscripts, collectively known as the Dead Sea Scrolls, have transformed our understanding of Second Temple Judaism and have shed ancient light on the text and interpretation of the Hebrew Bible.

One of the major focuses of this book is the *text* of the Genesis creation account in the Dead Sea Scrolls. Among the scrolls found in the Qumran caves are roughly twenty copies of Genesis. These fragmentary texts represent the oldest known copies of Genesis. Six of these copies contain portions of text from the creation account. 1QGen consists of a number of small fragments, with fragment 1 containing only a few words from Gen 1:18–21. On the other hand, 4QGen[b] contains the most material of the creation account, preserving text from Gen 1:1–28 and 2:14–19. 4QGen[d]

1. The Bedouin discovered the first scrolls sometime during the winter of 1946–1947, though it is difficult to verify exactly when. For a thorough account of this initial discovery, see Trever, *The Untold Story of Qumran*, 101–13; *The Dead Sea Scrolls: A Personal Account*, 96–110.

consists of a single moderately sized fragment, preserving text from Gen 1:18–27. 4QGen[g] is another significant copy, preserving text from Gen 1:1–11, 13–22, and 2:7 (or 2:19). In contrast, all that remains of 4QGen[h1] is a single tiny fragment with three words (and a partial fourth word) from Gen 1:8–10. Last, 4QGen[k] consists of several small fragments, preserving text from Gen 1:9, 14–16, 27–28, and 2:1–3. These ancient copies of Genesis provide valuable information for understanding the condition of the biblical text during the Second Temple period.[2] Also, these scrolls reveal ancient scribal practices in the copying of the biblical text.

The other major focus of this book is *interpretation* of the Genesis creation account in the Dead Sea Scrolls. Several non-biblical texts from Qumran contain the most ancient surviving interpretations of the Genesis creation account, dating from the mid-second century BC to the first century AD.[3] Concerning the nature of these interpretations of the creation account, John J. Collins observed, "They are not formal interpretations, where a passage is cited and then explained. Rather they allude to the biblical text in the process of expounding their teaching. Nonetheless, they imply an exegetical understanding of the texts in question."[4]

A liturgical text known as *Words of the Luminaries* (4Q504) reworks the biblical account of the creation of Adam within the historical section of the prayer for the first day of the week. The text reveals certain understandings regarding the creation of Adam in the likeness of God's glory, Adam's knowledge and dominion in the garden, Eden as a land of glory, the prohibition in the garden, and Adam's punishment for disobedience. The *Paraphrase of Genesis and Exodus* (4Q422) selectively reworks biblical passages, juxtaposing the creation account with the Flood and plagues narratives for hortatory or homiletical purposes. This fragmentary text addresses several aspects of interpretation, including the creation of the universe by the word of God, the role of the Holy Spirit in creation, the creation of Adam with dominion, the prohibition in the garden, and Adam's rebellion.

2. The Second Temple period generally refers to the period of Jewish history beginning with the dedication of the Second Temple around 516 BC and ending with the destruction of the Second Temple by the Romans in AD 70. Some scholars begin this period as early as the return of Jews from Babylon to Jerusalem around 539 BC and end it as late as the conclusion of the Bar Kokhba revolt against the Romans in AD 135.

3. Texts included here are 4Q504 (c. 150 BC), 4Q422 (c. 100–50 BC), 4QInstruction (4Q416 mid-first century BC; 4Q417 late first century BC; 4Q423 AD 1–50), 4Q303 (50–1 BC), 4Q265 (c. AD 25–50), and 4QJub[a]=4Q216 (c. 125–100 BC).

4. Collins, "Interpretations of the Creation of Humanity in the Dead Sea Scrolls," 30.

Several copies of a wisdom text known as *Musar le-Mebin* or 4QInstruction (4Q416, 4Q417, and 4Q423) employ material from the creation account in the context of instruction. The composition reveals certain understandings concerning the divinely ordered cosmos and the association of the Garden of Eden narrative with human choice. *Meditation on Creation* (4Q303–305) is a fragmentary wisdom text that employs language and themes from the creation account in the context of what appears to be an admonition. Though fragmentary, the text addresses the motif of Adam and the knowledge/insight of good and evil. A diverse text known as *Miscellaneous Rules* (4Q265) employs the Garden of Eden narrative in order to explain the etiology of certain purification laws in Leviticus. In doing so, the text presents Eden as an archetype of the sanctuary. A pseudepigraphal text known as *Jubilees* (4QJub[a]) reworks the creation week narrative. Within this unique retelling, the author presents the angels as being created on day one, the Garden of Eden as being created on day three, and God's election of Israel as occurring on the seventh day (the first Sabbath). These texts from Qumran reveal various aspects of how the Genesis creation account was *understood* and *employed* during the Second Temple period.

Notable Research on the Genesis Creation Account in the Dead Sea Scrolls

There are several notable works dealing with the text of the Genesis creation account in the Dead Sea Scrolls. 1QGen was published in a relatively quick manner in 1955 by Dominique Barthélemy in the first volume of the *Discoveries in the Judaean Desert* (DJD) series. This edition includes a brief physical description, transcription of the biblical text, and a few textual notes.[5] The Genesis texts from Cave 4, however, would not be officially published until decades later in 1994 by James R. Davila in volume XII of the DJD series. The publication of each text includes a physical description, paleographical and orthographical discussion,[6] transcription of the text,

5. Barthélemy, DJD I, 49–50.

6. Paleography is the study of the development of ancient scripts based on the understanding that handwriting changes over time. Joseph Naveh noted the nature and significance of paleography for the study of ancient manuscripts: "Paleography . . . is the study of ancient scripts which traces the development of letter forms so that documents (both inscriptions and manuscripts) may be read correctly and, if necessary, dated" (*Early History of the Alphabet*, 6). Hence, paleographical study ensures a more faithful reading of an ancient text and enables the dating of a manuscript to a certain period based upon the

textual notes, and plates of the text.[7] However, in 1990, just a few years prior to the DJD edition, Davila had already provided a groundbreaking analysis of the text of the Genesis creation account at Qumran in a book chapter titled, "New Qumran Readings for Genesis One."[8] Due to the general attestation to the Masoretic Text (MT) tradition in the Qumran Genesis texts, Davila's treatment of these texts was selective. In this chapter, he focused on the individual variant readings from MT in the Qumran Genesis texts. Notably, these new readings attest to a Hebrew *Vorlage* for readings found in the Septuagint.[9] Then, in 1998, Ronald Hendel published *The Text of Genesis 1–11: Textual Studies and Critical Edition*. In the second chapter, which examines in detail the textual variants in the creation account, Hendel incorporated the textual evidence from Qumran. He also recognized that the individual variant readings found in the Qumran Genesis texts attest to the reliability of the Septuagint translation from a Hebrew *Vorlage*

styles and shapes of the letters. Scholars have used this technique for dating the Dead Sea Scrolls from early on. Frank M. Cross designated three major paleographical periods for the scrolls: Archaic (250–150 BC), Hasmonean (150–30 BC), and Herodian (30 BC–AD 68). Cf. Cross, "The Development of Jewish Scripts," 133–202; "Paleography," 629–34; VanderKam, *The Dead Sea Scrolls Today*, 35. The reliability of paleography for dating the scrolls appears to have been confirmed by carbon-14 testing of a number of scrolls during the 1990s. Cf. Bonani et al., "Radiocarbon Dating of Fourteen Dead Sea Scrolls," 843–49; Jull et al., "Radiocarbon Dating of Scrolls," 11–19.

Orthography is the study of word spellings. Tov observed, "Orthography (spelling) is the realization in writing of the spoken word and, accordingly, it is possible to represent a specific word in different spellings. In fact, many words are written in different ways within the same language, at different periods, or in concurrent dialects without any difference in meaning" (*Textual Criticism of the Hebrew Bible*, 221). A common spelling practice in many Qumran texts is the addition of *matres lectionis*, which aid in the reading/pronunciation of a word. In this practice, the additional consonant functions as a "vowel letter" (e.g. ו indicates both *o* and *u* vowels). For example, the spelling of אלהים (*Elohim* "God") found in MT often (but not always) occurs with the fuller spelling אלוהים in many Qumran texts. For further study, see Tov, *Textual Criticism of the Hebrew Bible*, 108–09, 220–29; Davila, "Orthography," 625–28.

7. For the scrolls containing text from the creation account (4QGen[b], 4QGen[d], 4QGen[g], 4QGen[h1], and 4QGen[k]), see Davila, DJD XII, 31–78.

8. Davila, "New Qumran Readings for Genesis One," 3–11.

9. Ibid., 11. Davila concluded, "The most important general implication of the new Qumran material presented in this study is that we must take the LXX of Genesis very seriously as a source for a Hebrew textual tradition alternate to the MT. We have strong reason to believe that the translators of Genesis treated their Vorlage with respect and rendered the Hebrew text before them into Greek with great care and minimal interpretation."

that differs from MT.[10] These publications have significantly added to our understanding of the history of the text of the Genesis creation account.

The official publication of the non-biblical scrolls containing interpretation of the Genesis creation account, like many of the scrolls from Cave 4, was considerably delayed.[11] As a result, it was not until the 1990s that scholarly studies of these individual texts began to flourish. With access to these Qumran texts, scholars would soon give attention to various issues within each of these texts, including interpretations of the creation account. While considerable work has been done on interpretations of the creation account within these individual texts since the 1990s, what about "big-picture" studies dealing with the interpretations of the creation account in the Qumran texts as a whole? In this regard, there are a few notable studies.

Esther Chazon contributed a chapter, titled "The Creation and Fall of Adam in the Dead Sea Scrolls," in the 1997 publication, *The Book of Genesis in Jewish and Oriental Christian Interpretation*. In this chapter, Chazon examined the presentation of the Adam narrative in several Qumran texts: *Words of the Luminaries* (4Q504), *Paraphrase of Genesis and Exodus* (4Q422), and *Musar le-Mebin* (4QInstruction). She also included brief discussion on the book of *Jubilees*.[12] The two-fold purpose of her study was "first, to analyze the distinctive interpretation of this biblical story displayed in these works and second, to explore a possible literary relationship between them."[13] There is no discussion on *Meditation on Creation* (4Q303) or *Miscellaneous Rules* (4Q265).

In a 2005 work, *Biblical Interpretation at Qumran*, John J. Collins produced a chapter, titled "Interpretations of the Creation of Humanity in the

10. For example, Hendel noted, "In Gen 1:9, there are two significant textual variations between M and G, for both of which 4QGenesis texts provide new evidence. In each case, *both* the M and G readings are attested at Qumran. An important implication of this new evidence concerns the text-critical value of G: in these cases, it is now clear that the G translator has accurately rendered a Hebrew *Vorlage* that differs from M. . . . The Qumran reading indicates the reliability of the G translation of its *Vorlage* of Genesis" (*The Text of Genesis 1–11*, 24, 26).

11. *Words of the Luminaries* (4Q504) was officially published in 1982, while *Paraphrase of Genesis and Exodus* (4Q422), *Musar le-Mebin* (4QInstruction), *Meditation on Creation* (4Q303–305), *Miscellaneous Rules* (4Q265), and *Jubilees* (4QJub[a]) were all published in the 1990s.

12. Another text included in her study is *Ben Sira* 17:1–10. Also, Chazon employs the previous designation of *Sapiential Work A* for the text known as *Musar le-Mebin* (4QInstruction).

13. Chazon, "The Creation and Fall of Adam in the Dead Sea Scrolls," 13.

Dead Sea Scrolls." In this treatment, Collins examined the presentation of the creation of humanity in *Ben Sira* and then in Qumran texts, primarily focusing on *Musar le-Mebin* (4QInstruction) and the Instruction on the Two Spirits in the *Community Rule* (1QS).[14] However, only a brief mention is made of *Words of the Luminaries* (4Q504), *Paraphrase of Genesis and Exodus* (4Q422), and *Meditation on Creation* (4Q303). There is no discussion concerning interpretation in *Miscellaneous Rules* (4Q265) or *Jubilees* (4QJub[a]).

These studies by Chazon and Collins make valuable contributions toward developing more comprehensive understandings of certain aspects of interpretation of the creation account in the Qumran texts as a whole. These chapters, however, represent relatively brief treatments of the topic. Further, these studies are selective in the scope of texts they address and in the focus of interpretive issues they cover within these texts. Other aspects of interpretation within these texts and other Qumran texts are not addressed. Thus, the necessity for a more comprehensive treatment of the Qumran texts dealing with interpretation of the creation account remains.

Contribution of Current Research

The purpose of this current study is to provide a more comprehensive analysis of the *text* and *interpretation* of the Genesis creation account in the Dead Sea Scrolls within a single volume. This research includes: 1) text-critical analysis of the biblical texts containing the creation account, 2) analysis of certain scribal practices in these texts, and 3) a text-by-text literary analysis of the non-biblical Qumran texts containing interpretation of the creation account.

14. Collins sees in these two Qumran texts the creation of two kinds of humans (spiritual and fleshly) with access to the knowledge of good and evil, which reflects a particular understanding of the two creation accounts in Genesis 1–3 and the origin of evil ("Interpretations of the Creation of Humanity in the Dead Sea Scrolls," 35–41).

CHAPTER TWO

THE TEXT OF THE GENESIS CREATION ACCOUNT AT QUMRAN

The Qumran Genesis Manuscripts

THE PROMINENCE OF GENESIS at Qumran is attested by the large number of Genesis manuscripts recovered in the surrounding caves. At least nineteen, possibly twenty, fragmentary manuscripts of Genesis were found in caves 1, 2, 4, 6, and 8.[1] The majority of the Genesis manuscripts were found in Cave 4. These texts are the oldest known copies of Genesis. The oldest manuscript, 6QpaleoGen (containing text from Gen 6:13–21), is written in paleo-Hebrew script and is dated 250–150 BC.[2] The latest manuscript, 4QGen^{b} (containing text from Gen 1:1–28; 2:14–19; 4:2–11), is dated AD 50–68+. Between all the Qumran manuscripts, portions of thirty-three of the fifty chapters of Genesis are represented.[3] However, none of the in-

1. At least nineteen individual Genesis manuscripts have been identified. There is question, for example, about 4QGen$^{h\text{-}title}$, which consists of only a single small fragment containing the title (ברשית, spelled without the א) on the recto side of the skin. The leather of 4QGen$^{h\text{-}title}$ is similar to 4QGen^{c} and 4QGen^{k}, with all three dated to the same time period as well. It is possible, as Davila has suggested, that a) this title was originally part of one of those manuscripts or b) the Genesis text that this title was originally part of has been lost (Davila, DJD XII, 64). If 4QGen$^{h\text{-}title}$ represents a distinct manuscript, then there would be twenty Genesis manuscripts attested at Qumran.

2. See Crawford, "Genesis in the Dead Sea Scrolls," 353; Brooke, "Genesis 1–11 in the Light of Some Aspects of the Transmission of Genesis in Late Second Temple Times." Another text written in paleo-Hebrew, 4QpaleoGen^{m} (containing text from Gen 26:21–28), is dated c. 150 BC. This text is close to 6QpaleoGen in date.

3. Gen 1–6, 12–13, 17–19, 22–24, 26–27, 32–37, 39–43, 45–50. Cf. Ulrich (ed.), *The*

dividual Genesis manuscripts from Qumran are well preserved. Notably, all the manuscripts containing enough material for analysis attest to the Masoretic Text tradition.[4] A number of these manuscripts also contain some orthographic (spelling) differences and some individual textual variants from the traditional text. Some of the variant readings found in the Qumran Genesis manuscripts reveal the existence of Hebrew *Vorlagen* (base texts) for the readings found in the Septuagint.

The Qumran Genesis Manuscripts		
Manuscript	Date	Extant Genesis Text
1QGen	30–1 BC	1:18–21; 3:11–14; 22:13–15; 23:17–19; 24:22–24
2QGen	30 BC–AD 68	19:27–28; 36:6, 35–37
4QGen-Exod[a]	125–100 BC	22:14; 27:38–39, 42–43; 34:17–21; 35:17–36:13; 36:19–27; 37: 5–6, 22–27; 39:11–40:1; 45:23; 47:13–14; 48:2–4, 15–22; 49:1–5
4QGen[b]	AD 50–68+	1:1–28; 2:14–19; 4:2–11; 5:13 or 14
4QGen[c]	AD 25–68	40:12–13; 40:18–41:11
4QGen[d]	50–25 BC	1:18–27
4QGen[e]	50–25 BC	36:43–37:2; 37:27–30; 40:18–41:8; 41:35–44; 42:17–19; 43:8–14; 49:6–8
4QGen[f]	c. 50 BC	48:1–11
4QGen[g]	50–25 BC	1:1–11, 13–22; 2:7 or 19
4QGen[h1]	50–25 BC	1:8–10
4QGen[h2]	100–50 BC	2:17–18
4QGen[h-para]	125–100 BC	12:4–5
4QGen[h-title]	AD 1–68	title
4QGen[j]	50–25 BC	41:15–18, 23–27, 29–36, 38–43; 42:15–22; 42:38–43:2, 5–8; 45:14–22, 26–28

Biblical Qumran Scrolls, 783–84; Scanlin, *The Dead Sea Scrolls and Modern Translations of the Old Testament*, 141–42. Also included in this list is a small fragment likely containing text from 13:1–3 (see Eshel and Eshel, "New Fragments from Qumran," 144–46).

4. Davila, "Book of Genesis," 299; Crawford, "Genesis in the Dead Sea Scrolls," 354; VanderKam and Flint, *The Meaning of the Dead Sea Scrolls*, 104–05.

Manuscript	Date	Extant Genesis Text
4QGen^{k}	AD 1–30	1:9, 14–16, 27–28; 2:1–3; 3:1–2
4QpaleoGen-Exod^{l}	100–50 BC	50:26
4QpaleoGen^{m}	c. 150 BC	26:21–28
4QpapGen^{o} / Jubilees?		1:9–10, 28–29
4QGen^{n}	150–100 BC	50:3
6QpaleoGen	250–150 BC	6:13–21
8QGen	50–25 BC	13:1–3; 17:12–19; 18:20–25

Six of the Qumran Genesis manuscripts contain text from the creation account: 1QGen, 4QGen^{b}, 4QGen^{d}, 4QGen^{g}, 4QGen^{h1}, and 4QGen^{k} (see table above). 1QGen was officially published early on in 1955 by Dominique Barthélemy in volume I of the *Discoveries in the Judaean Desert* series. The other five texts (4QGen^{b}, 4QGen^{d}, 4QGen^{g}, 4QGen^{h1}, and 4QGen^{k}) were officially published decades later in 1994 by James R. Davila in volume XII of the series. These texts were also published in 2010 in *The Biblical Qumran Scrolls*, edited by Eugene Ulrich. The following survey examines these Qumran Genesis texts containing the creation account. Several of these texts contain only orthographical differences from the Masoretic Text, while a few contain some individual variant readings that are of interest.

1QGen

1QGen was the first of the Genesis manuscripts to come to light. The discovery of this text was part of the culmination of scholars finally locating the cave where the Bedouin had uncovered the original seven Dead Sea Scrolls in 1947. For various reasons, the location of the cave, now known as Cave 1, remained elusive for scholars until early 1949.[5] G. Lankester Harding and Roland de Vaux then led an archaeological excavation of Cave 1 from February 15 to March 5, 1949, in which new exciting finds were brought to

5. One reason was the dangerous political climate of that region in 1948, along with travel restrictions (removed in January 1949), which made it extremely difficult for scholars to visit the cave.

light.[6] Among the numerous fragments of some seventy manuscripts found in the Cave 1 excavation was this copy of Genesis (1QGen).

6. de Vaux, *Archaeology and the Dead Sea Scrolls*, 49; Trever, *The Untold Story of Qumran*, 145–46, 176–77; VanderKam, *The Dead Sea Scrolls Today*, 14; Flint, *The Dead Sea Scrolls*, 11–12. The new finds from this excavation included broken pieces of cylindrical "scroll" jars and lids, bowls, lamps, pieces of cloth, phylactery cases, and fragments of some seventy manuscripts. Some of the manuscript fragments found were actually pieces broken off from the scrolls the Bedouin had previously removed from the cave. These finds confirmed that this was the cave in which the Bedouin found the original seven scrolls.

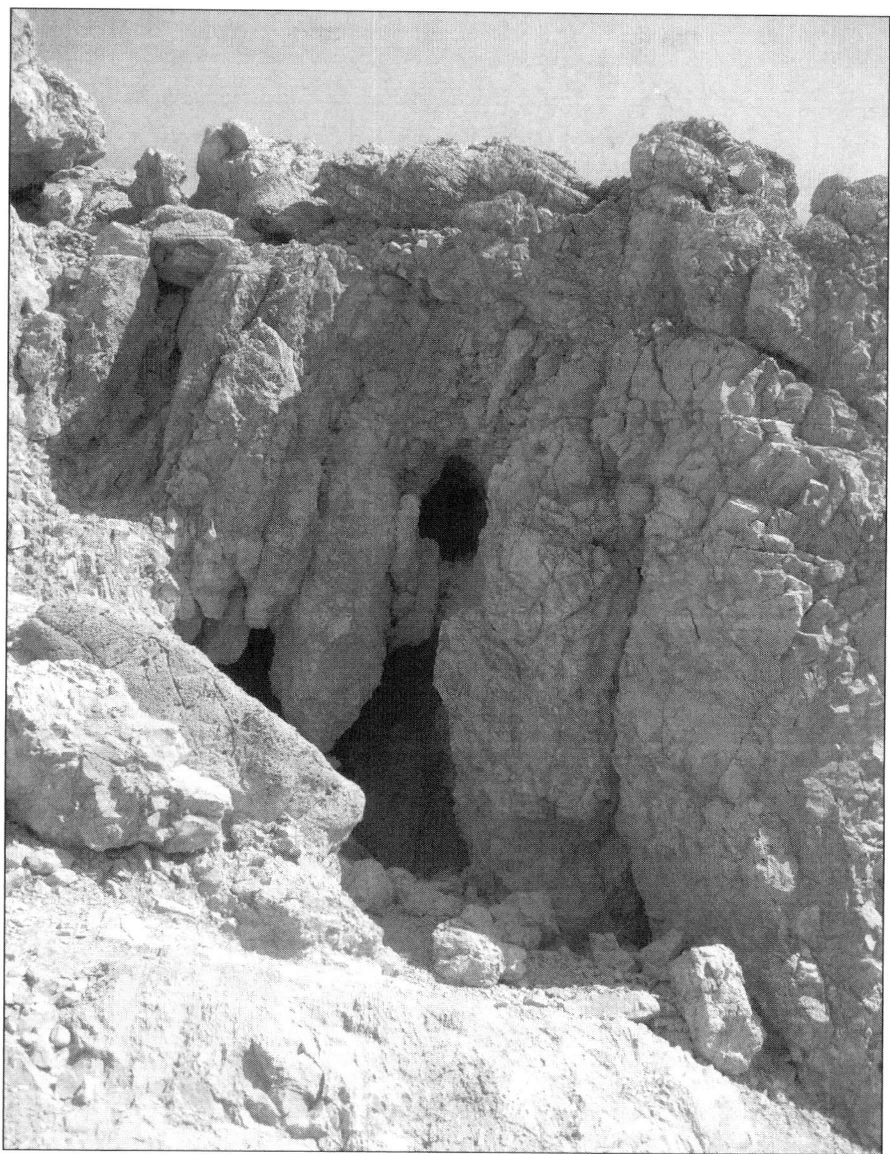

Qumran Cave 1. The original entrance to the cave is the small upper hole.
The larger opening was made later. (Photograph by Jeremy D. Lyon)

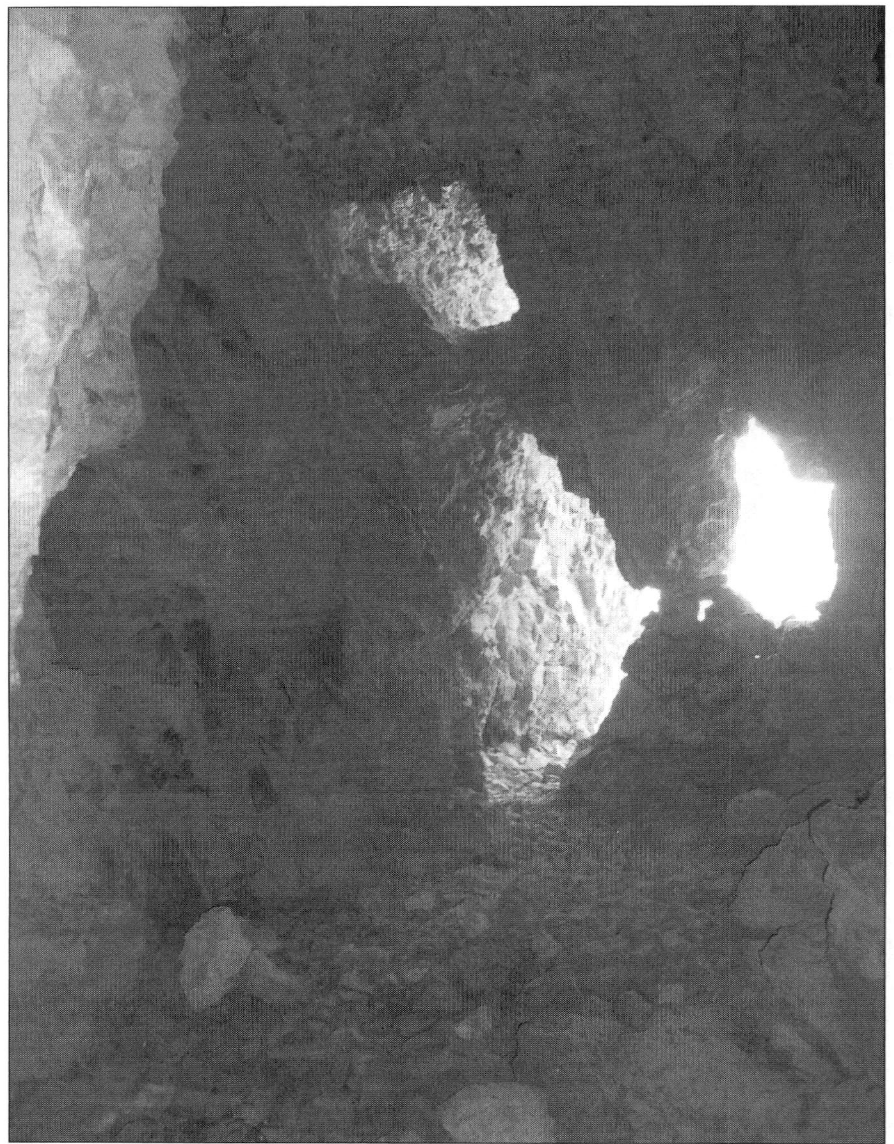

The view from inside Cave 1 (Photograph by Jeremy D. Lyon)

1QGen consists of numerous small fragments of text dated to the first century BC.[7] The five larger fragments of 1QGen, though still rather small,

7. Armin Lange noted the paleography of 1QGen as early Herodian formal script,

contain text from Genesis 1:18–21; 3:11–14; 22:13–15; 23:17–19; 24:22–24. The remaining fragments are even smaller, with some containing only part of a single word and others containing one or two words. It appears, as Barthélemy suggested, that some of these smaller fragments are the broken remains of the larger fragments.[8]

Due to the extremely fragmentary nature of 1QGen, an analysis of the text is necessarily limited. However, the small amount of remaining text reflects the Masoretic Text tradition, with only one small textual variant and a few spelling differences.[9] Fragment 1 is the only fragment containing text from the creation account.

1QGen, frag 1 (Genesis 1:18–21)
] אל]הים כי [טוב 19 [
20] יש]רצו המים שר[ץ [
] 21 ויאמר א]ל[הים [

Fragment 1 contains only a small portion of Genesis 1:18–21. The small and damaged nature of this fragment has made it difficult to discern the exact reading of one word. On line 2, Barthélemy reads ישרוצו, while Ulrich reads ישרצו.[10] With the aid of computer imaging, the horizontal stroke of the ר is visible, followed by three letters. While it is difficult to determine with certainty, it appears that ישרוצו is the reading preserved. This full type of spelling (ישרוצו) is common in Qumran texts, while the spelling ישרצו is found in the Masoretic Text and Samaritan Pentateuch.[11]

---

dating to 30–1 BC (*Handbuch der Textfunde vom Toten Meer: Band 1*, 43).

8. Barthélemy, DJD I, 49. According to Barthélemy, "L'appertenance de tous les fragments est assez certaine. Les fragments 6–19 sont trop brefs pour être identifies avec sécurité, mais il est intéressant de noter que 15, 14, 18, 6, 11, 9 trouvent place aisément dans Gen 228–13, c'est-à-dire immédiatement avant le f. 3, tandis que 17, 16, 12, 7 s'insèrent très bien en Gen 2423–24, c'est-à-dire aux abords du f. 5. Si ces rapprochements ne sont pas illusoires, ils suggéreraient que ces petits fragments sont les restes brisés d'un nombre très restreint de morceaux plus importants."

9. A small textual variant is found in fragment 3 (Gen 22:14): ויקרא אברהם את שם המקום (את not in MT).

10. Barthélemy, DJD I, 49; Ulrich (ed.), *The Biblical Qumran Scrolls*, 5.

11. For discussion on Qumran orthography, see Tov, *Textual Criticism of the Hebrew Bible*, 107–09.

4QGen^b

As many as sixteen fragmentary copies of Genesis were found in Cave 4 in 1952. While 4QGen^b is labeled as one of the Genesis texts from Cave 4, uncertainty remains as to whether Bedouin found this manuscript in Cave 4 or another Judean Desert cave.[12] This fragmentary manuscript is written in late Herodian, or possibly post-Herodian script (AD 50–68+).[13] 4QGen^b preserves text from Genesis 1:1–28; 2:14–19; 4:2–11; 5:13 or 14.[14] The text of 4QGen^b is identical to the Masoretic Text, with only a single orthographical variant in Genesis 1:15 (4QGen^b למארת; MT למאורת).

12. Frank Moore Cross raised the possibility, based on paleography, that 4QGen^b may be post-Herodian (after AD 68) and thus, not from Qumran. For example, see Cross, "The Development of the Jewish Scripts," 178. James R. Davila noted that Cross pointed this possibility out to him. Davila later provided several points concerning the questionable provenance of 4QGen^b, including: 1) the paleography (dating it to late Herodian or post-Herodian), 2) the manuscript being poorly prepared (unusual for a Qumran manuscript), 3) the virtually identical text with MT (reminiscent of biblical scrolls from Wadi Murabbaʿat), 4) the discovery of most scrolls from Cave 4 by Bedouin (thus, removed from their archaeological context), and 5) the fragments removed from Cave 4 in a controlled excavation (none have been identified as a fragment of 4QGen^b). See Davila, DJD XII, 31; "New Qumran Readings for Genesis One," 4–5. Consequently, Davila suggested, "It may be that 4QGen^b was actually discovered in another Judean Desert cave (perhaps in Wadi Murabbaʿat?) and that the Bedouin accidentally mixed it in with a group of Cave 4 manuscripts" ("New Qumran Readings for Genesis One," 5). It is certainly possible that 4QGen^b may not have come from Qumran, but from another site in the Judean wilderness. However, this has not been necessarily demonstrated.

13. Davila, "New Qumran Readings for Genesis One," 4; DJD XII, 31. See also Cross, "The Development of the Jewish Scripts," 178.

14. The reason for uncertainty as to 5:13 or 14 is that fragment 3 preserves only a single word (קינן) found in both verses.

Qumran Cave 4 (Photograph by Jeremy D. Lyon)

The largest fragment (frag. 1), measuring 37.5 cm wide and 19.5 cm high, preserves portions of two columns of text.[15] The first column preserves 30 lines, containing text of much of the creation account (Gen 1:1–25). The partially preserved second column contains text from Gen 2:14–19. The top, left, and right margins for the first column are preserved. A smaller fragment (frag. 2) contains a few more fragmentary lines of text from the first column (Gen 1:25–28). Thus, from these material remains, the missing text can easily be reconstructed, with the first column originally containing 40 lines of text.[16] This size of a writing block and height of the leather indicates 4QGen[b] was among the category of very large scrolls in antiquity.[17]

15. Davila, DJD XII, 31.

16. Ibid.

17. Emanuel Tov has categorized the writing block sizes of the Judean Desert scrolls: small (4–14 lines), medium (15–24 lines), large (25–34 lines), and very large (35–60 lines) (*Scribal Practices and Approaches Reflected in the Texts Found in the Judean Desert*, 84–89).

The preserved text of Gen 1:1–28 and 2:14–19 from the first two columns of 4QGen[b]
(Courtesy of the Leon Levy Dead Sea Scrolls Digital Library; Israel Antiquities Authority)

4QGen^b, frag. 1 i (Genesis 1:1–25a)

1בראשית ברא אלהי[ם את השמים ואת הארץ 2ו]הארץ[היתה]
תהו ובהו וחשך על פנ[י תהום ורוח אלהים מר]חפת[על פני המים]
3ויאמר אלהים יהי אור [ויהי אור 4וירא אלהים]את הא[ור כי טוב]
ויבדל אלהים בין האור[ובין החשך 5ויקרא א]להים לאו[ר יום ולחשך]
ק[רא לי]לה ויהי ערב[ויהי בקר יום אחד [*vacat*] [
6[ויאמר א]להים י[הי רקיע בתוך המים ויהי מב]דיל בין [מים למים 7ויעש]
[אלהים את הרקיע וי]בד[ל]ב[י]ן המים אשר מתחת לרק[יע ובין המים]
אשר מעל לרקיע ויהי כן 8ויקרא אלהים לרקיע שמ[ים ויהי ערב]
[ו]יהי בקר יומ שני *vacat*] [
9ויאמר אלהים יקוו המים מתחת השמים אל מקום אחד ותראה היב[שה]
ויהי כן 10ויקרא אלהים ליבשה ארץ ולמקוה המים קרא ימים וירא
אלהים כי טוב 11ויאמר אלהים תדשא הארץ דשא עשב מזריע זרע עץ
פרי עשה פרי למינו אשר זרעו בו על הארץ ויהי כן 12ותוצא הארץ דש[א]
עשב מז[ריע זרע למינהו ו]עץ עשה פרי אשר זרעו בו למינהו וירא
אלהים כי טוב 13ו[יהי ערב] ויהי בקר יום שלישי *vacat*
14ויאמר אלהים יהי [מא]רת ברקיע השמים להבדיל בין היום ובנ[ין]
הלילה והיו לאתת ול[מועדים ולימים וש]נים 15והיו למארת ברקיע
השמים להאיר על האר[ץ ויהי כן 16ויעש אלהים את שני]המארת
הגדלים את המאור הגדל למ[משלת היום ואת המאור] הקטן לממשלת
הלילה ואת הכוכבים 17ויתן[אתם אלהים ברקיע ה]שמים להאור
על הארץ 18ולמשל ביום ובלילה[ולהבדיל בי]ן האור ובין החשך וירא
אלהים כי טוב 19ויהי ערב ויהי בקר יום רביעי *vacat*
20ויאמר אלהים ישרצו המים שרץ נפש חיה ועוף יעופף על הארץ
על פני רקיע השמים 21ויברא אלהים את התנינים הגדלים ואת
כל נפש החיה הרמשת אשר שרצו המים למינהם ואת כל עוף[כנף]
למינהו וירא אלהים כי טוב 22ויברך אתם אלהים לא[מ]ר[פרו ורבו ומלאו]
את המים בימים והעוף ירב בארץ 23וי[הי ערב ויהי בקר יום חמישי]
vacat] [
24ויאמר אלהים תוצא[הארץ נפש חיה למינה בהמה ורמש וחיתו ארץ]
למינה [ויהי כן] 25ויע[ש [

4QGen^b is a significant copy of Genesis for several reasons. First, of the Qumran Genesis manuscripts, 4QGen^b preserves the most material of the creation account (1:1–28). Second, it is rare that we have such a relatively intact text of the creation account preserved from this period of antiquity. Last, but not least, this two thousand year old text is the same as our text today.

4QGen^d

4QGen^d was among the numerous Genesis manuscripts discovered in Cave 4 in 1952. The manuscript is written in a late Hasmonean script from the middle of the first century BC (50–25 BC).[18] All that remains of the original manuscript is a single fragment, measuring 10.7 cm wide and 10.8 cm high.[19] 4QGen[d] has eleven lines of text in the preserved column, containing text from Genesis 1:18–27.

This single fragment preserves some valuable clues for reconstructing this manuscript. For example, the preservation of the top and bottom margins allows us to measure the exact height of the column (or writing block). This column of text measures 8 cm in height, which indicates 4QGen[d] was among the category of smaller scrolls from Qumran.[20] Also, the preservation of the left margin with the stitching on the left edge of the fragment indicates this writing block, containing 1:18–27, was the last column of the first leather sheet. Based on the size of this column and the amount of text contained, it is likely that this first leather sheet originally contained three columns of text (with the first two columns containing 1:1–17). Determining the original length of the entire scroll is perhaps more difficult to state with certainty. However, George Brooke's reconstruction of 4QGen[d] indicates that this manuscript may have originally been approximately 2 meters in length, consisting of four or five sheets of leather, with 12 to 15 columns of text.[21] Based on the material remains, which indicate this was a small manuscript, it is unlikely that 4QGen[d] originally contained all of Genesis.[22] It seems likely, as Brooke has suggested, that this manuscript initially contained only the first four or five chapters of Genesis.[23]

18. Davila, "New Qumran Readings for Genesis One," 5.

19. Davila, DJD XII, 43.

20. The writing block in 4QGen[d], containing only eleven lines of text, is considered small among the Judean Desert scrolls as categorized by Tov (*Scribal Practices and Approaches Reflected in the Texts Found in the Judean Desert*, 84–85).

21. Brooke, "4QGenesis[d] Reconsidered," 57. More specifically, Brooke noted a range for the scroll as ". . . between 1.8 and 2.25 m in length."

22. Emanuel Tov noted, "4QGen[d], with merely eleven lines and 4QExod[e] with eight lines definitely did not contain the complete books" (*Scribal Practices and Approaches Reflected in the Texts Found in the Judean Desert*, 98); George Brooke also concluded, "But it has already become clear from the consideration of the possible reconstruction of the manuscript and the dimensions of the layout of its writing block, that 4QGen[d] was a small manuscript, relatively short, that could not have contained the whole of the book of Genesis" ("4QGenesis[d] Reconsidered," 59).

23. Brooke, "4QGenesis[d] Reconsidered," 60–61.

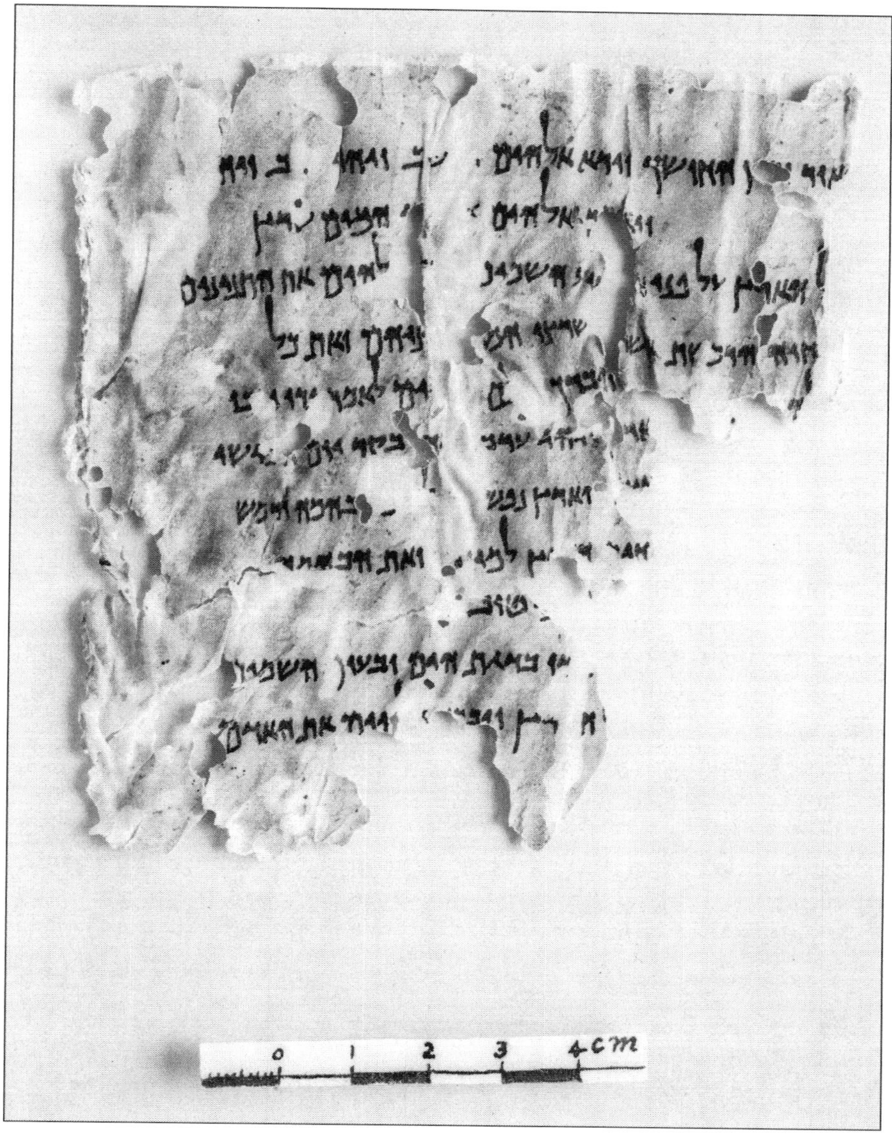

The preserved text of Gen 1:18–27 in 4QGen[d] (Courtesy of the Leon Levy Dead Sea Scrolls Digital Library; Israel Antiquities Authority)

4QGen^d (Genesis 1:18–27)

top margin

] האור וב[י]ן החושך וירא אלהים כ[י]טוב 19ויהי [ע]רב ויה[י]
] [*vacat* 20ויאמר אלהים י[שר]צו המים שרץ
] ע]ל הארץ על פני רקיע השמים[21וי]בר[א א]להים את התנינים
] ה]חיה הרמשת אשר שרצו המי[ם למ]יניהם ואת כל
] א]לה[ים כ]י[טוב] 22ויברך [א]תם[א]להים לאמר פרו ורבו
] ב]ארץ 23ויהי ערב[ו]יה[י] בקר יום חמישי
] *vacat?* ה]וצ[א]הארץ נפש[חיה] למ[י]נ[ה] בהמה ורמש
]]חית ה[א]רץ למינה ואת הבהמה
] אלהי]ם כי טוב *vacat*
26] וי]רדו בדגת הים ובעוף השמים
] ע]ל ה[א]רץ 27ויברא אלהים את האדם

bottom margin

The preserved text of 4QGen^d is identical to the Masoretic Text, containing only four orthographical differences: Gen 1:18 (line 1 החושך; MT החשך), Gen 1:21 (line 3 התנינים; MT התנִנם), Gen 1:21 (line 4 למיניהם; MT למינהם), and Gen 1:22 (line 5 א֯תם; MT אתם). In each case, the difference is simply the full spelling, characterized by the addition of *matres lectionis* commonly employed in Qumran texts.

The damaged right side of the column is missing some text. Thankfully, reconstructing fragmentary biblical texts is aided by the fact that these texts are *known* texts, in which we have a grid to work from. This is analogous to putting together the pieces of a jigsaw puzzle, in which we are aided by the image of the puzzle on the cover of the box. The missing text of 4QGen^d is reconstructed here.

A Reconstruction of 4QGen^{d} (Gen 1:18–27)
Based on the Material Remains and a Text Reflecting MT

top margin

[ובלילה ולהבדיל בין]האור וב[י]ן החושך וירא אלהים כ[י]טוב 19ויהי [ע]רב ויה[י]

[בקר יום רביעי] *vacat* 20ויאמר אלהים י[שר]צו המים שרץ

[נפש חיה ועוף יעופף ע]ל הארץ על פני רקיע השמים [21וי]בר[א א]להים את התנינים

[הגדלים ואת כל נפש ה]חיה הרמשת אשר שרצו המי[ם למ]יניהם ואת כל

[עוף כנף למינהו וירא א]לה[ים כ]י[טוב] 22ויברך [א]תם [א]להים לאמר פרו ורבו

[ומלאו את המים בימים והעוף ירב ב]ארץ 23ויהי ערב[ו]יה[י] בקר יום חמישי

[*vacat* 24ויאמר אלהים ת]וצ[א]הארץ נפש[חיה] למ[י]נ[ה] בהמה ורמש

[וחיתו ארץ למינה ויהי כל 25ויעש אלהים את]חית ה[א]רץ למינה ואת הבהמה

[למינה ואת כל רמש האדמה למינהו וירא אלהי]ם כי טוב *vacat*

[26ויאמר אלהים נעשה אדם בצלמינו כדמותינו וי]רדו בדגת הים ובעוף השמים

[ובבהמה ובכל הארץ ובכל הרמש הרמש ע]ל ה[א]רץ 72ויברא אלהים את האדם

bottom margin

Based on the preserved margins of this column and the preserved portion of text reflecting MT, the lacunae (missing portions) of the right side of the column can be reconstructed rather straightforwardly. The reconstructed lines of text, along with the lengths of the various lacunae, indicate no textual variants from MT for this column of text. Thus, in addition to the preserved portion of text in 4QGen^{d}, the reconstructed portion of text also attests to the Masoretic Text type.[24]

4QGen^{g}

4QGen^{g} is another copy of Genesis found in Cave 4 in 1952. This manuscript is also written in a late Hasmonean script from the first century BC (50–25 BC).[25] 4QGen^{g} consists of only a few fragments, preserving portions of Genesis 1:1–11, 13–22; 2:7 or 19. The largest fragment (frag. 1), measuring 8.7 cm wide and 9.3 cm high, preserves Gen 1:1–11, while fragment 2, measuring roughly the same size, preserves Gen 1:13–22.[26] A very small third fragment contains portions of two words from either Gen 2:7 or

24. Concerning 4QGen^{d}, Davila concluded, "Where its text is preserved or can be reconstructed it is identical to the MT . . ." ("New Qumran Readings for Genesis One," 5).

25. Davila, DJD XII, 57.

26. Ibid.

19. The reason for uncertainty as to 2:7 or 19 is that this fragment preserves only [הוה]ויצר י ("then Yahweh formed"), found in both.

Fragment 1 preserves text from Gen 1:1–11 and fragment 2 preserves text from Gen 1:13–22. (Courtesy of the Leon Levy Dead Sea Scrolls Digital Library; Israel Antiquities Authority, photo: Shai Halevi)

4QGen^g, frags. 1 and 2 (Genesis 1:1–11, 13–22)

1בראש[ית ברא]אלהים את השמים ואת הארץ [2 [
[ע]ל[פני תהו]ם ורוח אלהים מרחפת על פני המים[[
] 4וי]רא אלהים]את האור כי טוב ויבדל אלה[ים [
5ויקרא ////////// אלהים לאור יומם ולחשך קר[א [
יום אחד *vacat* [
6ויאמר אלהים יהי רקיע בתוך המים ויהי מב]דיל [
אלהים את הרקיע ויבדל בין המים אשר מתח[ת [
מעל לרקיע ויהי כן 8ויקרא אלהים לרקיע ש[מים [
יום שני *vacat* [
9ויאמר אלהים יקאו המים מתחת לשמים] [
]] ויהי כן 10ויקרא אלהים ליבשה א[רץ [
]] כי טוב *vacat* 11ויאמ[ר [

text missing (end of fragment 1)

ויהי בקר יום שלשי] *vacat* [
14ויאמר ^אלהים^ יהי מארות ברקי[ע [
ובין הלילה ויהיו לאתות ולמועדים ל[ימים ושנים 15והיו למאורת [
ברקִע השמים להאיר על הארץ ויהי כ[ן 16 [
את שני המארות הג[ד]לים את המאור ה[גדול [
[המ]אור הקטון לממשל[ת] הלילה ואת הכוכב[ים 17 [
]]השמים ל[האיר] על הארץ 18ולמשול ב[יום [
] האו]ר ובין [החש]ך וירא אלהים כי טוב]19 [
] רבי]עי *vacat*] [
]20 א]ל[הים ישרצו] המים שרץ נפש חיה וע[וף [
]] 21ויברא אלהים את התנינים[[
]] הרמשת אשר שרצו המים ל[מינהם [
]] אלהים כי טוב 22ויבר[ך [
] בימ]ים והעוף ירבה ב[ארץ [

text missing (end of fragment 2)

Several clues aid in the reconstruction of 4QGen^g. Fragment 1 preserves twelve lines of text (and possibly traces of a few letters from a thirteenth line along the bottom edge of the fragment), while fragment 2 preserves fourteen lines of text. Concerning the margins, the top and right margins are clearly preserved in fragment 1, while it appears that a small part of the right and bottom margins are preserved in fragment 2. However, the bottom margin of fragment 1 and the top margin of fragment 2 are not preserved. Thus, one particular question is raised concerning any attempt at a reconstruction—do fragments 1 and 2 represent a single column of text or two separate, contiguous columns of text? According to Davila, it is likely that these two fragments represent two columns with each containing 14 lines. His conclusion is based on the consistently longer lines in fragment 1 (58–65 letter-spaces per line) than those of fragment 2 (43–54 letter-spaces per line) and the comparable size of the two fragments.[27] While Davila may be correct, the lack of a bottom margin for fragment 1 and a top margin for fragment 2 makes it difficult to determine with certainty. Whether these two fragments represent a single column or two columns of text, it is significant that much of the creation account is preserved in 4QGen^{g}.

While the text of 4QGen^{g} generally attests to the Masoretic Text type, there are several orthographical and textual variants from MT. The spelling differences are minor, with 4QGen^{g} simply containing the fuller spelling in most cases: Gen 1:9 (frag. 1, line 10 יקאו; MT יקוו), Gen 1:14 (frag. 2, line 2 מארות; MT מארת), Gen 1:14 (frag. 2, line 3 לאותות; MT לאתת), Gen 1:16 (frag. 2, line 5 המארות; MT המארת), Gen 1:16 (frag. 2, line 6 הקטון; MT הקטן), Gen 1:18 (frag. 2, line 7 ולמשול; MT ולמשל), Gen 1:21 (frag. 2, line 11 התנינים; MT התנינם). In two instances, MT contains the fuller spelling: Gen 1:13 (frag. 2, line 1 שלשי; MT שלישי) and Gen 1:14 (frag. 2, line 3 ולמעדים; MT ולמועדים).[28] In addition to these minor orthographical differences, 4QGen^{g} contains several textual variants of interest.

In Genesis 1:5 of the Masoretic Text, the word יום (*yom* "day") is used with two different meanings: 1) daytime (ויקרא אלהים לאור יום "Then God called the light day") and 2) a twenty-four hour period (ויהי־ערב ויהי־בקר יום אחד "And it was evening and it was morning, the first day"). Interestingly, where MT reads ויקרא אלהים לאור יום (Then God called the light day), 4QGen^{g} employs יומם (daytime) instead of יום (day).[29] As Brooke observed, 4QGen^{g} makes a distinction between the two uses of יום in 1:5, using יומם (daytime) for the period of light and יום for the twenty-four hour period.[30] While יומם in 4QGen^{g} is the secondary reading, how did this variant arise? Davila believes that this variant arose through a scribal error, namely the dittography of the letter *mem* (מ) in a manuscript that did not distinguish

27. Ibid.

28. Concerning all the orthographical differences found in 4QGen^{g} (Gen 1:9, 13, 14, 16, 18, 21), the preserved text of 4QGen^{b} uniformly agrees with MT. In Gen 1:14, the three orthographical differences found in 4QGen^{g} are attested in 4QGen^{k}. In Gen 1:21, the single orthographical difference found in 4QGen^{g} is attested in 4QGen^{d} also.

29. The MT reading (יום) is also attested by the Samaritan Pentateuch and the Septuagint, while the 4QGen^{g} reading (יומם) is reflected in the Syriac Peshitta and the Aramaic Targumim.

30. Brooke, "The Rewritten Law, Prophets, and Psalms," 34.

between the medial form (מ) and final form (ם).[31] This is certainly possible. However, Brooke suggests what appears to be a more likely solution—that יומם "was an exegetical variant from the outset; . . . clearly dependent upon a particular understanding of the undifferentiated text of Genesis as received."[32]

A few other minor textual variants are preserved in the extant text of 4QGen^g^. In Genesis 1:9, 4QGen^g^ reads מתחת לשמים where the Masoretic Text, Samaritan Pentateuch, and 4QGen^b^ all read מתחת השמים.[33] Another textual variant may be preserved in Genesis 1:14. According to Davila and Ulrich, 4QGen^g^ reads ל[ימים] where MT reads ולימים.[34] However, only the first letter of this word is partially preserved as the manuscript is broken off at this point. While this partially damaged letter could be the bottom half of a ל, it is also possible this letter is a ו. If this letter is a ו, then the extant text of 4QGen^g^ does not differ from the reading of ולימים found in MT. Last, in Genesis 1:22, 4QGen^g^ and the Samaritan Pentateuch read ירבה where the Masoretic Text and 4QGen^b^ read ירב. These textual variants found in 4QGen^g^ are minor and in each case do not affect the essential meaning of the biblical text. In addition to these variants found in the extant portions of 4QGen^g^, there is also the possibility, based on a reconstruction of several damaged lines of text (frag. 2, lines 2, 4, 13–14), that this manuscript may have contained additional variant readings from MT.[35]

31. Davila, "New Qumran Readings for Genesis One," 5–6. Dittography is "the accidental repetition of a letter, a group of letters, a word, or a group of words" (Würthwein, *The Text of the Old Testament*, 109).

32. Brooke, "The Rewritten Law, Prophets, and Psalms," 34; see also Brooke's discussion in *Reading the Dead Sea Scrolls*, 4–5.

33. In addition, the Septuagint and Aramaic Targumim reflect the reading in MT.

34. Cf. Davila, DJD XII, 59; Ulrich (ed.), *The Biblical Qumran Scrolls*, 4.

35. For example, in fragment 2, line 2, the opening of Genesis 1:14 is preserved in the first part of the line: ויאמר אלהים יהי מארות ברקי[ע] (Then God said, "Let there be lights in the firmament . . ."). The rest of the line is missing due to scroll damage. The latter part of this verse picks up at the beginning of line 3: ובין הלילה ויהיו לאתות ולמעדים ו[לימים ושנים] (. . . and between the night. And they will be for signs and for seasons, and [for days and years]). If the missing portion of the text (השמים להבדיל בין היום ". . . the heavens to divide between the day") in line 2 is reconstructed based on MT and 4QGen^b^, then the line appears to have been a little short compared to the average length of lines in the column. Thus, one possibility is that 4QGen^g^ contained the additional phrase להאיר על הארץ (to give light upon the earth) between השמים and להבדיל, which is attested by the Samaritan Pentateuch and the Septuagint (εις φαυσιν επι της γης). The addition of this phrase would have made the length of line 2 slightly long, but within range of the other lines of the column. If this additional phrase was contained in 4QGen^g^, it is possible the

4QGen^{h1}

4QGen^{h1} is a very small fragment found among the thousands of fragments from Cave 4. The manuscript was written in a late Hasmonean or early Herodian script (50–25 BC).[36] This single fragment, measuring only 2.3 cm high and 1.7 cm wide,[37] preserves a few words from Genesis 1:8–10. The right margin of the column is preserved, with only the first word of four lines preserved or partially preserved. The first line preserves part of a word from the latter part of 1:8 with only a partial ש, representing either שמים or שני. The second line opens with the beginning of 1:9 (ויאמר), while the third line preserves מקוה from 1:9. The fourth line preserves ליבשה from 1:10. In addition to the right margin, it appears that part of the bottom margin is preserved. If this is the case, then the first column of this manuscript can be reconstructed as originally containing thirteen lines of text.[38]

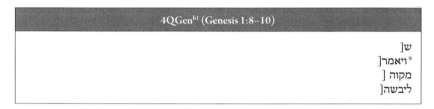

4QGen^{h1} (Genesis 1:8–10)
ש]
9 ויאמר]
מקוה [
ליבשה]

The preservation of only three words (and a partial fourth word) in 4QGen^{h1} prohibits any conclusive judgments as to the text type of this manuscript. Nonetheless, 4QGen^{h1} is a very small fragment that preserves a significant textual variant. Genesis 1:9 of the Masoretic Text reads: ויאמר אלהים יקוו המים מתחת השמים אל־מקום אחד (Then God said, "Let the waters beneath the heavens be gathered into one place"). The MT reading of מקום

scribe accidentally inserted this phrase at this point in 1:14 following ברקיע השמים, while looking at 1:15, which contains this phrase following ברקיע השמים. Another possibility for explaining the length of the lacuna (missing text) in line 2 is that there were blank spaces on the line, due to rough patches of leather that were unsuitable for writing. A prime example of this is found in 4QGen^{g} (frag. 1, line 4), where the scribe left a blank space of roughly eight letter-spaces between ויקרא and אלהים, due to an uneven surface (cf. Tov, "The Biblical Texts from the Judaean Desert," 161n14). In the end, both options (insertion of an additional phrase or blank spaces due to rough patches of leather) appear equally viable. For further discussion of this and other examples, see Davila, "New Qumran Readings for Genesis One," 6–7.

36. Davila, "New Qumran Readings for Genesis One," 7.

37. Ibid.

38. Davila, DJD XII, 61.

(place) in 1:9 is attested in the Samaritan Pentateuch and 4QGen[b].[39] However, the Septuagint reads συναγωγην (gathering). Interestingly, 4QGen[h1] reads מקוה (gathering) instead of מקום (place), which provides us with a Hebrew *Vorlage* for the Septuagint reading of συναγωγην (gathering).

This textual variant in 4QGen[h1] also raises the issue whether מקום or מקוה is the original reading. Davila views מקום as original and מקוה as a scribal harmonization of the text, based on his understanding that 1:9 originally contained מקויהם (gatherings) in the latter part of the verse (see discussion on 4QGen[k]). He concludes, "If we assume that מקום was the original reading earlier in the verse, it is easy to see how a harmonizing scribe could have miswritten מקוה instead under the influence of מקויהם. On the other hand, it is very difficult to explain why מקום would have been substituted for an original מקוה."[40] Ronald Hendel acknowledges the possibility that מקום is original, but also provides an explanation for מקוה as original and מקום as a scribal error involving graphic confusion of the final ם and ה. He argues that the direction of change from מקוה to מקום is more likely: ". . . the word מקוה is uncommon in Hebrew, whereas מקום is very common. It is a natural tendency for scribes to mistake an uncommon word for a common word, particularly when facilitated by graphic confusion. The reverse change, from a common word to an uncommon word, is far less frequent."[41] Thus, alternative explanations have been provided concerning whether מקום or מקוה is original. Regardless of which reading is original, the reading preserved in 4QGen[h1] indicates that the Septuagint translator(s) accurately copied from a Hebrew *Vorlage* that differed from MT.

4QGen[k]

4QGen[k] is the last of the fragmentary Genesis manuscripts from Cave 4 that preserves portions of the creation account. This manuscript, written in Herodian script, is dated AD 1–30.[42] 4QGen[k] consists of only five small fragments that preserve portions of Genesis 1:9, 14–16, 27–28, 2:1–3, and 3:1–2. Fragment 1, containing only a few words from 1:9, preserves the right margin.

39. In addition, the Aramaic Targumim, Syriac Peshitta, and Latin Vulgate reflect the reading in MT.

40. Davila, "New Qumran Readings for Genesis One," 11.

41. Hendel, *The Text of Genesis 1–11*, 25.

42. Davila, DJD XII, 75; "New Qumran Readings for Genesis One," 7.

There is evidence of stitching along the outer edge of the right margin,[43] indicating there was an uninscribed handle sheet (protective sheet) at the beginning of the manuscript.[44] Fragment 2 is the largest fragment, measuring 4.5 cm high and 8.5 cm wide.[45] This fragment, containing portions of 1:14–16, preserves the bottom margin. Fragments 3 and 4 preserve only a few words and, in each case, do not preserve any margins. Fragment 5, containing text from 3:1–2, also preserves the bottom margin.

Concerning the reconstruction of the columns of text from these five fragments, the bottom margin preserved in fragments 2 and 5 indicates two possibilities. Fragment 2, containing 1:14–16, could be the bottom of column I, indicating 20 lines per column.[46] In this case, fragment 1 (1:9) would be in the middle of column I and fragment 5 (3:1–2) would represent the bottom of column IV. However, there is not enough text or margins preserved concerning the preceding material of 1:1–13 to place fragment 2 (1:14–16) at the bottom of column I with certainty. Thus, another option is that fragment 2 could represent the bottom of column II, indicating 10 lines per column.[47] In this case, fragment 1 (1:9) would be at the bottom of column I and fragment 5 would represent the bottom of column VIII. The bottom margin preserved in fragments 2 and 5 certainly narrows the options for reconstructing the columns of text. Nonetheless, the lack of preserved text and margins makes it difficult to determine with any certainty whether the original layout of the columns contained 10 or 20 lines of text.[48]

43. The stitching holes are clearly visible (see PAM image M43.008).

44. Cf. Tov, *Scribal Practices and Approaches Reflected in the Texts Found in the Judean Desert*, 79, 110, 114, 117. Tov also notes, "A separate uninscribed handle sheet (protective sheet, *page de garde*) was often stitched before the first inscribed sheet" (p. 114).

45. Davila, DJD XII, 75.

46. This size of writing block (20 lines) would place 4QGen^{k} among the category of medium sized scrolls (15–24 lines) in antiquity.

47. This size of writing block (10 lines) for 4QGen^{k} is comparable to 4QGen^{d} (11 lines per column), placing it among the category of small scrolls (4–14 lines) in antiquity. If George Brooke's conclusions regarding the original length of 4QGen^{d} are generally correct (see Brooke, "4QGen^{d} reconsidered"), then it also possible that 4QGen^{k} did not originally contain all of Genesis.

48. Davila, DJD XII, 75. Davila briefly discusses the two possibilities for the reconstruction of the columns of text. He does not draw a conclusion concerning which option (10 or 20 lines per column) is preferable.

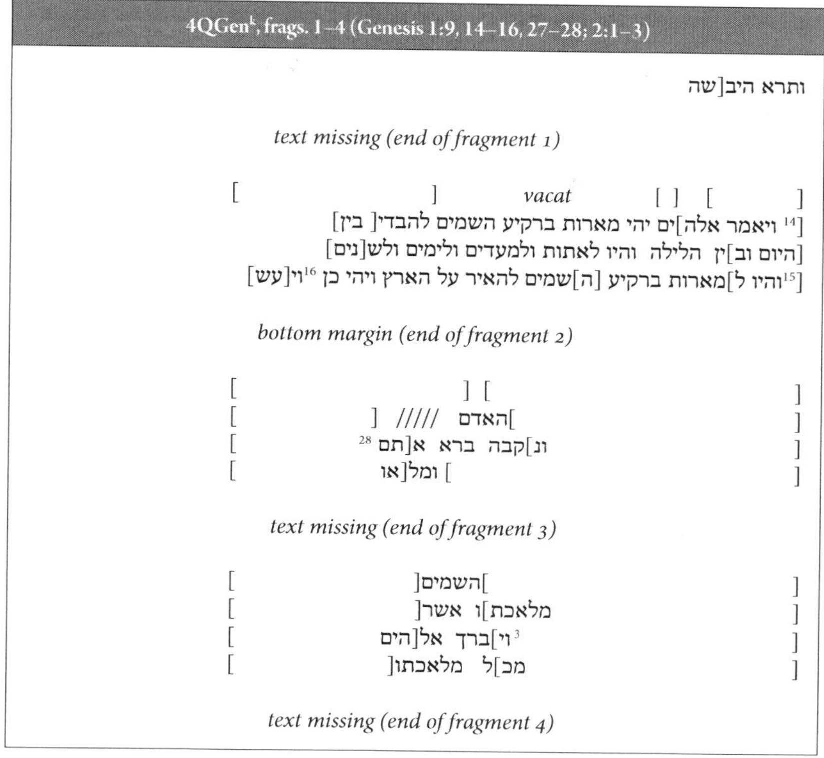

4QGen^k, frags. 1–4 (Genesis 1:9, 14–16, 27–28; 2:1–3)

ותרא היב[שה

text missing (end of fragment 1)

[ ] *vacat* [ ] [ ]
[14 ויאמר אלה]ים יהי מארות ברקיע השמים להבדי[בין]
[היום וב]ין הלילה והיו לאתות ולמעדים ולימים ולש[נים]
[15והיו ל]מארות ברקיע [ה]שמים להאיר על הארץ ויהי כן 16וי[עש]

bottom margin (end of fragment 2)

[ ] [ ]
[ ]האדם ///// [ ]
[ונ]קבה ברא א[תם 28]
[ ] ומל[או]

text missing (end of fragment 3)

[ ]השמים[ ]
[מלאכת]ו אשר[ ]
[3וי]ברך אל[הים]
[מכ]ל מלאכתו[ ]

text missing (end of fragment 4)

The preserved text of 4QGen^k contains a few orthographical and textual variants from the Masoretic Text. The orthographical differences are all found in fragment 2: Gen 1:14 (line 2 מארות; MT מארת), Gen 1:14 (line 3 לאתות; MT לאתת), Gen 1:14 (line 3 ולמעדים; MT ולמועדים), Gen 1:15 (line 4 למארות; MT למאורת).[49] A textual variant is found in both fragment 1 (Gen 1:9) and 2 (Gen 1:14).

The variant reading preserved in fragment 1 is of particular interest. The Masoretic Text of Genesis 1:9 records God's declaration: יקוו המים מתחת השמים אל־מקום אחד ותראה היבשה ("Let the waters under the heavens be gathered together into one place, and let the dry land appear"). The verse then concludes with the observation, ויהי־כן ("and it was so"). The Septuagint, however, contains additional text describing the accomplishment of God's command: και συνηχθη το υδωρ το υποκατω του ουρανου εις τας

49. The spellings of לאתות ,מארות, and ולמעדים found in 4QGen^k are also attested by 4QGen^g. The spellings in MT are attested by 4QGen^b, with the exception of למאורת (4QGen^b למארת).

συναγωγας αυτων και ωφθη η ξηρα (And the water beneath the heaven was collected into its gatherings, and the dry land appeared). Is this addition to the text of 1:9 in the Septuagint the result of the translator(s) harmonizing the text in order to preserve a certain pattern in the creation account?[50] Or is the addition found in the Septuagint due to a Hebrew *Vorlage* (base text) from which the translator(s) carefully copied? Fragment 1 of 4QGen^k preserves only two words from Genesis 1:9: ותרא היב[שה] (and the dry land appeared). Notably, ותרא (and it appeared) in 4QGen^k is a niphal *wayyiqtol* verb, whereas ותראה (and let it appear) in MT is a niphal jussive verb. This indicates that 4QGen^k included the additional text in 1:9 that is found in the Septuagint. Consequently, 4QGen^k appears to demonstrate that the longer reading preserved in the Septuagint is based on a Hebrew *Vorlage*.[51]

50. In this case, the general pattern in Genesis 1 for other acts of creation includes God's declaration (command) and the accomplishment of God's command. Another pattern in Genesis 1 is the statement that "God saw that it was good" (cf. 1:4, 10, 12, 18, 21, 31), which is included for each of the days of creation in MT, except for day two. LXX preserves the additional phrase "God saw that it was good" for day two, where MT does not include it. This is a possible example of harmonization in LXX in order to preserve the pattern in Genesis 1.

51. Davila also concluded that the Septuagint reading was not the result of harmonization, but was based on a Hebrew *Vorlage* ("New Qumran Readings for Genesis One," 10).

The Text of Genesis 1:9		
Masoretic Text & 4QGen[b]	4QGen[h1] & 4QGen[k]	Septuagint
ויאמר אלהים יקוו המים מתחת השמים אל מקום אחד ותראה היבשה ויהי כן	ויאמר [אלהים יקוו המים מתחת השמים אל] מקוה [אחד ותראה היבשה ויהי כן] [ויקוו המים מתחת השמים אל מקויהם] ותרא היב[שה]	Και ειπεν ο Θεος συναχθητω το υδωρ το υποκατω του ουρανου εις συναγωγην μιαν και οφθητω η ξηρα και εγενετο ουτως και συνηχθη το υδωρ το υποκατω του ουρανου εις τας συναγωγας αυτων και ωφθη η ξηρα
Then God said, "Let the waters under the heavens be gathered into one place, and let the dry land appear." And it was so.	Then God said, "Let the waters under the heavens be gathered into one gathering, and let the dry land appear." And it was so. [Then the waters beneath the heavens were gathered into their gatherings] and the dr[y land] appeared.	And God said, "Let the water beneath the heaven be gathered into one gathering, and let the dry land appear." And it was so. And the water beneath the heaven was collected into its gatherings, and the dry land appeared.

The other textual variant preserved in 4QGen[k] is found in fragment 2, line 2. In the Masoretic Text, the latter part of Genesis 1:14 reads: והיו לאתת ולמועדים ולימים ושנים (and let them be for signs and for seasons, and for days and years). The first three nouns in the list include the ל preposition, while the final noun (שנים) does not include it.[52] Where MT reads ושנים (and years), 4QGen[k] reads ולש[נים] (and for years). The inclusion of the ל preposition with the final noun in 4QGen[k] is attested in the Septuagint (και εις ενιαυτους "and for years").[53] In light of the textual variant in 1:9, this minor textual variant in 1:14 further attests to the existence of a Hebrew *Vorlage* for the Septuagint.

52. The MT reading (ושנים) is attested in the Aramaic Targumim.

53. In addition, the Samaritan Pentateuch and Syriac Peshitta reflect the reading in 4QGen[k].

The Text of the Genesis Creation Account at Qumran: Conclusions

1QGen, 4QGen^{b}, 4QGen^{d}, 4QGen^{g}, 4QGen^{h1}, and 4QGen^{k} represent the oldest extant copies of the Genesis creation account, dating from the first century BC to the mid-first century AD. Though fragmentary, these Qumran copies are valuable for textual studies for several reasons. First, the text tradition preserved in the medieval Masoretic Text is attested in these Qumran Genesis manuscripts containing the creation account.[54] 4QGen^{b} and 4QGen^{d}, for example, are virtually identical to MT, demonstrating the faithful scribal transmission of the text over the centuries.[55] Thus, when we read the text of the creation account today, which is based on MT, we are reading the same text that people were reading during the Second Temple period. Second, some of the variant readings preserved in these Qumran Genesis scrolls reveal the existence of a Hebrew *Vorlage* (base text) for readings found in the Septuagint. The variant readings in 4QGen^{h1} and 4QGen^{k}, for example, indicate that the Septuagint translator(s) carefully copied from a Hebrew text tradition that differed from MT.[56] Third, these Qumran Genesis scrolls attest to the variety of text traditions that existed during the Second Temple period. In other words, the text tradition preserved in MT existed *alongside* other text traditions at Qumran.[57] The text of the Genesis

54. Davila, "Book of Genesis," 299; Crawford, "Genesis in the Dead Sea Scrolls," 354; VanderKam and Flint, *The Meaning of the Dead Sea Scrolls*, 104–05.

55. 4QGen^{b}, which preserves the most material of the creation account (1:1–28), is virtually identical to MT, with only one orthographical variant. 4QGen^{d}, preserving text from Gen 1:18–27, is also virtually identical to MT, with only a few spelling differences. It is widely recognized that the Qumran biblical scrolls, in general, attest to the reliable transmission of the biblical text. For example, VanderKam noted, "Many of the new scrolls do belong to the same textual tradition as the Masoretic Text. They are, however, centuries older and thus demonstrate in a forceful way how carefully Jewish scribes transmitted that text across the years" (*The Dead Sea Scrolls Today*, 162–63). Similarly, Stegemann observed that the biblical manuscripts from Qumran ". . . now constitute a testimonial to a professionalism of the highest excellence on the part of the Jewish copyists . . . The text of the Bible as we have it from the Middle Ages is virtually identical to the text a thousand years before" (*The Library of Qumran*, 86).

56. Based on 4QGen^{h1} and 4QGen^{k}, Davila also concluded, ". . . we must take the LXX of Genesis very seriously as a source for a Hebrew textual tradition alternate to the MT. We have strong reason to believe that the translators of Genesis treated their Vorlage with respect and rendered the Hebrew text before them into Greek with great care and minimal interpretation" ("New Qumran Readings for Genesis One," 11).

57. Arie van der Kooij noted that the textual variety attested in the biblical scrolls from Qumran does not mean that the biblical text was 'fluid' in the sense of a "continuing

creation account, in particular, reflects the overall picture of textual variety in the biblical manuscripts from Qumran.

process of textual change and reworking." On the contrary, "the available evidence strongly suggests that an essentially uniform textual tradition existed *alongside* a pluriform tradition in Palestinian Judaism." This is confirmed by the fact that "the later MT is attested by a large number of biblical texts dating to the period before 70 CE which have been found in the Dead Sea region" ("The Textual Criticism of the Hebrew Bible Before and After the Qumran Discoveries," 170). Lawrence Schiffman observed, "The proto-Masoretic text type was dominant, even though alongside it were texts of sectarian-type as well as a few proto-Samaritan or Septuagintal-type texts" (*Reclaiming the Dead Sea Scrolls*, 180).

CHAPTER THREE

SCRIBAL PRACTICES IN THE DEAD SEA SCROLLS AND THE LITERARY STRUCTURE OF THE GENESIS CREATION ACCOUNT

Introduction

THE BIBLICAL QUMRAN SCROLLS, dated 250 BC to AD 68, have unquestionably transformed our understanding of the text of the Hebrew Bible.[1] In addition, these scrolls have provided us a unique window into scribal practices during the Second Temple period, showing how ancient scribes prepared, wrote, copied and made corrections in preserving biblical texts. But what kind of new information can we glean from the scribal clues left

1. Prior to the discoveries of the Dead Sea Scrolls between 1947 and 1956, the Hebrew textual witnesses dating earlier than the medieval period were extremely scarce (e.g. the tiny Nash papyrus). The biblical scrolls from Qumran, dated 250 BC to AD 68, take the dating of available biblical manuscripts back a thousand years or more. Remarkably, many of these ancient scrolls closely match the medieval Masoretic Text tradition, which modern Hebrew and English Bibles are based upon, confirming the biblical text has been faithfully preserved for all these centuries. Not only that, some of the biblical scrolls attest to a Hebrew text tradition underlying the Septuagint, validating it as a faithful translation of a Hebrew text tradition that existed during the Second Temple period. Further, another text tradition attesting to the Samaritan Pentateuch is found among the biblical scrolls. Thus, the biblical Qumran scrolls also attest to the variety of text traditions that existed during that time. The biblical scrolls from Qumran appear to indicate that a stable, uniform text tradition (proto-MT) existed alongside a pluriform text tradition prior to the end of the first century AD.

behind in these copies of the biblical texts? Interestingly, several Genesis manuscripts from Qumran provide a good example of scribal practices in the transmission of the biblical text which may shed light on their understanding of the literary structure of the creation account. In order to better understand and appreciate the textual observations in the Qumran Genesis manuscripts, we will first take a look at some of the techniques employed by the scribes in these ancient texts from the Judean desert.

Ancient Scribal Methods in the Dead Sea Scrolls

Various scribal rules or practices were followed in the production of scrolls during the Second Temple period.[2] The preparation of the scroll itself included technical procedures such as the manufacturing of the leather sheets and the ruling of horizontal lines with a sharp instrument. The writing or copying of the text itself onto the scroll also included technical procedures such as the various scribal markings, notations of corrections, writing of Divine names,[3] and sense divisions (e.g. the breaks between words, paragraphs, or books).[4] The external Talmudic tractate *Maseket Sopherim* (Tractate for Scribes), dated to the seventh or eighth century AD, also presents detailed rules for the production of biblical manuscripts.[5] Though this tractate is considerably later in date, much of the scribal guidelines recorded therein appear to come from the latter part of the Second Temple period and are similar to the scribal practices observed in the Dead Sea Scrolls.[6]

2. For a standard work on scribal practices, see Tov, *Scribal Practices and Approaches Reflected in the Texts Found in the Judean Desert*; see also "Copying of a Biblical Scroll," 189–209.

3. For example, in manuscripts written in Jewish square script, the Divine name יהוה (YHWH) is commonly written in Paleo-Hebrew script.

4. For example, in Paleo-Hebrew texts, dots were used instead of spaces to indicate word divisions. During the Second Temple period, the use of spacing to mark word divisions in the Hebrew manuscripts is distinct from the Greek monumental inscriptions and uncial texts with no word divisions. *See* Pfann, "Scripts and Scribal Practice," 1204–05; Tov, "Scribal Practices," 828–29.

5. Bar-Ilan, "Writing in Ancient Israel and Early Judaism," 28; Strack and Stemberger, *Introduction to the Talmud and Midrash*, 228; Yeivin, *Introduction to the Tiberian Masorah*, 7.

6. Bar-Ilan, "Writing in Ancient Israel and Early Judaism," 28; Pfann, "Scripts and Scribal Practice," 1204.

A common scribal feature in the Qumran scrolls is the subdividing of the text into units that were demarcated by means of spacing.[7] The Qumran texts were subdivided into large units and segmentations of the larger units into smaller units. In other words, the available writing space on a line was intentionally left blank to indicate paragraph divisions or subdivisions within paragraphs. This intentional blank space used for paragraph divisions is also referred to as a *vacat* and is usually indicated as such in published transcriptions of the Qumran texts. Different techniques of spacing were employed to indicate a major section break (paragraph division) or a subdivision within a larger unit.[8]

A major division between sections was indicated by a blank space extending from the last word in a line to the end of that line (see III.1). The new section would then commence at the beginning of the next line at the right-hand margin. In some cases, the beginning of the new section on the next line is indented from the right-hand margin. This major division, or 'open section,' indicates a new section "thematically distinct from the section which immediately precedes it."[9]

III.1 Division of Large Units in a Text (Open Section)[10]	
Section "A"	xxxxxxxxxxxxxxxxxxxxxxxxxxxxxxxxxxxxxxxxxxxxxx
section break →	xxxxxxxxxxxxxxxxxxxxxxxxxxxx
Section "B"	xxxxxxxxxxxxxxxxxxxxxxxxxxxxxxxxxxxxxxxxxxxxxx xxxxxxxxxxxxxxxxxxxxxxxxxxxxxxxxxxxxxxxxxxxxxx

This method of dividing large units of text is most common in the Qumran texts, but whenever the writing concluded near the end of the line, there would not be a sufficient space to indicate a major division (section

7. Tov, *Scribal Practices and Approaches Reflected in the Texts Found in the Judean Desert*, 143.

8. While the scribal use of sense divisions is generally consistent in the Qumran texts, there is some diversity in the way scribes employed sense divisions.

9. Siegel, "The Scribes of Qumran," 73. See also Martin, *The Scribal Character of the Dead Sea Scrolls*. In this early study (1958), shortly after the discoveries of the Qumran scrolls, Martin already noted that this method of dividing major sections "is used to mark off the beginning of a new theme" (p. 122).

10. Tables III.1 to III.4 are adaptations from Tov, *Scribal Practices and Approaches Reflected in the Texts Found in the Judean Desert* 145–47. The tables represent Hebrew texts which go from right to left.

break) between units. In this case, two options were available to indicate major divisions. One method employed by scribes was to place a sufficient space at the beginning of the next line to indicate that the previous line should have ended with a space (*vacat*).[11] Thus, the line beginning with this space, or indentation, would represent the beginning of a new distinct section (see III.2). The length of indentation from the right-hand margin was typically a few blank letter spaces, but there are also cases of considerably longer spaces at the beginning of the line.[12]

III.2 Division of Large Units in a Text (Open Section)	
Section "A"	xxxxxxxxxxxxxxxxxxxxxxxxxxxxxxxxxxxxxxxxxx
section break →	xxxxxxxxxxxxxxxxxxxxxxxxxxxxxxxxxxxxxxxxxx
Section "B"	xxxxxxxxxxxxxxxxxxxxxxxxxxxxxxxxxxxxxx xxxxxxxxxxxxxxxxxxxxxxxxxxxxxxxxxxxxxxxxxx

Another technique employed by scribes was to leave a complete line empty to indicate a major division (see III.3).

III.3 Division of Large Units in a Text (Open Section)	
Section "A"	xxxxxxxxxxxxxxxxxxxxxxxxxxxxxxxxxxxxxxxxxx xxxxxxxxxxxxxxxxxxxxxxxxxxxxxxxxxxxxxxxxxx
section break →	
Section "B"	xxxxxxxxxxxxxxxxxxxxxxxxxxxxxxxxxxxxxxxxxx xxxxxxxxxxxxxxxxxxxxxxxxxxxxxxxxxxxxxxxxxx

The segmentation of a larger unit into smaller units was generally designated by a sufficient space in the middle of the line with the writing of the following related unit beginning on that same line (see III.4). This 'closed section' is "thematically related to what immediately precedes it."[13]

11. Tov, *Scribal Practices and Approaches Reflected in the Texts Found in the Judean Desert*, 146.

12. For examples of longer indentations, see 1QapGen (XX, 24; XXI, 8; XXII, 18), 1QH^{a}, 1QIsa^{a} (XLIV, 16), 11QPs^{a} (XXVI, 4; XXVII, 12).

13. Siegel, "The Scribes of Qumran," 73–74.

III.4 Segmentation of Large Units into Smaller Units (Closed Section)
xxxxxxxxxxxxxxxxxxxxxxxxxxxxxxxxxxxxxxxxxxxx
xxxxxxxxxxx   xxxxxxxxxxxxxxxxxxxxxxxx
xxxxxxxxxxxxxxxxxxxxxxxxxxxxxxxxxxxxxxxxxxxx
xxxxxxxxxxxxxxxxxxxxxxxxxxxxxxxxxxxxxxxxxxxx

Thus, the scribes inserted both large and small section breaks according to the content in the text. The large section breaks (open sections) generally indicate thematically distinct sections and the small section breaks (closed sections) typically indicate thematically related sections within larger units. Consequently, as Emanuel Tov noted, the scribes "must have had a good understanding of the composition."[14]

The Qumran Genesis Manuscripts

The scribal practice of denoting units in the text by means of spacing is illustrated nicely in the layout of the creation account in several fragmentary Genesis manuscripts from Qumran (4QGen^{b}, 4QGen^{d}, 4QGen^{g}, 4QGen^{h1}, and 4QGen^{k}). These ancient manuscripts were among the roughly 600 fragmentary manuscripts found in Cave 4 by Bedouin in 1952. These texts were officially published decades later in 1994 by James R. Davila in volume XII of the Discoveries in the Judaean Desert series.[15] These Qumran Genesis texts were also published in 2010 in *The Biblical Qumran Scrolls*, edited by Eugene Ulrich.[16] Two of the manuscripts (4QGen^{b} and 4QGen^{g}) preserve a significant amount of text from the creation account, providing a nice overall picture of the layout. The other three manuscripts (4QGen^{d}, 4QGen^{h1}, and 4QGen^{k}) are more fragmentary, providing less textual data. The following survey reveals a general literary structure exhibited in these Qumran manuscripts by various means of spacing.

14. Tov, "Copying of a Biblical Scroll," 201.

15. Ulrich, Cross, Davila, et al. *Qumran Cave 4, VII: Genesis to Numbers*. Here after, DJD XII. Davila published the ten Genesis manuscripts in this volume.

16. Ulrich, ed. *The Biblical Qumran Scrolls*. The three-volume paperback edition was published in 2013.

4QGen[b]

This manuscript is written in late Herodian, or possibly post-Herodian script (AD 50–68+).[17] 4QGen[b] preserves text from Gen 1:1–28; 2:4–19; 4:2–11; 5:13 or 14.[18] The largest fragment (frag. 1), measuring 37.5 cm wide and 19.5 cm high,[19] contains text of much of the creation account (1:1–25).

17. Frank Moore Cross raised the possibility, based on paleography, that 4QGen[b] may be post-Herodian (after AD 68) and thus, not from Qumran. See Cross, "The Development of the Jewish Scripts," 178. In addition, James R. Davila raised legitimate points concerning the provenance of 4QGen[b], including the manuscript being poorly prepared (unusual for a Qumran manuscript), the paleography, and the virtually identical text with MT (reminiscent of biblical scrolls from Wadi Murabbaʿat). See Davila, DJD XII, 31. It is certainly possible that 4QGen[b] may not have come from Qumran, but from another site in the Judean wilderness. This possibility, however, does not adversely affect in any way the task at hand to observe the literary structure of the text as exhibited by the scribal practices found therein.

18. The reason for uncertainty as to 5:13 or 14 is frag. 3 preserves only a single word (קינן) found in both.

19. Davila, DJD XII, 31.

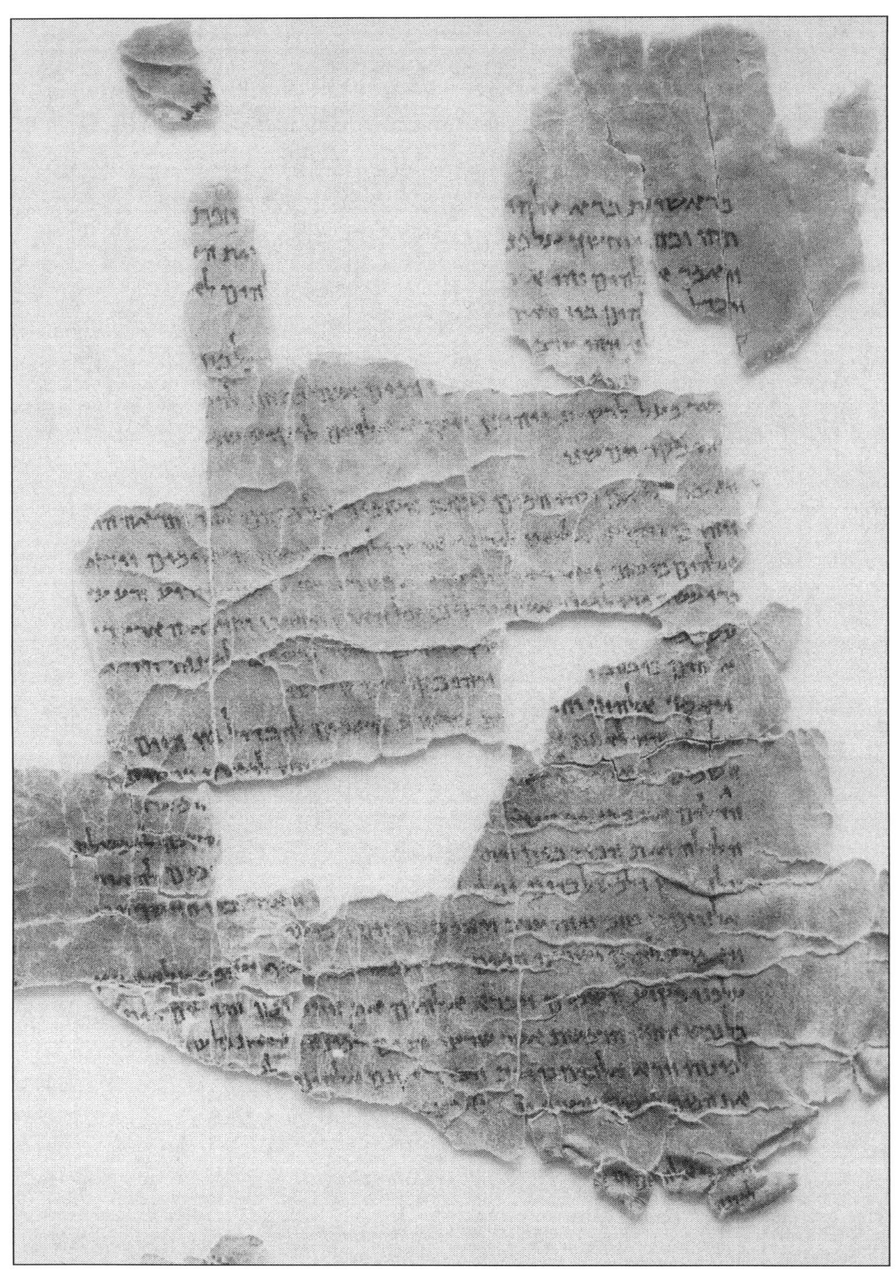

Column I of 4QGen[b] (Courtesy of the Leon Levy Dead Sea Scrolls Digital Library; Israel Antiquities Authority)

4QGen^b, frag. 1 i (Genesis 1:1–25a)	
	1בראשית ברא אלהי[ם את השמים ואת הארץ 2ו]הארץ[היתה]
Day 1	תהו ובהו וחשך על פנ[י תהום ורוח אלהים מר]חפת[על פני המים]
	3ויאמר אלהים יהי אור [ויהי אור 4וירא אלהים]את הא[ור כי טוב]
	ויבדל אלהים בין האור[ובין החשך 5ויקרא א]להים לאו[ר יום ולחשך]
section break →	ק[רא לי]לה ויהי ערב[ויהי בקר יום אחד] *vacat* [
	[6ויאמר א]להים י[הי רקיע בתוך המים ויהי מב]דיל בין [מים למים 7ויעש]
Day 2	[אלהים את הרקיע וי]בד[ל]ב[י]ן המים אשר מתחת לרק[יע ובין המים]
	אשר מעל לרקיע ויהי כן 8ויקרא אלהים לרקיע שמ[ים ויהי ערב]
section break →	[ו]יהי בקר יום שני] *vacat* [
	9ויאמר אלהים יקוו המים מתחת השמים אל מקום אחד ותראה היב[שה]
	ויהי כן 10ויקרא אלהים ליבשה ארץ ולמקוה המים קרא ימים וירא
	אלהים כי טוב 11ויאמר אלהים תדשא הארץ דשא עשב מזריע זרע עץ
Day 3	פרי עשה פרי למינו אשר זרעו בו על הארץ ויהי כן 12ותוצא הארץ דש[א]
	עשב מז[ריע זרע למינהו ו]עץ עשה פרי אשר זרעו בו למינהו וירא
section break →	אלהים כי טוב 13ו[יהי ערב] ויהי בקר יום שלישי *vacat*
	14ויאמר אלהים יהי [מא]רת ברקיע השמים להבדיל בין היום וב[ין]
	הלילה והיו לאתת ול[מועדים ולימים וש]נים 15והיו למארת ברקיע
	השמים להאיר על האר[ץ ויהי כן 16ויעש אלהים את שני]המארת
Day 4	הגדלים את המאור הגדל למ[משלת היום ואת המאור] הקטן לממשלת
	הלילה ואת הכוכבים 17ויתן[אתם אלהים ברקיע ה]שמים להאור
	על הארץ 18ולמשל ביום ובלילה[ולהבדיל בי]ן האור ובין החשך וירא
section break →	אלהים כי טוב 19ויהי ערב ויהי בקר יום רביעי *vacat*
	20ויאמר אלהים ישרצו המים שרץ נפש חיה ועוף יעופף על הארץ
	על פני רקיע השמים 21ויברא אלהים את התנינים הגדלים ואת
Day 5	כל נפש החיה הרמשת אשר שרצו המים למינהם ואת כל עוף[כנף]
	למינהו וירא אלהים כי טוב 22ויברך אתם אלהים לא[מ]ר[פרו ורבו ומלאו]
	את המים בימים והעוף ירב בארץ 23וי[הי ערב ויהי בקר יום חמישי]
section break →	] *vacat* [
Day 6	24ויאמר אלהים תוצא[הארץ נפש חיה למינה בהמה ורמש וחיתו ארץ]
	למינה [ויהי כן] 25ויע[ש]

In 4QGen^b, a major division (open section) was placed after 1:5, 8, 13, 19, and 23, dividing the text according to the days of creation week. In the case of 1:5 (end of day one), 1:8 (end of day two), 1:13 (end of day three), and 1:19 (end of day four), the major division between sections was indicated by a sufficient blank space extending from the last word of the verse to the end of the line. Each of the new sections then commence at the beginning of the next line at the right-hand margin (see III.1). In the case of the major division after 1:23 (end of day five), the text reached the end of the line, leaving insufficient space to indicate a major section break.[20] Thus,

20. The majority of verse 23 is a reconstruction of the text, which would have concluded near the end of that line. This is evidenced by the completely blank line left by the

the scribe opted to leave the next line completely blank, with the following section (day six) commencing at the beginning of the next line (see III.3). In this manner, each day of the creation week ends with an open section.

*4QGen^d^*

This manuscript is written in a late Hasmonean script from the middle of the first century BC (50–25 BC).[21] 4QGen^d^ consists of a single fragment, measuring 10.7 cm wide and 10.8 cm high.[22] 4QGen^d^ has eleven lines of text in the preserved column, with the top and bottom margins.[23] This fragment preserves text from Gen 1:18–27.

4QGen^d^ (Genesis 1:18–27)		
Day 4	*top margin*	
	האור וב[י]ן החושך וירא אלהים כ[י]טוב 19ויהי [ע]רב ויה[י]	]
section break →	[*vacat* 20ויאמר אלהים י[שר]צו המים שרץ	]
Day 5	ע]ל הארץ על פני רקיע השמים[21וי]בר[א א]להים את התנינים	]
	ה]חיה הרמשת אשר שרצו המי[ם למ]יניהם ואת כל	]
	א]לה[ים כ]י[טוב] 22ויברך [א]תם[א]להים לאמר פרו ורבו	]
section break →	ב]ארץ 23ויהי ערב[ו]יה[י] בקר יום חמישי	]
Day 6 creation of land animals	*vacat?* וצ[א]הארץ נפש[חיה] למ[י]נ[ה] בהמה ורמש	]
	]חית ה[א]רץ למינה ואת הבהמה	]
	אלהי]ם כי טוב *vacat*	]
creation of man	וי]רדו בדגת הים ובעוף השמים	26]
	ע]ל ה[א]רץ 27ויברא אלהים את האדם	]
	bottom margin	

In 4QGen^d^, only portions of days 4, 5, and 6 are extant. A section break was placed after 1:19, 23, and 25. The section break after 1:19 (end of day four) is placed in the middle of the line with the new section, beginning in 1:20, commencing on that same line.[24] In the case of the major division

scribe on the next line. Verse 24 then begins on the following line.

21. Davila, "New Qumran Readings for Genesis One," 5.

22. Davila, DJD XII, 43.

23. According to George Brooke, it is likely that this manuscript originally contained only the first four or five chapters of Genesis. See Brooke, "4QGenesis^d^ Reconsidered," 51–70.

24. The missing part of the text at the beginning of this line can be easily reconstructed

after 1:23 (end of day five), the text reached the end of the line, leaving insufficient space to indicate a major section break. Thus, the scribe opted to place a sufficient space at the beginning of the next line to indicate that the previous line should have ended with a space. The line beginning with this space, or indentation, represents the start of a new distinct section with 1:24 (see III.2).[25] The section break after 1:25 is marked by a blank space extending from the last word in the line to the end of that line. In this case, the section break is placed in the middle of day six after the creation of the land animals and before the creation of mankind.

4QGen^{g}

This manuscript is written in a late Hasmonean script (50–25 BC). 4QGen^{g} consists of only a few fragments, with the largest fragment measuring 8.7 cm wide and 9.3 cm high.[26] These fragments preserve portions of Gen 1:1–11, 13–22; 2:7 or 19.[27] Thus, like 4QGen^{b}, 4QGen^{g} also contains text of much of the creation account (1:1–11, 13–22).

with the end of 1:19 (בקר יום רביעי). The extant portion of the line picks up with the section break after 1:19. This is not necessarily a smaller sense division (closed section) within a larger unit, since in some cases, as Tov has noted, "the two systems of sense division were of equal value, distinguished merely by their place on the line" (*Scribal Practices and Approaches Reflected in the Texts Found in the Judean Desert*, 144). Further, scribes were to some degree individualistic in denoting sense divisions and, consequently, they did not always consistently employ these two systems of sense divisions.

25. While the beginning of this line is missing due to damage of the scroll, there is more than sufficient space available to reconstruct the first two words of 1:24 (ויאמר אלהים) with an indentation at the beginning of the line at the right-hand margin.

26. Davila, DJD XII, 57.

27. The reason for uncertainty as to 2:7 or 19 is frag. 3 preserves only ויצר י[הוה], found in both.

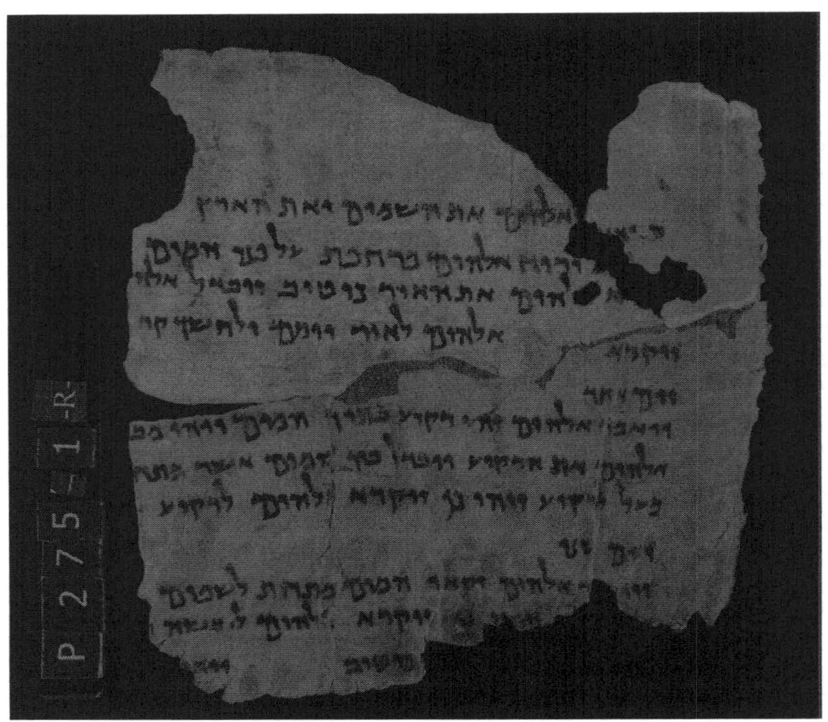

Fragment 1 of 4QGen[g] (Courtesy of the Leon Levy Dead Sea Scrolls Digital Library; Israel Antiquities Authority, photo: Shai Halevi)

4QGen^g, frags. 1 and 2 (Genesis 1:1–11, 13–22)		
Day 1	1בראש[ית ברא]אלהים את השמים ואת הארץ [2	[
	[ע]ל[פני תהו]ם ורוח אלהים מרחפת על פני המים]	[
	] 4וי]רא אלהים]את האור כי טוב ויבדל אלה[ים	[
	5ויקרא ////////// אלהים לאור יומם ולחשך קר[א	[
section break →	יום אחד *vacat*	[
Day 2	6ויאמר אלהים יהי רקיע בתוך המים ויהי מב]דיל	[
	אלהים את הרקיע ויבדל בין המים אשר מתח[ת	[
	מעל לרקיע ויהי כן 8ויקרא אלהים לרקיע ש]מים	[
section break →	יום שני *vacat*	[
Day 3	9ויאמר אלהים יקאו המים מתחת לשמים [	[
	]] ויהי כן 10ויקרא אלהים ליבשה א[רץ	[
	]] כי טוב *vacat* 11ויאמ[ר	[
	text missing (end of fragment 1)	
section break →	ויהי בקר יום שלשי] *vacat*	[
Day 4	14ויאמר ^אלהים^ יהי מארות ברקי[ע	[
	ובין הלילה ויהיו לאתות ולמועדים ל[ימים ושנים 15והיו למאורת	[
	ברקִע השמים להאיר על הארץ ויהי כ[ן 16	[
	את שני המארות הג[ד]לים את המאור ה[גדול	[
	[המ]אור הקטון לממשל[ת] הלילה ואת הכוכב[ים 17	[
	]]השמים ל[האיר] על הארץ 18ולמשול ב[יום	[
	] האו]ר ובין [החש]ך וירא אלהים כי טוב [19	[
section break →	] רבי]עי *vacat*]	[
Day 5	20] א]ל[הים ישרצו] המים שרץ נפש חיה וע[וף	[
	] [21ויברא אלהים את התנינים]	[
	]] הרמשת אשר שרצו המים ל[מינהם	[
	]] אלהים כי טוב 22ויבר[ך	[
	] בימ]ים והעוף ירבה ב[ארץ	[
	text missing (end of fragment 2)	

4QGen^g preserves the better part of the text covering the first five days. However, unlike 4QGen^b, it does not preserve the portion of text dealing with the end of day five and the beginning of day six. In 4QGen^g, a major division (open section) was placed after 1:5 (end of day one), 1:8 (end of day two), 1:13 (end of day three), and 1:19 (end of day four), dividing the text according to the days of creation week. In each case, the major division between sections was indicated by a sufficient blank space extending from the last word of the verse to the end of the line. Each of the new sections then commence at the beginning of the next line at the right-hand margin (see III.1). In the case of the section break after 1:13, part of the manuscript is missing on the first line of fragment 2 after ויהי בקר יום שלישי (and it was morning, a third day). It is almost certain that there was a *vacat* (section break) on this line after the end of verse 13, since there would have been more than sufficient space on the line and, furthermore, the next line below opens with the beginning of verse 14.[28]

Besides the major divisions (open sections) according to the days of creation, 4QGen^g also contains a smaller sense division (closed section) after 1:11, designated by a sufficient space in the middle of the line with the writing of the following related unit (1:12–13) beginning on that same line (see III.4). In this manner the larger unit of material covering day three (1:9–13) is subdivided. In light of 4QGen^d, it is tantalizing to wonder if another small division (closed section) was originally present here in 4QGen^g after the creation of land animals (1:25) and before the creation of mankind (1:26–27) within the larger unit of the day six material (1:24–31). Unfortunately, this portion of the text has been lost.

4QGen^h1

This manuscript was written in a late Hasmonean or early Herodian script (50–25 BC).[29] 4QGen^h1 consists of a single small fragment (2.3 cm high and 1.7 cm wide),[30] preserving a few words from Gen 1:8–10. Thus, only a small amount of textual data is available from 4QGen^h1.

4QGen^h1 (Genesis 1:8–10)	
Day 2 section break →	*vacat*]ש
Day 3	9 ויאמר] מקוה] ליבשה]

Significantly, the right margin of the column is preserved, along with the first word of four lines of text. The first line preserves part of a word from the latter part of 1:8 with only a partial ש, representing either שמים

28. While it is possible some sort of text could have been present in the now missing part, it is highly unlikely in light of the general practice of scribal reproduction of biblical scrolls found at Qumran.

29. Davila, "New Qumran Readings for Genesis One," 7.

30. Ibid.

or שני. In either case, the end of this line would have been blank.[31] This is confirmed by the fact that the second line opens with the beginning of 1:9 (ויאמר) at the right-hand margin.

Reconstruction of 4QGen[h1] (Gen 1:8–10)	
Option "A"	
Day 2 section break →	ש]מים ויהי ערב ויהי בקר יום שני *vacat*
Day 3	9ויאמר] אלהים יקוו המים מתחת השמים אל מקוה [אחד ותראה היבשה ויהי כן 10ויקרא אלהים ליבשה] ארץ ולמקוה המים קרא ימים וירא אלהים
Option "B"	
Day 2 section break →	ש]ני *vacat*
Day 3	9ויאמר] אלהים יקוו המים מתחת השמים אל מקוה [אחד ותראה היבשה ויהי כן 10ויקרא אלהים ליבשה] ארץ ולמקוה המים קרא ימים וירא אלהים

Thus, this small fragment likely contained a large division (open section) between 1:8 (end of day two) and 1:9 (beginning of day three). Not too much can be inferred from such a small amount of extant text. At the least, 4QGen[h1] attests to the scribal practice of denoting units in a text by means of spacing and this section break after 1:8 is consistent with the division of the creation account according to days observed in the other Qumran texts.

4QGen^k

This manuscript is written in Herodian script (AD 1–30).[32] 4QGen^k consists of only a few small fragments, preserving portions of Gen 1:9, 14–16, 27–28; 2:1–3; 3:1–2. The largest fragment (frag. 2) contains text from 1:14–16 and provides only a small amount of textual data for analysis.

31. The editor of 4QGen[h1] noted the major division (פ) after 1:8 in MT and that "the scribe of 4QGen[h1] similarly left the end of the line blank after v. 8" (Davila, DJD XII, 61).

32. Davila, DJD XII, 75.

4QGen^k, frag. 2 (Genesis 1:14–16)	
section break →	[ ] *vacat* [ ] [ ]
Day 4	[14 ויאמר אלה]ים יהי מארות ברקיע השמים להבדי[ן בין] [היום וב]ין הלילה והיו לאתות ולמעדים ולימים ולש[נים] [15 והיו ל]מארות ברקיע [ה]שמים להאיר על הארץ ויהי כן 16 וי[עש] *bottom margin*

The bottom margin is preserved in this fragment which is helpful in determining that the blank space above the preserved text is not a top margin. Rather, it is evident that the blank line above the preserved text is a section break following the end of day three in 1:13, confirmed by the fact that 1:14 begins on the next line at the right-hand margin. The only question that remains concerning the line in which the section break occurs is if any text was initially present at the beginning of that line prior to the blank space or if the entire line was left blank (with the previous line containing the end of 1:13). Either way, this would have been a large division (open section) between 1:13 (end of day three) and 1:14 (beginning of day four). It is acknowledged that in the case of 4QGen^k not too much can be drawn from such fragmentary textual data.[33] However, at the least, we have another witness to the scribal practice of denoting units in a text by means of spacing and this section break after 1:13 is consistent with the division of the creation account according to days observed in the other Qumran texts.

Qumran and the Structure of the Creation Account

In this survey of the Qumran Genesis manuscripts, the scribal practice of dividing the text into units by means of spacing has been observed in the creation account. A major division (open section) was placed after each day of creation week, dividing the text according to days. Consequently, these Qumran texts indicate that in the Second Temple period scribes understood the creation account as being structured according to days.

This general scribal practice of employing section breaks is also present in the medieval Masoretic Text tradition. Notably, in the Leningrad

33. For example, we cannot extrapolate how the creation account as a whole was divided in this particular text due to the lack of extant text. Divisions in the text could have been present at the same places or in different places within the text.

Codex (AD 1008) the open section breaks (major divisions) in the creation account are identical to 4QGen[b] and 4QGen[g]. Thus, this understanding of the structure of the creation account was preserved by the Masoretes.

Genesis 1 in the Leningrad Codex (Photograph by Bruce and Kenneth Zuckerman, West Semitic Research, with the collaboration of the Ancient Biblical Manuscript Center. Courtesy Russian National Library (Saltykov-Shchedrin).)

Modern Hebrew Bibles such as *Biblia Hebraica Stuttgartensia* also preserve the open section breaks in the creation account (observed in the Qumran Genesis manuscripts and the medieval Masoretic Text) with a פ

(for פתוחה – *petuchah* "open section"). While these divisions in the text of the creation account have apparently been preserved for over two millennia, one is led to ask, "How far back do these divisions in the text go?"

In the case of the Masoretic Text tradition, the section breaks in the creation account represent scribal transmission of a structure already present in the text long before, as evidenced by the Qumran Genesis manuscripts. However, in the case of the Qumran texts, do these section breaks represent the scribal transmission of a structure already present in the text or do they represent an element of interpretation by the scribes of the Qumran texts? Generally speaking, the divisions in the text were copied by the scribes from their *Vorlage* (base text). At times, however, scribes changed the divisions in the text based on their understanding of the content.[34] It is difficult to determine in some cases whether the scribes of the Qumran texts have copied the divisions (section breaks) in the text from their *Vorlage* or changed the divisions based on their own understanding of the text. In the case of the Qumran Genesis manuscripts, the general attestation to the division of the creation account according to days may represent scribal transmission of a structure already present in the text *or* an element of interpretation by the scribes of the Qumran texts. Either way, a certain structure for the creation account is being determined for the reader of the text.

The possibility that these sense divisions represent scribal transmission of a structure already present in the text leads to another question. When were these divisions of the text first used? Scholars have noted parallel ancient documents preceding our earliest extant biblical documents that already attest to the practice of dividing texts into units.[35] Thus, Tov concluded, ". . . in the wake of ancient parallels, it stands to reason that some kind of sense division was already embedded in the earliest biblical scrolls, probably spacing."[36] Consequently, it is possible that these divisions in the text were employed by the original authors/editors of the biblical texts, reflecting their understanding.[37] Nonetheless, it is difficult to determine if the divisions of the text in the biblical Qumran scrolls reflect original sense divisions due to: 1) the differences in section divisions between

34. Tov, *Scribal Practices and Approaches Reflected in the Texts Found in the Judean Desert*, 150.

35. For example, see the Elephantine papyri from the fifth century BC.

36. Tov, *Scribal Practices and Approaches Reflected in the Texts Found in the Judean Desert*, 155.

37. See Oesch, *Petucha und Setuma*.

parallel manuscripts of the same biblical compositions at Qumran and 2) differences in section divisions between the biblical Qumran texts and MT. In the case of the Qumran Genesis texts, however, there is a uniformity of structure according to days represented in the six manuscripts preserving portions of the creation account. In addition, these major divisions according to days are preserved exactly in MT. Thus, it is possible that the major divisions according to days in the creation account reflect original sense divisions. However, certainty regarding the origin (original author/editor or later scribes) of these sense divisions in the creation account remains elusive due to the fact that there are no extant Genesis texts earlier than the Qumran Genesis manuscripts. Whether the sense divisions in the creation account were part of the original structure intended at the compositional level by the author/editor of the text, or were inserted by later scribes (prior to Qumran) or the scribes of the Qumran texts, they represent an early understanding of the structure of the text.

These major divisions in the creation account also provide an occasion to take another look at a particular discussion concerning Gen 1:1–5 and the literary boundary of day one. Some hold that verse one describes the initial creative act of the heavens and the earth on day one. Verse two, beginning with a *waw* disjunctive, then functions like a parenthetical statement, describing the initial state of "the heavens and the earth" as they were created in verse one. Verse three then moves the narration forward with a *wayyiqtol* verb, describing God's creation of light. In this view, the first five verses (1:1–5) constitute the creative acts of day one.[38] The following verses (1:6–31) then record the forming and filling of the heavens and the earth with the creation of the firmament (day two), dry land and plants (day three), the sun, moon, and stars (day four), sea creatures and flying creatures (day five), and land animals and man (day six). However, some hold that day one of creation week begins in verse two. Within this view, verse one is understood as either: a) an introductory heading, summarizing the content of the creation account[39] or b) a statement recording the initial creation of the universe (including the sun, moon, stars, animals, etc.).[40] Yet, others hold that the first two verses serve as a preface to day one which

38. For example, see Leupold, *Exposition of Genesis*, vol. 1, 42; Young, *Studies in Genesis One*, 87–89, 103–05; Fields, *Unformed and Unfilled*, 222.

39. For example, see Cassuto, *A Commentary on the Book of Genesis: From Adam to Noah*, 13, 19–30.

40. For example, see Sailhamer, *The Pentateuch as Narrative*, 82–89.

begins in verse three. Within this view also, verse one is variously understood as either: a) an introductory heading[41] or b) a statement recording the initial creation of "the heavens and the earth."[42] The beginning of day one in either verse two or verse three allows for an undisclosed period of time prior to day one of creation week. Concerning this discussion of the literary boundary of day one, what can be gleaned from the Qumran Genesis manuscripts?

4QGen[b] and 4QGen[g] preserve the opening verses of the creation account and in both cases the first major section break occurs after 1:5, which seems to indicate that 1:1–5 was understood as constituting the creative acts of day one. However, the lack of a section break (open or closed) after Gen 1:1 or 1:2 does not necessarily demonstrate that the first five verses were understood as constituting the creative acts of day one. It is conceivable that a section break (open or closed) was not placed after 1:1 or 1:2 due to the small amount of text involved prior to the first major section break after 1:5 and/or due to the natural flow of the opening five verses of the creation account. However, in the creation account of the Qumran Genesis manuscripts, section breaks regularly occur within smaller intervals of text compared to the typically larger section divisions in many Qumran scrolls. Thus, the small amount of text prior to the first major section break (after 1:5) was not, by necessity, a deterrent for placing a section break after 1:1 or 1:2. Also, the natural flow of the opening five verses can just as easily point to the fact that they are to be read as a single unit constituting the creative acts of day one. In light of the section breaks observed in the creation account, it appears more problematic to imagine that the author or scribe understood 1:1 and/or 1:2 to be distinct from 1:3–5, without indicating this in any way. The section breaks in the Qumran Genesis manuscripts provide positive evidence for a particular literary structure of the creation account according to days, with no suggestion that 1:1–2 were separated from 1:3–5. Taken straightforwardly, the positive textual evidence indicates that the first five verses were understood as constituting the creative acts of day one.

41. For example, see Waltke, *Genesis: A Commentary*, 58–60.

42. For example, see Collins, *Genesis 1–4*, 42–43.

Concluding Remarks

An important aspect to understanding a biblical text is the compositional strategy or arrangement of the material itself. Notably, several Qumran Genesis manuscripts (4QGen^{b}, 4QGen^{d}, 4QGen^{g}, 4QGen^{h1}, 4QGen^{k}), preserving portions of the creation account, exhibit the ancient scribal practice of denoting units in a text by means of spacing. A major division was placed after each day of creation week, dividing the text according to days. It is possible that the major divisions (open sections), according to days in the creation account, reflect original sense divisions. At the least, these Qumran texts reflect an ancient understanding of the creation account during the Second Temple period. There is no doubt, however, that the section divisions observed in the Qumran texts are of great value to modern biblical scholarship. In reference to Josef M. Oesch's work on section divisions in ancient texts, James Barr observed that ". . . a detailed investigation of an apparently dry and technical textual matter can lead to far-reaching consequences for the understanding of the Bible."[43] Indeed, we are used to thinking of interpretation as something that happens within texts (e.g. rewritten texts) or in dialogue with texts (e.g. *pesharim*), but the Genesis texts from Qumran highlight how interpretation also happens around the text at a scribal level.[44] Thus, the sense divisions reflected in the Qumran Genesis manuscripts invite further analysis of the literary structure of the creation account.

43. Barr, review of Oesch, *Petucha und Setuma*, 472.

44. This basic observation was noted by Andrew Perrin after reading an earlier version of this chapter.

CHAPTER FOUR

QUMRAN INTERPRETATION OF THE GENESIS CREATION ACCOUNT

WORDS OF THE LUMINARIES (4Q504)

Discovery of 4Q504

A LITURGICAL WORK KNOWN as the *Words of the Luminaries* (4Q504) was discovered in 1952 among the roughly 600 manuscripts (represented by thousands of fragments) in Cave 4. This manmade cave is situated in the soft sandstone marl terrace upon which Khirbet Qumran sits and also lies within close proximity to the site itself (within the Sabbath limit of 1,000 cubits). In March of 1952, scholars had conducted a cave survey in which they explored over 200 caves in the limestone cliffs around Qumran. However, they did not explore the sandstone marl terrace upon which Khirbet Qumran sits.[1] And this proved to be significant. Several months later, the Bedouin, who had also been exploring the region for more scrolls,

1. Cf. de Vaux, *Archaeology and the Dead Sea Scrolls*, 52. Roland de Vaux noted, "During this exploration we restricted our research to the rock cliffs and did not examine the marl terrace stretching in front of them. The reason was that the nature of the terrain is such as to exclude in this marl terrace the presence of any natural caves suitable for human use. All that we noticed were cavities eroded by water which were archaeologically barren. In this we erred. Six months after we had left the Bedouin returned, and discovered a cave artificially hollowed out in the marl terrace and containing an immense number of manuscript fragments (Cave 4Q)."

found the cave and they were able to remove thousands of fragments before scholars were informed and uncovered their clandestine activity. An official excavation of the cave, led by Roland de Vaux, was then conducted September 22–29, 1952, in which hundreds more fragments were found.[2] The thousands of scroll fragments found by the Bedouin were then obtained by the Palestine Archaeological Museum in Jerusalem through several large purchases over the next few years.[3] A preliminary publication of 4Q504 appeared soon after in 1961.[4] However, it would not be until 1982 that the official edition of 4Q504 was published by Maurice Baillet in volume 7 of the *Discoveries in the Judaean Desert* series.

Physical Description of 4Q504

4Q504 is a fragmentary Hebrew text written in Jewish script. Paleographic analysis indicates that 4Q504 was written in an early Hasmonean hand, dating the manuscript to the middle of the second century BC (c. 150 BC).[5] While many scrolls from Cave 4 are extremely deteriorated and damaged, 4Q504 is relatively well preserved, consisting of forty-eight (or forty-nine) fragments.[6] These extant fragments contain prayers for each day of the

2. Accounts of the discovery and subsequent excavation of Cave 4 include: de Vaux, *Archaeology of the Dead Sea Scrolls*, 52; Trever, *The Untold Story of Qumran*, 148–49; Cross, *The Ancient Library of Qumran*, 32–34; Fields, "Discovery and Purchase," 211; VanderKam and Flint, *The Meaning of the Dead Sea Scrolls*, 16–18.

3. The Palestine Archaeological Museum was able to obtain the thousands of fragments from Cave 4 through funding from the Jordanian government, the Vatican Library, University of Oxford, University of Manchester, University of Heidelberg, McGill University, McCormick Theological Seminary of Chicago, and All Souls Church of New York. Cf. Zias, "Palestine Archaeological Museum," 635.

4. Baillet, "Un recueil liturgique de Qumran, Grotte 4: 'Les Paroles des Luminaires.'"

5. Baillet, DJD VII, 137; Davila, *Liturgical Works*, 239; Falk, "Words of the Luminaries," 1960. Baillet provided a more detailed discussion of the paleography and date of 4Q504 in his preliminary publication in 1961 ("Un recueil liturgique de Qumran, Grotte 4: 'Les Paroles des Luminaires,'" 235–38). Concerning the date of 4Q504, Geza Vermes stated that Baillet "attributes to it an exaggeratedly early date, the mid-second century BCE" (*The Complete Dead Sea Scrolls in English*, 377). Vermes, however, did not provide any reasons for rejecting Baillet's date. Esther Chazon, on the other hand, noted, "Even if we take into account that paleographical dating is approximate and that allowance must be made for a span of years, it is reasonable to place this copy in the second century" ("*4QDibHam*: Liturgy or Literature?" 455n19).

6. Baillet notes forty-nine fragments (DJD VII, 137, plates XLIX–LIII), while Davila counts forty-eight (*Liturgical Works*, 239). In an updated edition of 4Q504, Parry and

week. Fragments 1 and 2 are fairly large and contain portions of seven columns of text covering the prayers for the fifth and sixth days of the week, along with the Sabbath. Fragments 3–8, though not as large, are moderate in size, covering the prayers for the first through fourth days of the week. In particular, fragment 8 preserves portions of 15 lines of text from the first column, containing the prayer for the first day of the week which recalls the creation of Adam. The verso side of this fragment preserves the title of the work: דברי המארות (*Words of the Luminaries*). The rest of the fragments are much smaller and, thus, are more difficult to place. Based on the material remains, it is likely that 4Q504 originally consisted of at least twenty columns of text,[7] with about 22 lines each.[8] The final column was written on the back of the scroll. Part of this column is preserved on the verso side of fragment 2.

4Q504: A Qumran Composition?

Is 4Q504 a Qumran sectarian composition? It is apparent that 4Q504 is a *Jewish* composition. For example, it is a Hebrew text found in the Judean Desert. In addition, this liturgical text recalls various periods of Israel's history. However, it is unlikely that 4Q504 was composed at Qumran based on two particular observations.[9] First, based on the paleographic dating of 4Q504 to around 150 BC, this manuscript was likely composed before the sectarian group settled at Qumran.[10] Second, this manuscript does not contain any distinct sectarian language or theology that is found in the

Tov also count forty-eight fragments (*The Dead Sea Scrolls Reader*, 5:240–60).

7. According to Davila, the manuscript originally likely consisted of 20 columns (*Liturgical Works*, 239). Parry and Tov indicate the manuscript originally contained 23 columns (*The Dead Sea Scrolls Reader*, 5:240–60).

8. Davila, *Liturgical Works*, 239. The amount of text preserved in fragments 1–6 appears to confirm this. See Baillet, DJD VII, plates XLIX–LII; Parry and Tov, *The Dead Sea Scrolls Reader*, 5:240–54.

9. See Chazon, "Is *Divrei Ha-Me'orot* a Sectarian Prayer?" 3–17; "Words of the Luminaries," 989; Falk, "Words of the Luminaries," 1960; Davila, *Liturgical Works*, 242.

10. While this may be the case, the origin of the sectarian movement itself also predated their occupation at Qumran. Thus, the dating of the manuscript alone does not rule out the possibility that 4Q504 could have been composed by the sectarian group prior to their settlement at Qumran. The dating of the manuscript does appear to rule out the possibility that 4Q504 was originally composed at Qumran.

sectarian texts at Qumran.[11] Rather, as Daniel Falk observed, these prayers "reflect typical Jewish concerns for Israel's covenant with God."[12]

While this Jewish document was likely not composed by the Qumran community (יחד), it was evidently preserved and used for liturgical purposes at Qumran. The content in the text may not be uniquely sectarian, but neither is it inconsistent with Qumran thought.[13] In other words, 4Q504 was usable material at Qumran. Also, 4Q504 was found in Cave 4, which gives evidence of having been a dwelling space directly connected to the Qumran site.[14] The manuscript was likely present in the Qumran community before it was conveniently and hastily placed in this nearby cave as the Roman legion approached in AD 68. Further, a second copy of the *Words of the Luminaries*, labeled 4Q506, was found in Cave 4 and is dated to around AD 50.[15] This copy was written roughly two hundred years after 4Q504 and, according to Esther Chazon, attests to "this liturgy's long life at Qumran, where it would have been integrated into the daily prayer ritual of the Qumran community."[16] James Davila also noted, "The fact that copies

11. However, the extant text of 4Q504 is incomplete, making it difficult to determine with absolute certainty whether the text originally would have had any sectarian language or not. Perhaps, the strongest indication that 4Q504 did not contain any distinct sectarian language or theology is its absence in the extant text containing the prayer for the sixth day, covering the Second Temple period (cf. frags. 1–2).

12. Falk, "Words of the Luminaries," 1960.

13. James Davila also made this observation, stating, "There are no explicitly sectarian literary characteristics in the text . . . but neither is there anything in the content that would have been unacceptable to the members of the Qumran community" (*Liturgical Works*, 242).

14. See de Vaux, *Archaeology and the Dead Sea Scrolls*, 52–57. Early on, Roland de Vaux set forth several evidences indicating Cave 4 was a dwelling space connected to the Qumran site: 1) The cave lies in close proximity (within a hundred meters) to the Qumran site. 2) The cave was artificially hollowed out and contained objects used for habitation. 3) Storage jars, lids, bowls, jugs, a lamp, and scrolls were found in the cave, belonging to the same period the community inhabited Khirbet Qumran. 4) The pottery in the cave belongs to the same types found in the Qumran site. See also Crawford, "A View from the Caves," 30–39, 69. Sidnie White Crawford has also provided a number of evidences: 1) The cave lies in close proximity (within the Sabbath limit of 1,000 cubits) to the Qumran site. 2) The cave was well lit and ventilated with flat floors and storage niches. 3) Storage jars, lamps, bowls, cooking utensils, and scrolls were found in the cave. 4) There were also trails leading from the Qumran site to the marl terrace caves, which include Cave 4.

15. Baillet, DJD VII, 170; Chazon, "Words of the Luminaries (4Q504–506)," 1349; Falk, "Words of the Luminaries," 1960.

16. Chazon, "Words of the Luminaries (4Q504–506)," 1349.

of it were made over a period of as much as two centuries makes it likely that it was put to use by the sectarians . . . ."[17] Thus, it appears that 4Q504 was not composed at Qumran, but was accepted and used by the Essenes at Qumran.[18]

History of Research on 4Q504

This brief survey of the history of research on 4Q504 will focus on some of the primary contributions to the study of this text. Attention is given, in particular, to select studies that are relevant to the current discussion on Qumran interpretation of the Genesis creation account.

Maurice Baillet

A preliminary publication of 4Q504 was produced in 1961 by Maurice Baillet in an article, "Un recueil liturgique de Qumran, Grotte 4: 'Les Paroles des Luminaires.'" Though he discussed various aspects of the manuscript, he published only fragments 1 and 2.[19] The publication of all the fragments would have to wait until 1982, when Baillet's official edition of 4Q504 was produced in volume 7 of the *Discoveries in the Judaean Desert* series. This edition includes a general description of the text, a transcription of the text, notes on the readings, a translation of the text, line-by-line commentary on the entire text, and plates of the text. Particularly relevant to this study on Qumran interpretation of the creation account is the material pertaining to fragment 8. Baillet's publications provided the foundation for subsequent 4Q504 studies, which began to surface in the early 1990s.

17. Davila, *Liturgical Works*, 242.

18. Whether or not the sectarian community employed the text in the manner intended by its author, this manuscript contains particular understandings of the creation account attested at Qumran.

19. The publication of fragments 1 and 2 included a transcription and translation of the text, notes on the text, line-by-line commentary on the text, and plates. Other aspects of the manuscript, such as paleography and orthography, among other things, were discussed.

Esther Chazon

Esther Chazon made significant contributions to the study of 4Q504, beginning with her 1991 dissertation, "תעודה ליטורגית מקומראן והשלכותיה: 'דברי המארות'."[20] That same year, Chazon published an article, "4QDibHam: Liturgy or Literature?" showing that 4Q504 is a deliberate literary composition that was liturgical in function. In 1992, she published a chapter titled, "Is *Divrei Ha-Me'orot* a Sectarian Prayer?" Then, in 1997, Chazon included a discussion of 4Q504 in a book chapter titled, "The Creation and Fall of Adam in the Dead Sea Scrolls." She discussed the juxtaposition of the Eden and Flood accounts in the prayer for the first day, noting that "sin and its concomitant punishment form the theme which binds this historical section together."[21] Thus, she concluded that "the reminiscences of past sin and punishment motivate the petition" in 4Q504.[22] Her study of 4Q504 in this chapter reveals how the creation account was employed in this liturgical text. Chazon has also published other works on 4Q504, including general articles in the *Encyclopedia of the Dead Sea Scrolls* (2000) and the *Eerdmans Dictionary of Early Judaism* (2010).

Daniel K. Falk

In 1998, Daniel Falk published *Daily, Sabbath, and Festival Prayers in the Dead Sea Scrolls*, in which, he included a chapter on 4Q504. Falk addresses the date and provenance of the text, the form and content of the prayers, and the liturgical use of the text. Another treatment of 4Q504 appeared in 2013 in the multi-volume work, *Outside the Bible: Ancient Jewish Writings Related to Scripture.*[23] Falk introduces the text with a summary of the content, literary structure, and its significance as the earliest known collection of daily prayers. The primary value of this work is the line-by-line commentary on the text of 4Q504, accompanying the translation.

20. Chazon's research was conducted at the Hebrew University of Jerusalem.

21. Chazon, "The Creation and Fall of Adam in the Dead Sea Scrolls," 15.

22. Ibid., 21.

23. Falk, "Words of the Luminaries," 1960–84.

James R. Davila

In 2000, James Davila published *Liturgical Works*, which contains commentary on various liturgical texts from Qumran, including 4Q504. Davila introduces the text with a general description of the manuscript and its structure and content. Most pertinent to this study on Qumran interpretation of the creation account is his line-by-line commentary on the text.

Content and Literary Structure of 4Q504

The *Words of the Luminaries* (4Q504) is a liturgical work containing prayers for each day of the week. The title of this composition, דברי המארות (*Words of the Luminaries*), is preserved on the outside of the scroll on the back of the first column (fragment 8). There are several possibilities for the meaning of המארות (the luminaries) in the title.[24] The Hebrew Bible uses the term in various ways, including as a reference to the heavenly bodies (sun, moon, and stars) that regulate times, seasons, days, and years (Gen 1:14–19). This particular meaning of the term is attested in the Qumran sectarian literature (cf. 1QS X:3). However, other Qumran texts also use this term in reference to angels (cf. 1QH[a] IX:11; 1QM X:11).[25] Another suggestion is that this term refers metaphorically to the priests, that is, "those through whom the 'light of God' was made manifest."[26] This idea is attested at Qumran (1QS II:1–3) and in other Second Temple period literature (*Sir* 45:17; *Test Levi* 4:3; 18:2–4), including the New Testament (Matt. 5:14–16). In the context of 4Q504, Chazon's proposal appears most likely—that the title "relates to the scroll's liturgical function in daily communal prayer."[27] דברי refers to the words of the prayers and המארות refers to the days/times assigned for these prayers as determined by the heavenly bodies.[28] In this vein, Falk notes that the title "probably implies that the

24. See Baillet, DJD VII, 138–39.

25. Baillet noted, "Cependant, vu le lien étroit entre les astres et les anges, il est vraisemblable que les luminaires sont considérés ici comme des êtres pensants, et donc doués de la parole. Se reporter par example à 4Q511. On sait aussi que les étoiles symbolisent des anges en I Hen 861, 3 881" (DJD VII, 138).

26. Wise et al., *The Dead Sea Scrolls: A New Translation*, 522. This was also suggested as a possibility by Baillet (DJD VII, 139).

27. Chazon, "Words of the Luminaries," 989.

28. Ibid. Chazon added, "The title might further allude to recitation at the time of the interchange of the luminaries in the morning and evening, a standard time for prayer in

prayers are words to be recited at times determined by the lights in the sky, presumably, at sunset and sunrise."[29]

General Structure of 4Q504

Though the manuscript is fragmentary, there is enough text preserved to discern the basic structure of the composition. 4Q504 consists of a petitionary prayer for each day of the week and a doxological prayer for the Sabbath. Each prayer contained a title, indicating the day of the week it was to be recited (titles for the fourth day and Sabbath are extant).

The six weekday prayers follow the same basic structure. Each prayer begins with the phrase זכור אדוני (Remember, Lord), which introduces a request for the Lord to remember wonders He has performed. The prayer then recalls certain historical events, followed by a petition to God for either physical deliverance (third, fourth and sixth days) or spiritual strengthening (first and fifth days).[30] A closing benediction blesses God and concludes with the response "Amen, Amen." In addition to this shared structure, the historical recollections for the weekday prayers progress in chronological order, beginning with the creation and Fall of Adam in the prayer for the first day and ending with events in the post-exilic period in the prayer for the sixth day.

The Sabbath prayer differs from the weekday prayers in genre, content, and structure. The Sabbath prayer is doxological in nature. The extant text indicates this prayer consisted of multiple hymns or a single hymn with multiple stanzas, containing invitations to praise God for His creation. The hymn(s) for the Sabbath prayer (instead of a petition) underscores the Sabbath as being holy and set apart from the rest of the week. Chazon observed that the theme of creation in the Sabbath hymn(s) ". . . does bring this weekly liturgy full circle."[31]

---

both sectarian and nonsectarian circles."

29. Falk, "Words of the Luminaries," 1963; See also Davila, *Liturgical Works*, 240–41.

30. Chazon, "'דברי המארות': תעודה ליטורגית מקומראן והשלכותיה"; see also "Words of the Luminaries," 989.

31. Chazon, "Words of the Luminaries (4Q504–506)," 1349.

Type of Liturgy	Literary Structure for 4Q504
	Prayers for Days 1–6
Petitionary Prayer / Communal Lament	*Title:* indicates the day the prayer is to be recited *Introductory Request:* "Remember, Lord . . ." *Historical Recollections:* recalls historical events that justify the petition *Petition:* requests God for deliverance (physical and/or spiritual) *Benediction:* invokes blessing to God *Response:* "Amen, Amen"
	Prayer for the Sabbath Day
Thanksgiving Hymn(s)	*Title:* "Thanksgiving Hymns/Praises for the Sabbath day" *Invitations to praise God for His creation:* "Give thanks to [the Lord]," "[bless] His holy name forever . . . ," ". . . sing joyously to God"

Structure for the Prayer on the First Day

Particular to our study is the prayer for the first day, contained in fragments 8, 9, 6, and 4. The first column of the scroll (frags. 8, 9) begins with the introductory request, [זכו]ר אד[ו]נ[י] (Remember, Lord), asking God to remember "wonders from of old and awesome deeds" that He has done (frag. 8, lines 1–3). The prayer then recalls the creation and Fall of Adam (frag. 8, lines 4–10), retelling portions of Genesis 1:26–3:19. This retelling includes God's forming Adam in His image (Gen 1:26–27; 2:7) and breathing the breath of life into him (Gen 2:7), the planting of the Garden of Eden (Gen 2:8) and Adam's dominion in it (Gen 2:15; cf. 1:28), the prohibition given to Adam (Gen 2:16–17; 3:11), and the subsequent disobedience and punishment of Adam (Gen 3:19). This is followed by a recollection of the Flood (frags. 8 and 9) and then the Exodus from Egypt (frag. 6). The juxtaposition of these historical events (Creation/Fall, Flood, and Exodus) is attested elsewhere at Qumran in *Paraphrase of Genesis and Exodus* (4Q422). Based on these historical recollections, the petition to God is then made (frag. 4). The extant portion of text includes the petition for God to "Redeem us and [please] forgive our iniquities and si[ns]" (lines 6–7). Next, the extant text of lines 8–10 contains content concerning the "Torah which [You] commanded by the hand of Mos[es]." Perhaps this portion of text originally contained a request for God to "teach us/make known to us the Torah." Last, is the petition for God to "Circumcise the foreskin of [our heart] . . . Strengthen our heart to . . . walk in Your ways" (lines 11–13). The prayer then concludes with the benediction and response: "[Blessed be] the Lord who has made know[n] . . . [ ] Amen, Amen" (lines 14–15). An outline of the prayer for the first day provided here maintains a degree of tentativeness due to the fragmentary nature of this manuscript.

Structure for the Prayer on the First Day	
Introductory Request	"Remember, Lord" (frag. 8, line 1)
Historical Recollections	• Creation and Fall of Adam (frag 8) • The Flood (frags. 8 and 9) • The Exodus/Wilderness (frag. 6)
Petition to God	• "Redeem us and [please] forgive our iniquities and si[ns]" (frag. 4, lines 6–7) • [Make known to us (?)] "Torah which [You] commanded by the hand of Mos[es]." (frag. 4, lines 8–10) • "Circumcise the foreskin of [our heart] . . . Strengthen our heart to . . . walk in Your ways" (frag. 4, lines 11–13).
Benediction and Response	"[Blessed be] the Lord who has made know[n] . . . [ ] [ ] Amen, Amen" (Frag 4, lines 14–15).

The Introductory Request of the Prayer for the First Day

The opening lines of column I recount the creation of Adam at the beginning of the prayer for the first day. The extant text of the first line begins with the request, [זכו]ר אד[ו]נ[י] כיא מעפ[ ] (Remember Lord that from . . .). The exact reading of the first line is difficult to determine with certainty due to the damaged or missing portion of text. The fourth word is cut off with only part of the first three letters preserved. The remains of the third letter was understood by Baillet to represent a מ, hence rendering the text as מעמ[ ].[32] However, based on an enlargement of an electronic image of

32. Baillet, DJD VII, 162; See also Parry and Tov, *The Dead Sea Scrolls Reader*, 5:240.

fragment 8, the third letter could also represent a פ, thus rendering the text as [ר]מעפ (from dust).[33] Chazon suggested a possible reading (with partial reconstruction) for line 1: [זכו]ר אד[ו]נ[י] כיא מעפ[ר יצרתנו] (Remember Lord that from dust You formed us).[34] This reconstruction was also adopted by Falk.[35] This reading of line 1 dovetails with line 4, both of which appear to refer to the creation of humanity from dust as recorded in Genesis 2:7.

> *4Q504* (I:1) "Remember Lord that from dust ([ר]מעפ) . . ."
>
> *4Q504* (I:4) "[Adam] our [fa]ther You formed (יצרתה) . . ."
>
> Genesis 2:7 "And the Lord God formed (וייצר) man of the dust (עפר) of the ground . . ."

Further, this reading of line 1 appears to be bookended with the latter part of this historical recollection in line 9: [בשר הואה ולעפר ה[ואה ישוב] (he is flesh and to dust h[e returns]).[36] Thus, it seems that the likely reading for line 1 is: [זכו]ר אד[ו]נ[י] כיא מעפ[ר יצרתנו] (Remember Lord that from dust You formed us).

The extant text of line 2 reads: [ ]קתנו ואתה חי עול[מים]. The first part of the initial word in the line is missing. One possible reconstruction for the missing text at the beginning of the line is: [ולעפר תשו]קתנו ([and to dust is] our [des]ire).[37] This language is found in a similar context in a sectarian text known as the *Community Rule* (1QS XI:22): ולעפר תשוקתו (and to dust is his desire). The previous line in 1QS (XI:21) speaks of man as being מעפר (from dust). Likewise, this reconstruction in 4Q504, column I, line 2, is preceded by a reference to man being formed מעפר (from dust). The second part of line 2 reads: ואתה חי עול[מים] (but You live for[ever]). The depiction of humanity as being formed from dust (line 1) and returning to dust (line 9; also line 2a?) is contrasted here with God's eternality ("but You live for[ever]," line 2b). Line 3 then recalls that this eternal God has done "wonders from of old and awesome deeds." Thus, the first three lines form the introductory request for God to remember: a) "from dust

33. See PAM 42.439 image.

34. Chazon, "'תעודה ליטורגית מקומראן והשלכותיה: 'דברי המארות," 144.

35. Falk, "Words of the Luminaries," 1963.

36. The fragmentary nature of this column makes it difficult to determine precisely where this historical recollection ends and the next one begins. What appears to be a small *vacat* in line 10 may indicate the end of this section.

37. תשוקה refers to "desire" or "longing." Cf. BDB, 1003; HALOT, 1801–02. This term occurs only three times in the Hebrew Bible (Gen 3:16; 4:7; Song of Songs 7:10).

You formed us," b) "but You are eternal," and c) You have done "wonders from of old and awesome deeds." Some of God's wondrous acts in history are then recited, beginning with the creation of Adam.

The Creation of Adam in the Likeness of God's Glory

Line 4 begins the retelling of the creation of Adam: [אדם א]בינו יצרתה בדמות כבוד[כה] ([Adam] our [fa]ther You formed in the likeness of [Your] glory). This line combines elements from Genesis 1:26 and 2:7. The opening words, "Adam our father You formed (יצרתה)," allude to Genesis 2:7: "Then the LORD God formed (וייצר) man of the dust (עפר) of the ground." Though the first part of line 4 is no longer extant, the allusion to 2:7 suggests the possibility that this line may have contained another reference to Adam being made "from dust" (מעפר). The identification of Adam as "our father" is not explicitly stated in Genesis 1–3 (though it is presumed in Gen 3:20). In this way, the prayer acknowledges that the Jewish people are descendants of Adam, the first human. This idea is attested elsewhere in Second Temple period literature (cf. *Jub* 2:23; *Wis* 10:1).[38]

The second part of line 4, בדמות כבוד[כה] (in the likeness of [Your] glory), alludes to Gen 1:26: "Then God said, 'Let Us make man in Our image, according to Our likeness (כדמותנו).'" This language also echoes Genesis 5:1, which reiterates that God made Adam "in the likeness (בדמות) of God." Concerning the use of this phrase, "in the likeness of Your glory," Falk has suggested, "By the time of these prayers, Jews respectfully avoided speaking directly about God in human terms, and so used indirect expressions like 'glory' of God."[39] This reference to Adam being formed in the likeness of God's glory (line 4) supplements, quite strikingly, the contrast between humans made from dust and the eternal God (lines 1–2). Like the biblical account, this prayer presents Adam as made from dust, yet elevated to a privileged status in God's creation. The idea that Adam somehow shared in (or perhaps reflected) the glory of God is attested in antiquity. Other Qumran texts such as the *Community Rule* (1QS IV:23) and *Damascus Document* (CD III:20) refer to the "glory of Adam" (כבוד אדם). In addition,

38. *Jubilees* 2:23: "There were twenty-two chief men from Adam until Jacob . . ." (Translation from Kugel, "Jubilees," 292); *Wisdom of Solomon* 10:1: "Wisdom protected the first-formed father of the world, when he alone had been created" (Translation from Enns, "Wisdom of Solomon," 2179).

39. Falk, "Words of the Luminaries," 1964.

the pseudepigraphal work known as *3 Baruch* (or *Apocalypse of Baruch*)[40] refers to Adam's sin and subsequent loss of the "glory of God" (*3 Apoc Bar* 4:16): ". . . just as Adam through this tree was condemned and was stripped of the glory of God."[41]

The Creation of Adam with Knowledge

Line 5 continues this retelling of Genesis 2:7: [נשמת חיים נ]פחתה באפו [. . .] ובינה ודעת ([the breath of life] You [br]eathed into his nostrils, and understanding and knowledge [. . .]). There is missing text at the end of this line, immediately following the phrase ובינה ודעת (and understanding and knowledge). The use of second person verbs in the immediately surrounding context (יצרתה line 4, נפחתה line 5, המשלתה line 6) indicates some sort of second person verb was likely present, denoting the giving of understanding and knowledge to Adam. In the official DJD edition, Baillet reconstructed the text as ובינה ודעת [מלאתה אותו] (with knowledge and understanding [You filled him]).[42] Parry and Tov also adopted this reconstruction.[43] Chazon recognized this reconstruction as a possibility,[44] but also suggested other possible options: a) נתתה בלבו (You gave his mind),[45] b) שמתה בלבו (You placed in his mind),[46] c) למדתה אותו (You taught him),[47] and d) חוננתה לו (You gave graciously/showed favor to him).[48]

This idea of God giving Adam knowledge *prior to* his eating from "the tree of the knowledge of good and evil" (cf. Gen 2:17; 3:5–7) is not explicitly stated in the biblical creation account. However, the Genesis account does indicate that Adam indeed had knowledge, for example, of God's blessings

40. *3 Baruch* is generally dated to the late first-century or second-century AD.

41. Translation from Zingerman, "3 Baruch," 1594.

42. Baillet, DJD VII, 162. Cf. *Ben Sira* 17:7: "He filled them with knowledge and understanding . . ." (Translation from Wright III, "Wisdom of Ben Sira," 2254).

43. Parry and Tov, *The Dead Sea Scrolls Reader*, 5:240–41.

44. Chazon, "'תעודה ליטורגית מקומראן והשלכותיה: 'דברי המארות," 145.

45. Cf. *Ben Sira* 17:6: "Discretion and tongue and eyes, ears and a mind for thinking He gave them" (Translation from Wright III, "Wisdom of Ben Sira," 2254).

46. Cf. 4Q511, frag. 28: שמתה דעת בסוד עפרי (You have placed knowledge in the foundation of my dust).

47. Cf. Psalm 94:10: המלמד אדם דעת (He who teaches man knowledge).

48. Cf. 11QPs[a] XIX:14: רוח אמונה ודעת חונני (Graciously give me a spirit of faithfulness and knowledge).

and commands (Gen 1:28–30), his role in serving God in the Garden (Gen 2:15), and God's prohibition (2:16–17) among other things. All of Adam's knowledge concerned that which was "good" as God had originally intended. Then, after Adam ate from the prohibited tree (Gen 3:6), he and his wife would know not only "good," but also "evil" (cf. Gen 3:7–5:5).[49] Consistent with the biblical account, this retelling in 4Q504 introduces this idea of the creation of Adam with "understanding and knowledge" in line 5, prior to the prohibition (line 8) and subsequent punishment for his disobedience (line 9). This retelling makes no mention of Adam possessing knowledge of both good *and evil* prior to his disobedience.[50]

Knowledge appears to be a major theme in this prayer for the first day. The prayer begins by recalling God's creation of Adam with knowledge (דעת) (frag. 8, line 5). A reference is then made to God's knowledge: "And You, You know (ידעתה)" (frag. 8, line 10). In the petitionary part of the prayer, a reference is made to God's knowledge of man's thoughts: "[Fo]r You are the God of knowledge (אל הדעות), [and] every thought [of our hearts] is be[fore Y]ou" (frag. 4, lines 4–5a). The prayer then acknowledges that God gives knowledge to people: "These things we know (ידענו) because You graciously gave u[s Your] H[oly] Spirit" (frag. 4, line 5b). The closing benediction reiterates this theme of knowledge: "[Blessed be] the Lord who has made know[n to us] . . . Amen, Amen" (frag. 4, lines 14–15). Thus, this theme of "knowledge" also forms bookends around the prayer, apparently linking the people praying this prayer to Adam their father (cf. frag. 8, lines 4–5). Just as God gave knowledge to Adam who dwelt in Eden, so also God has given knowledge to his descendants who dwelt in the Promised Land.

The Creation of Adam with Dominion

Line 6 reads: [בג]ן עדן אשר נטעתה המשלת[ה אותו] ([In the Gard]en of Eden which You planted, Yo[u] gave [him] dominion). This line draws from

49. This knowledge of "evil" included: pain (3:16), a relationship of conflict (3:16), a cursed creation (3:17–19), toil (3:17), death of animals (3:21), expulsion from the Garden of Eden (3:22–24), murder of their own son (4:1–15), Adam's own death (5:5). It can be argued that if Adam would not have disobeyed God, then he would have not "known" evil such as he experienced.

50. Unlike 4Q504, another Second Temple period text known as *Ben Sira* teaches that from the beginning (prior to Adam's disobedience) God "filled them with knowledge and understanding, and showed them good and evil" (*Sir* 17:7).

Gen 1:26, 28; 2:8, 15. In particular, המשלתה (You gave dominion/caused to rule) alludes to Gen 1:26, 28:

> Then God said, "Let Us make man in Our image, according to Our likeness; **let them have dominion** (וירדו) over the fish of the sea, over the birds of the air, and over the cattle, over all the earth and over every creeping thing that creeps on the earth." . . . Then God blessed them and God said to them, "Be fruitful and multiply; fill the earth and subdue it; **and have dominion** (ורדו) over the fish of the sea, over the birds of the air, and over every living thing that moves on the earth."

Notably, 4Q504 (frag. 8, line 6) employs the verb משל while the Genesis account uses רדה. The use of משל instead of רדה, in the context of creation, occurs in Psalm 8:7 (MT): "You have made him to have dominion (תמשילהו - root משל) over the works of Your hands." In addition, other Qumran texts employ משל in the context of the creation of man. 4Q287 (frag. 4, line 2) reads: "and You have given mankind dominion (ותמשל)." Similarly, 4Q381 (frag. 1, line 7) states: "And by His Spirit, He appointed them to rule (למשל) over all of these on the earth." A wisdom text known as 4QInstruction makes reference to the Garden of Eden, followed by the statement, "And over it, He has given you dominion (המשילכה), to work it and keep it" (4Q423 frag. 2, line 2). The phrase "and over it" (ובו) refers to the "garden" mentioned in the previous line.[51] This passage in 4Q423 refers to the dominion given to the *mebin* ("understanding "one"), who is likened to Adam, over the "Garden of Eden," which is said to produce wisdom.

4Q504 (frag. 8, line 6), indicates that Adam was given dominion "in the Garden of Eden" (בג]ן עדן]) which God planted (cf. Gen 2:8). Thus, 4Q504 reworks the giving of Adam's dominion (Gen 1:26–28) into the Eden narrative (Gen 2–3). Though the fragmentary nature of the text precludes any certainty, 4Q504 appears to limit the focus on Adam's dominion to the Garden of Eden, whereas the Genesis account states that God gave Adam dominion "over all the earth" (cf. Gen 1:26, 28).

The Garden of Eden as a Land of Glory

Lines 6–7 preserve a description of the Garden of Eden, along with Adam's role in it. Line 6 refers to the "Garden of Eden which You planted," alluding

51. The understanding of ובו (and over it) as a reference to the "garden" is reinforced by the following phrase, "to work it and keep it" (cf. Gen 2:15).

to Gen 2:8. The extant text of line 7 then describes the garden with language not directly found in the Genesis creation account: ולתהלך בארץ כבוד (and to walk in a land of glory).[52] What does this reference to the Garden of Eden as a "land of glory" entail? Though the term כבוד is often understood as "glory," it can also refer to "abundance" and/or "wealth" (cf. Gen 31:1; Isa 10:3; 61:6; 66:11–12; Ps 49:16–17 [MT 49:17–18]).[53] Accordingly, Chazon suggested that the phrase בארץ כבוד (in a land of glory) fits the description of the Garden of Eden in Gen 2:9–10.[54] That is, line 7 may reflect, at least in part, an understanding of the biblical description of Eden as a "land of abundance."

Another occurrence of the term כבוד (glory) within the context of this prayer for the first day may be instructive at this point. Line 4 already employed כבוד in reference to God's glory: "Adam our father, You formed in the likeness of [Your] glory (כבוד[כה])." This use of כבוד (glory) in line 4 suggests the possibility that the "land of glory" in line 7 refers to God's glory. In this case, Eden was understood as a land of God's glory or a land where God's glory dwelt. Not only was Adam formed in the likeness of God's glory (line 4), but he would have dominion in Eden (line 6) and walk in the presence of God in this "land of glory" (line 7). The author of 4Q504 may have imported this idea from outside the Bible. For example, there is a tradition preserved in 3 *Enoch* 5:1–6 that God's glory, in the form of the Shekinah, dwelt in the Garden of Eden until the generation of Enosh:

> 1b. From the day that the Holy One, blessed be He, banished the first man from the garden of Eden, the Shekinah resided on a cherub beneath the tree of life. . . . 3. The first man and his generation dwelt at the gate of the garden of Eden so that they might gaze at the bright image of the Shekinah . . . 4. anyone who gazed at the brightness of the Shekinah was not troubled by flies or gnats, by sickness or pain; malicious demons were not able to harm him, and even the angels had no power over him. 5. When the Holy One, blessed be He, went out and in from the garden to Eden, and from Eden to the garden, from the garden to heaven, and from heaven to the garden of Eden, all gazed at the bright image of His

52. The first few words of the line have been lost. Presumably, ולתהלך (and to walk) was connected to another verb in the lacuna.

53. See BDB, 458; HALOT, 457.

54. Chazon, "תעודה ליטורגית מקומראן והשלכותיה: 'דברי המארות'," 146.

Shekinah and were unharmed 6. until the coming of the generation of Enosh . . . .[55]

The author of 4Q504 may also have incorporated this idea of God's glory dwelling in Eden from other biblical texts which speak of God's glory dwelling in the tabernacle or temple (cf. Exod 29:42–43; 40:34–35; Lev 9:6, 23; Num 14:10; 16:19; Ps 26:8; 2 Chr 5:14; 7:1–3). Notably, in the Hebrew Bible there are a number of lexical and thematic links between the descriptions of the sanctuary (Exod 25–31; 35–40; 1 Kgs 7–8; 2 Chr 3–5) and the Eden narrative (Gen 2–3). Consequently, the sanctuary (tabernacle/temple) is depicted as a recreation of Eden. Thus, it is possible that this idea of God's glory dwelling in the sanctuary was retrofitted by the author of 4Q504 into the Eden narrative.

The Prohibition in the Garden of Eden

Lines 8–9 allude to the prohibition given to Adam and the subsequent punishment for his disobedience. The retelling of the prohibition is partially preserved in line 8: ותקם עליו לבלתי ס[ור] (And You charged him not to turn as[ide]). Based on the context of this prayer (lines 1–7), which follows the sequence of the Genesis account, this line alludes to the prohibition of eating from "the tree of the knowledge of good and evil" (Gen 2:16–17). The first part of line 8 employs the phrase ותקם עליו (And You charged him) rather than ויצו יהוה אלהים על־האדם (Then the Lord God commanded the man) as found in Genesis 2:16. The second part of the line, לבלתי ס[ור] (to not turn aside), is notable for two reasons. First, this line employs לבלתי, which is not found in the prohibition in Genesis 2:17. Chazon has noted that the use of לבלתי in this retelling of the prohibition foreshadows Adam's disobedience, employing language from God's accusation of Adam in Genesis 3:11 (לבלתי אכל).[56] The context of the accusation in 3:11 is that Adam has disobeyed God by eating from "the tree of the knowledge of good and evil." Second, this retelling of the prohibition in 4Q504 incorporates language (לבלתי סור) from other biblical texts in which the Israelites (Adam's descendants), who dwelt in the Land of Promise (linked to Eden), were commanded not to turn aside from God's commands. For example, in Joshua 23:6, Joshua addresses the Israelites who were dwelling in the Promised Land: "Therefore

55. Translation from Alexander, "3 (Hebrew Apocalypse of) Enoch," 259–60.

56. Chazon, "The Creation and Fall of Adam in the Dead Sea Scrolls," 15.

be very courageous to keep and to do all that is written in the Book of the Torah of Moses, lest you turn aside from it (לבלתי סור־ממנו) to the right hand or to the left."[57] Though the fragmentary nature of the text precludes certainty, the language in line 8 may further link the Israelites who dwelt in the land to Adam who dwelt in Eden. To turn aside from God's commands in either locale ultimately resulted in expulsion from the land (cf. Gen 2–3; Deut 28, 30, 32; Josh 23; 2 Kgs 25; 2 Chr 36).

Sin and Punishment

The text of 4Q504 moves quickly from the prohibition given to Adam in line 8 to his punishment for disobedience in line 9. Following the prohibition are lacunae (missing text) at the end of line 8 and the beginning of line 9. It is possible that a brief reference to Adam's act of disobedience was originally contained in this missing portion of text. Regardless, the extant text of line 9 assumes Adam's disobedience with a description of his punishment: בשר הואה ולעפר ה[ ] (he is flesh and to dust h[e returns]). This retelling of the punishment of Adam paraphrases Genesis 3:19: כי־עפר אתה ואל־עפר תשוב (For dust you are, and to dust you shall return).[58] Further, the phrase בשר הואה (he is flesh) is introduced into this recasting of Adam's punishment, likely alluding to Gen 6:3, 12.[59] Thus, Chazon has proposed that this phrase foreshadows the antediluvian sin and subsequent punishment (Gen 6–8).[60] This may be the case, considering the immediately following text—though fragmentary—recalls the Flood account.[61] This juxtaposition of the creation and Flood accounts may highlight the theme of human sin and Divine judgment. However, the recollection of the Flood account is poorly preserved, making it difficult to determine with any certainty the exact relationship of these two accounts in the prayer.

57. Cf. Deut 17:14–20; Jer 32:40.

58. Based on this, a possible reconstruction for the lacuna at the end of line 9 is: ולעפר ה[ואה ישוב] (and to dust h[e returns]).

59. Gen 6:3: "And the Lord said, 'My Spirit shall not strive with man forever, for he is indeed flesh (הוא בשר); yet his days shall be one hundred and twenty years"; Gen 6:12: "So God looked upon the earth, and indeed it was corrupt; for all flesh (כל־בשר) had corrupted their way on the earth."

60. Chazon, "The Creation and Fall of Adam in the Dead Sea Scrolls," 15.

61. For example, see line 14: [למלוא את ה]ארץ [ח]מס ולשפו[ך דם] ([to fill the] earth [with vio]lence and to she[d blood]). This line likely alludes to Gen 6:11–13.

Interpretation of the Creation Account in 4Q504: Conclusions

4Q504 preserves only a few lines of fragmentary text dealing with the creation and Fall of Adam. Nonetheless, this liturgical text from Qumran reveals various aspects of how the Genesis creation account was *understood* and *employed* during the Second Temple period. The author of 4Q504 reworks the biblical account of the creation of Adam (frag. 8, lines 4–9) within the historical section of the prayer for the first day of the week.

First, in similar fashion to the biblical account, Adam is presented as being made from dust (frag. 8, line 1), yet formed in the likeness of God's glory (frag. 8, line 4; cf. Gen 1:26; 2:7). This idea that Adam shared in, or reflected, God's glory is not explicitly stated in the Genesis account. Second, this retelling introduces the giving of knowledge to Adam prior to eating from "the tree of the knowledge of good and evil" (frag. 8, line 5; cf. Gen 2:17; 3:5–7). Knowledge is a dominant motif in the prayer and the author appears to link the people praying this prayer to Adam their father (frag 8, lines 4–5). Just as God gave knowledge to Adam who dwelt in Eden, so also He gave knowledge to his descendants dwelling in the Promised Land (cf. frag. 4, lines 14–15). Third, the author reworked the giving of Adam's dominion (Gen 1:26–28) into the Eden narrative (Gen 2:8, 15). 4Q504 appears to limit the focus of Adam's dominion to the Garden of Eden (frag. 8, line 6), whereas the biblical account states that God gave Adam dominion "over all the earth" (Gen 1:26, 28). Fourth, the Garden of Eden is depicted as a "land of glory" in which Adam walked before God (frag. 8, line 7). The author may have retrofitted the idea of God's glory dwelling in the sanctuary into the Eden narrative. Fifth, the language used in the retelling of the prohibition foreshadows Adam's disobedience (frag. 8, line 8; employing language from God's accusation in Gen 3:11) and recalls the later prohibition given to the Israelites in the Promised Land (e.g. Josh 23:6). To "turn aside" from God's commands in either locale would lead to expulsion from the land.

Even though Adam was created in the likeness of God's glory, given knowledge and dominion, and walked in a land of glory (Eden), he would return to the dust (from which he was made) as punishment for disobedience (frag. 8, line 9; cf. Gen 3:19). Chazon observed, "The resulting presentation emphasizes the magnitude of God's creation and empowerment of Adam and also brings Adam's subsequent disobedience into sharp relief."[62]

62. Chazon, "The Creation and Fall of Adam in the Dead Sea Scrolls," 15.

This recollection of the creation, fall, and subsequent punishment of Adam provides a historical basis for the petition to God in the prayer (frag. 4, lines 6–13). In the presentation of this prayer, the author also appears to link the Israelites dwelling in the Land of Promise to Adam (their father) who dwelt in Eden, the land of glory.

CHAPTER FIVE

QUMRAN INTERPRETATION OF THE GENESIS CREATION ACCOUNT

PARAPHRASE OF GENESIS AND EXODUS (4Q422)

Discovery of 4Q422[1]

Paraphrase of Genesis and Exodus (4Q422) is another manuscript dealing with the Genesis creation account that was found among the thousands of scroll fragments (representing some 600 manuscripts) from Cave 4 in 1952. However, due to the large volume of these fragmentary manuscripts and a number of other reasons, the publication of many of these manuscripts was significantly delayed. In fact, over forty years would pass before this manuscript was published in 1994 by Torleif Elgvin and Emanuel Tov in volume 13 of the *Discoveries in the Judaean Desert* series.[2] The portion of the manuscript dealing with Genesis was edited by Elgvin.

1. The sections of this chapter dealing with general introductory matters for 4Q422 were originally published in slightly different form in Lyon, *Qumran Interpretation of the Genesis Flood*, 120–40. These sections include: Discovery of 4Q422, Physical Description of 4Q422, 4Q422: A Qumran Composition?, History of Research on 4Q422, Literary Genre of 4Q422, and Content and Literary Structure of 4Q422.

2. Elgvin and Tov, "4QParaphrase of Genesis and Exodus" (hereafter, DJD XIII), 417–41, Pl. XLII–XLIII.

Physical Description of 4Q422

4Q422 is a poorly preserved manuscript consisting of thirty-three fragments.[3] Of these fragments, only eleven were reconstructed into three columns of text by Elgvin and Tov.[4] These columns contain what is often referred to as a "paraphrase" of Genesis (frags 1–9) and Exodus (frags 10a, e). Column I recounts creation and human rebellion (Genesis 1–3) while column II, consisting of six fragments (2–7), relates to the Flood (Genesis 6–9).[5] Column III reworks the first chapters of Exodus, including the plagues against Egypt. 4Q422 is a Hebrew text written in the Jewish script. Based on paleographical study, the scroll was written in an early Hasmonean hand, dating the scroll to the early part of the first century BC (c. 100–75 BC),[6] or perhaps as early as the latter part of the second century BC (c. 125–100 BC).[7]

The opening lines (1–5) of column I, now missing, were likely the beginning of the manuscript since lines 6–13 (frag. 1) cover the creation (Gen 1–2) and humanity's rebellion (Gen 3). Interestingly, the partially preserved left margin of column III (frag. 10e) has stitching marks at the end of the sheet, indicating that another sheet likely followed.[8] The first sheet measured roughly 52 cm in length. Based on measurements and the rolling of the scroll, Elgvin estimated the missing second sheet was only about 17 cm, containing one column of text.[9]

Reconstruction of the fragmentary 4Q422 scroll is aided by several factors. The partial preservation of the margins between columns I and II, II and III, and the left margin of column III helps to provide a framework. The PAM 42.820 image of 4Q422 presents the fragments according to

3. Feldman, "The Story of the Flood in 4Q422," 58. Here, I follow Feldman's count as he pointed out, "The DJD edition of 4Q422 counts thirty-four fragments. However, a small fragment joined to frag. 10e . . . was also edited there as an unidentified frg. P."

4. Elgvin and Tov, DJD XIII, 417–41, Pl. XLII–XLIII.

5. Fragments 8 and 9 possibly relate to the Flood, though the language could relate to the creation also. In addition, several of the 22 hitherto unassigned fragments appear to also contain language related to the Flood story (e.g. frags. C, D, G, L, P).

6. Elgvin and Tov, DJD XIII, 420; Vermes, *The Complete Dead Sea Scrolls in English*, 478.

7. Elgvin, "The Genesis Section of 4Q422," 196; Brooke, "Commentary on Genesis and Exodus (4Q422)," 663.

8. Elgvin and Tov, DJD XIII, 417. Stitching marks are clearly visible in the PAM 42.820 image.

9. Ibid., 420.

the four stacks in which they were found. Each horizontal row represents several fragments which were stuck together. Studying the shapes of these fragments which were stuck together is helpful in reconstructing this fragmentary scroll since the similar shape between fragments indicates close relationship. According to the scroll's editors, the matching shapes of these various fragments show that they ". . . represent layers of the original scroll which were rolled immediately upon one another."[10] This is further shown by a number of fragments (2, 3, 4, 8, 10d, 10e, and E) which reveal an additional layer of writing where ink from one layer has left an imprint on the backside of the scroll layer above it.[11] For example, only traces of ה and ב remain from the word המבול in fragment 4 (line 4), which are imprinted on the backside of fragment 10a. Thus, 4Q422 has been partially reconstructed based on a number of factors including the partial preservation of several margins, the similar shapes of fragments found stuck together in stacks, and the ink from the writing on one layer imprinted on the backside of another layer. Nonetheless, uncertainties remain as more of the text is missing than is extant. Also, a number of fragments remain unplaced in the reconstructed text. Thus, caution is prerequisite in studying the text of 4Q422.

4Q422: A Qumran Composition?

It is apparent that 4Q422 is a *Jewish* composition, since it: 1) is a Hebrew text found in Judea at Qumran, 2) dates to the Hasmonean period (placing it in the period of sectarian writing at Qumran), and 3) relates to and paraphrases texts from the Hebrew Bible. But, is 4Q422 a Qumran sectarian composition?

Elgvin acknowledges that 4Q422 has "no clear signs of sectarian theology," but then mentions several elements which may indicate that 4Q422 was composed within the Qumran community.[12] He points out: 1) several phrases occurring in both 4Q422 and sectarian texts (רוח קודשו "His Holy Spirit," מועדי יום ולילה "the set times of day and night," דורות עולם "generations of eternity" I:7; II:10–12; III:7), 2) the use of the Divine name אל instead of יהוה in paraphrasing Gen 7:16 (II:5) and Exod 9:12 (III:11), 3) the interchange (the Masoretic יֶרֶק of Exod 10:15 with ירוק in 4Q422 II:11) attested in 1QIsa[a] (indicating Qumran scribal practice since 1QIsa[a] was

10. Elgvin, "The Genesis Section of 4Q422," 181.

11. Ibid., 183.

12. Ibid., 196.

copied at Qumran), and 4) links with the sectarian 4QInstruction (formerly *Sapiential Work A*).[13] In other words, 4Q422 is not overtly a sectarian manuscript, but it might be, based on numerous affinities with sectarian literature. However, Ariel Feldman views 4Q422 strictly as a non-sectarian text and is doubtful that Elgvin's observations demonstrate otherwise.[14] In particular, Feldman does not see any of the observations linking 4Q422 to sectarian writings as being strictly sectarian in nature, but as common within Second Temple period Judaism.[15] While a sectarian provenance for 4Q422 may not be demonstrable at this point, it remains possible and plausible since it was found at Qumran (cave 4) and does display several affinities with sectarian writings (though not necessarily exclusive to sectarian literature).

Whether or not 4Q422 was composed at Qumran, it was certainly written by Jews during the Hasmonean period. While overtly sectarian theology may be absent, the content of 4Q422 is not inconsistent with Qumran ideology. Further, this text was found in cave 4, a dwelling space directly connected to the Qumran site. Thus, it is likely that 4Q422 was present in the Qumran community before it was conveniently placed in this nearby cave as the Romans approached Qumran in AD 68. In light of these observations, 4Q422 appears to have been acceptable for study and use at Qumran.

History of Research on 4Q422

The publication of 4Q422 and the subsequent research on this text did not commence until the mid-1990s. This brief survey of the history of research on 4Q422 will focus only on selected studies directly relevant to the current discussion on Qumran interpretation of the Genesis creation account. Several works on 4Q422 have been published, dealing primarily with the Flood section.[16] However, less attention has been given to the first column of 4Q422 dealing with the creation account.

13. Ibid.

14. Feldman, "The Story of the Flood in 4Q422," 57.

15. Ibid.

16. For example, some fuller treatments of the Flood section of 4Q422 include: Feldman, "The Story of the Flood in 4Q422," 57–77; Lyon, *Qumran Interpretation of the Genesis Flood*, 120–40. Other works address the Flood material of 4Q422 in less detail: Bernstein, "Noah and the Flood at Qumran," 199–231; Peters, *Noah Traditions in the Dead Sea Scrolls*, 139–44.

Torleif Elgvin

The official edition of 4Q422 was published in 1994 in volume 13 of the *Discoveries in the Judaean Desert* series by Torleif Elgvin and Emanuel Tov,[17] with the Genesis section of 4Q422 (cols. I and II) edited by Elgvin. This edition included a physical description of the text, discussion on the reconstruction of the fragmentary columns, paleographical and orthographical notes, a transcription and translation of the text, notes on the readings, line-by-line comments on the text, and plates of the text. In 1994, Elgvin also published an article, titled "The Genesis Section of 4Q422 (4QParaGenExod)," in the journal *Dead Sea Discoveries*.[18] Here, much of the same material was published and Elgvin provided some concluding remarks on the text. Elgvin's editorial work on this text is foundational and remains the standard for 4Q422 studies.

Esther Chazon

In 1997, Esther Chazon published a chapter titled "The Creation and Fall of Adam in the Dead Sea Scrolls," in which she: 1) discussed interpretation of the biblical creation account in several Qumran texts and 2) explored possible literary relationships between these texts.[19] Within the survey of several Qumran texts, she provides a relatively brief treatment of 4Q422, which is nonetheless insightful. Chazon understands the presentation of the creation of Adam and the subsequent rebellion, which is juxtaposed with the Flood account, to be focused on "the sin-punishment theme."[20]

Literary Genre of 4Q422

4Q422 is usually labeled as a "paraphrase" of Genesis and Exodus. However, this may not fully describe the genre of this composition for several reasons. First, the text is highly selective and does not appear to include a significant number of other stories from Genesis and Exodus.[21] Second, as

17. Elgvin and Tov, DJD XIII, 417–41, Pl. XLII–XLIII.

18. Elgvin, "The Genesis Section of 4Q422," 180–96.

19. Chazon, "The Creation and Fall of Adam in the Dead Sea Scrolls," 13–24.

20. Ibid., 17.

21. Cf. Elgvin and Tov, DJD XIII, 426. Perhaps more passages were selected from Exodus on the missing sheet. Even if this were the case, the point remains that 4Q422 is

Dorothy Peters contends, the Flood narrative in 4Q422 is "... more complex and exegetically developed than a simple paraphrase would allow."[22] 4Q422 reworks in detail the Flood story, interweaving new biblical material and often differing in its order. This rewritten text also introduces material not found in the biblical text. Much of the same can be said for the reworked creation account which also appears to interweave new biblical material. While Elgvin views 4Q422 as a paraphrase, he recognizes that theological interpretations were woven into the paraphrases of these biblical texts.[23] This was more the case in the retelling of Genesis than of Exodus. Third, the creation and Flood stories in 4Q422 appear to be employed for hortatory or homiletic purposes.[24] Elgvin even suggested that the Genesis section could be characterized as a "homiletic paraphrase."[25]

For the aforementioned reasons, among others, the label of "paraphrase" to describe 4Q422 does not appear to be sufficient. Martin Abegg understood this text as another example of "rewritten Bible," a popular method of biblical interpretation during the Second Temple period.[26] Feldman also understood 4Q422 as reworking the biblical narratives.[27] It is suggested here that 4Q422 is better described as a selective reworking of Scripture employing paraphrase, as well as insertions of other biblical material and additions not found in the biblical text, for didactic or homiletical purposes.

Content and Literary Structure of 4Q422

As reconstructed, 4Q422 consists of three fragmentary columns which contain a selective retelling of the opening chapters of Genesis (frags. 1–9) and Exodus (frags. 10a, e). Column I recounts creation and humanity's rebellion (Gen 1–3) while column II relates to the Flood account (Gen 6–9).

---

a highly selective text which is not a paraphrase of *the whole book* of Genesis or *the whole book* of Exodus.

22. Peters, *Noah Traditions in the Dead Sea Scrolls*, 140.

23. Elgvin, "The Genesis Section of 4Q422," 195.

24. This is similar to the function of the reworked Flood story in 4Q370 for admonitory purposes. Cf. Bernstein, "Noah and the Flood at Qumran," 212.

25. Elgvin, "The Genesis Section of 4Q422," 195.

26. Wise et al., *The Dead Sea Scrolls: A New Translation*, 495.

27. Feldman, "The Story of the Flood in 4Q422," 70–75.

Column III reworks the opening chapters of Exodus, including the plagues against Egypt.

Column I (Creation, Eden, and Human Rebellion)

The first five lines of column I are missing and, based on the content in lines 6–13, were likely the opening lines introducing the creation story. Lines 6–8 preserve some of this recounting of the creation story from Genesis 1:1–2:3. Line 6 records that God made (עשה), by His word (בדברו),[28] the heavens and the earth. In line 7, the phrase מלאכתו אשר עשה (His work which He had done) is taken from Genesis 2:2. The following phrase, ורוח קודשו (and His Holy Spirit), includes the role of God's Holy Spirit in the act of creating. Line 8 refers to כול הנפש החיה והרמשת על הארץ (every living creature and what moves on the earth), echoing Genesis 1:28 (ובכל־חיה הרמשת על־הארץ) in which the context is humanity's dominion over the animals. Lines 9–10 speak of Adam in the Garden of Eden, whom God caused to have dominion/rule (המשילו) over the fruit of the ground (line 9), along with a warning not to eat from the tree of the knowledge of good and evil (line 10; cf. Gen 2:16–17). Lines 11–13 speak of humanity's rebellion: "[. . . and] he rose up against Him and they forgot [. . .] . . . with an evil inclination and for work[s of wickedness]." The placement of the human rebellion immediately after line 10, which refers to Genesis 2:16–17, strongly suggests that this human rebellion in line 11 relates to Genesis 3.[29] The phrase ביוצר רע (with an evil inclination) (line 12) alludes to Genesis 6:5: וכל־יצר מחשבת לבו רק רע כל־היום (and every inclination of the thoughts of his heart was only evil continually) (cf. also 8:21). Thus, the phrases "with an evil inclination" and "works of wickedness" in line 12 appear to serve as a literary bridge from Genesis 3 to the Flood story in 4Q422.

Column II (The Flood)

The second column of 4Q422 is concerned with retelling the Flood story. Line 1 begins with what appears to be a description of God seeing the

28. García Martínez and Tigchelaar do not include the reconstructed בדברו in their transcription. See García Martínez and Tigchelaar, *The Dead Sea Scrolls Study Edition*, 884–85.

29. Elgvin and Tov, DJD XIII, 423.

wickedness of man as described in Genesis 6:5.[30] If this is the case, then the opening line of column II began the Flood story. Line 2a then reads "[righteous in] his generation up[on the earth]." The reading [ב]דורו (in his generation) led to Elgvin's reconstruction of [צדיק ב]דורו.[31] This reconstruction seems likely in light of Genesis 6:9: נח איש צדיק תמים היה בדרתיו (Noah was a righteous man, perfect in his generations).

Lines 2(a)–5 refer to the deliverance (נצלו; line 3) of Noah and his family in the ark. The last phrase of line 2a, [א]תו אל חיה, has been read by Elgvin as "to an animal"[32] and by Moshe Bernstein as "to living creatures."[33] However, Feldman has proposed reading אל as "God" (instead of "to") and חיה as "kept alive" (instead of "animal" or "living creature"). Feldman's reading, "with him God kept alive," seems to fit better with the context of נצלו (they were delivered) in line 3 and the following lines.[34] Line 4, taken from Genesis 7:7, refers to Noah's sons, his wife, and his sons' wives, who were delivered from "the waters of the Flood" (מי המבול).[35] The next line states, [ויס]גור אל בעדם (and God shut behind them), which echoes Genesis 7:16: ויסגר יהוה בעדו (and Yahweh shut him in). Notice here the substitution of the Divine name יהוה with אל in 4Q422, which is a common scribal practice at Qumran. The next phrase of line 5, [צו]העליו את כ[ו]ל, appears to refer to God giving commands to Noah, while Genesis 6:22 and 7:5–6 records that Noah did all God had commanded.

Lines 6–8 describe the Flood itself, employing biblical language. The phrase [כול] אשר בחרבה כל א[שר] (all that was on the dry ground all which) (line 6) is likely taken from Genesis 7:22.[36] The phrase [ארובות השמי[ם נפ[ת]חו (the windows of heaven were opened) (line 6) is taken from Genesis 7:11. Interestingly, the missing text preceding this phrase in 4Q422 may be represented by the phrase [מ]עינות רבה (great fountains), preserved in the unplaced fragment D.[37] The phrase תחת כול השמ[ים] (under all the

30. 4Q422 II:1: [. . .].וירא אל כיא רבה ו; Cf. Gen 6:5: .וירא יהוה כי רבה רעת האדם בארץ

31. Elgvin, "The Genesis Section of 4Q422," 189.

32. Ibid., 190; cf. DJD XIII, 426.

33. Bernstein, "Noah and the Flood at Qumran," 212.

34. Feldman, "The Story of the Flood in 4Q422," 63, 71.

35. 4Q422 II:4: [. . .]ומ מי המבול[שתו ונשי בניו מפני]א ואת בניו[את נוח . . .]; Cf. Gen 7:7: .ויבא נח ובניו ואשתו ונשי־בניו אתו אל־התבה מפני מי המבול

36. Gen 7:22: כל אשר נשמת־רוח חיים באפיו מכל אשר בחרבה מתו (All in whose nostrils was the breath of the spirit of life, all that was on the dry land, died).

37. Elgvin, "The Genesis Section of 4Q422," 191; see Feldman, "The Story of the Flood in 4Q422," 68.

heavens) alludes to Genesis 7:19 where the waters prevailed exceedingly upon the earth, covering all the high hills "under all the heavens" (תחת כל השמים). In lines 7–8, [ארבעים] יום וארב[עים] לילה היה ה[גשם] על [הארץ] (forty days and forty nights there was rain upon the earth) is adopted from Genesis 7:12.[38] The latter part of line 8 and the beginning of line 9 departs from the biblical Flood narrative, providing the purposes behind the Flood: "8. [the water]s were migh[ty] upon [the earth in order to] cleanse sin and in order to 9. make known the glory of the Mo[st High . . .]."

Lines 9–13 paraphrase Genesis 9, describing the post-Flood situation in language similar to Genesis 8–9 and even Genesis 1. The remaining few lines of column II are no longer extant.

Column III (Exodus)

The third column of 4Q422 contains a paraphrase of the first part of the book of Exodus, covering the plagues and a few of the events prior to them. Lines 1–7 briefly mention a few events leading up to the plagues: the two midwives (line 2), the Israelite sons thrown into the Nile (line 3), the sending of Moses to the people (line 4), possibly God's burning bush appearance (line 4), the sending of Moses and Aaron to Pharaoh (line 6), and the hardening of Pharaoh's heart (line 7). The author moved rapidly through these events using only a few words for each. Lines 7–12 (half the column) then describe the plagues in more detail.[39] But why does the author focus on the plagues in column III, immediately following the retelling of the Flood account in column II? Dorothy Peters suggested, "Its very juxtaposition with the creation and flood narratives highlights a thematic reversal of creation."[40] In addition, both the Flood and plagues narratives describe well known examples of God's judgment upon the wicked and deliverance of God's people.

38. Gen 7:12: ויהי הגשם על־הארץ ארבעים יום וארבעים לילה (And the rain was on the earth forty days and forty nights).

39. Tov, "The Exodus Section of 4Q422," 197–209. The list of plagues in 4Q422 III:7–12 includes all of those mentioned in the biblical narrative except for the plague of boils. Emanuel Tov observed that the sequence of the plagues is close to that of the Exodus account and Psalm 105. Concerning the author's employment of biblical texts, Tov notes that ". . . in the description of the plagues, the wording of 4Q422 depends in the first place on the historical Psalm 78, second on Psalm 105, and third on the account in Exodus" (197).

40. Peters, *Noah Traditions in the Dead Sea Scrolls*, 140.

General Structure of 4Q422

There is not a lot of space in these columns of text for a detailed retelling of the biblical accounts of creation, the Flood, and the Exodus. The author was selective and, as far as one can tell from this fragmentary text, omitted numerous details. The author reworked or alluded to a number of biblical passages in the retelling of these historical events.

A general description of the content of 4Q422 leads to discerning at least some literary patterns which make up this composition. Though fragmentary, a working general outline of 4Q422 may be proposed:

Outline of 4Q422		
Column I (Creation, Eden, Human Rebellion)	Column II (The Flood Story)	Column III (Book of Exodus, the Plagues)
• Creation (6–8) • Adam's rule in Eden (9–10) • Human rebellion (11–13) ביוצר רע (with an evil inclination) **Gen 6:5**	• Human wickedness (1) **(Gen 6:5)** • Righteous Noah and family delivered in the ark (2a–6) • Flood judgment (6–8) • Purposes of the Flood (8–9) למען (in order to) • Post-Flood covenant (9–13)	• The two midwives (2) • Israelite sons thrown into the Nile (3) • Moses sent to the people (4) • Moses and Aaron sent to Pharaoh (6) • Pharaoh's heart hardened (7) Purpose: למען (in order to) • Plagues judgment (7–12)
Creation → Human Rebellion ←	→ Human Rebellion → Judgment	Human rebellion → Judgment

Column I covers creation, Eden, and human rebellion. Interestingly, in column I, line 12, the author employed the biblical phrase ביוצר רע (with an evil inclination) in reference to the human rebellion in Genesis 3–4 (lines 10–12). The phrase ביוצר רע is adopted from Genesis 6:5 which originally referred to the antediluvian rebellion. Thus, the author links the human rebellion in Genesis 3–4 to the Flood story. Column II then opens with human rebellion (antediluvians) with a likely reference to Genesis 6:5 and then the Flood judgment. Column III then also mentions human rebellion (Pharaoh), followed by the plague judgments. In addition, there is an important lexical link between columns II (Flood judgment) and III (judgment with plagues), as both provide the purpose of judgment, introduced with למען (in order that). These "purpose" statements are central to understanding the message of 4Q422.

The Creation of the Universe by the Word of God

The extant text of the first column begins in line 6: צבאם עשה בדבר[ו] (their hosts He made by [His] word). Elgvin partially reconstructed this fragmentary line as [השמים והארץ וכול] צבאם עשה בדבר[ו] ([the heavens and the earth and all] their hosts He made by [His] word).[41] It should be noted that בדבר[ו] (by His word) is only partially preserved. The first two letters (בד) are fully preserved, while the upper portions of the next two letters (בר) are broken off. Even with the manipulation of digital imaging, it is difficult to determine with certainty the third (ב) and fourth (ר) letters of this word. However, a consideration of the extant lower portions of these two letters with the preserved first two letters of the word and the immediate context indicates this is perhaps the most reasonable reconstruction. The final letter (ו) is not preserved and thus, is reconstructed.

This line likely reworks Gen 2:1: ויכלו השמים והארץ וכל צבאם (And the heavens and the earth and all their hosts were finished).[42] Of particular interest is the inclusion in 4Q422 of the phrase עשה בדבר[ו] (He made by [His] word) which is not explicitly found in the Genesis creation account. If the reconstruction of בדברו is correct, an emphasis on the role of God's word in creating the heavens and the earth is present in 4Q422. The author introduces this idea with language found in Ps 33:6:

> *4Q422* (I:6): "[the heavens and the earth and all] their hosts (צבאם) He made (עשה) by [His] word ([בדבר[ו)"
>
> Psalm 33:6: "By the word (בדבר) of the LORD the heavens were made (נעשו), and all their hosts (צבאם) by the breath of His mouth."

Both 4Q422 (col. I, line 6) and Psalm 33:6 summarize the manner in which God created by His spoken word. In Genesis 1, the phrase ויאמר אלהים (then God said) is used ten times.[43] What follows each of these

41. Elgvin, "The Genesis Section of 4Q422," 184.

42. This language is likely also attested in 4Q304 (*Meditation on Creation B*): ואת הארץ וכ[ול צבאם] (and the earth and a[ll their hosts]).

43. The root אמר (to say) is used 11 times in Gen 1, with the other occurrence in the Qal Infinitive construct form (לאמר "saying") in 1:22.

declarations is the creation of light (1:3), the expanse (1:6–7), the dry land (1:9), plant life (1:11–12), luminaries in the heavens (1:14–16), marine life and birds (1:20–21), land animals (1:24–25), humans (1:26–27), the dominion mandate for humans (1:28), and the diets for humans, birds, and land animals (1:29–30). Thus, the Genesis creation account indicates that God created the physical universe and life itself through His spoken word. In 4Q422, the extant text of column I (lines 6–13) indicates that there was not a lot of space devoted to this retelling of the creation account.[44] Thus, the author was highly selective in reworking the biblical text, which may partially explain the use of the phrase עשה בדברו (He made by His word).

In addition, the phrase "He made by His word" may also reflect the ancient understanding where the "word" functions as God's *agent* in creating the universe. Most notably, the creation of the universe is ascribed to the מימרא (*Memra* "Word") in the Aramaic Targums (cf. *Tg. Neof.* Gen 1)[45] and the λογος (*Logos* "Word") in the New Testament (cf. John 1:1–3).[46] Elgvin concluded that ". . . in its interpretation of creation, 4Q422 might provide an early link to the Memra-theology of the Targums as well as the *logos* of John 1:1, 3."[47] While the phrase "He made by His word" in 4Q422 may represent this understanding, it is difficult to conclude with any certainty due to the fragmentary nature of this text.

The Role of the Holy Spirit in Creation

The extant text of line 7 reads: [אש]ר עשה ורוח קודש[ו] ([whi]ch He did. And [His] Holy Spirit). Elgvin partially reconstructed this line as [וישבת ביום השבעי מכול מלאכתו אש]ר עשה ורוח קודש[ו] ([Then He rested on the seventh day from all His work whi]ch He did. And [His] Holy Spirit).[48] If this reconstruction is correct, then the first part of this line likely recalls

44. For example, line 10 includes a retelling of the prohibition found in Gen 2:16–17. Lines 11–13 then introduce humanity's rebellion (cf. Gen 3).

45. In the Aramaic Targums, the מימרא (*Memra* "Word") often functions as God's agent, performing actions that the Hebrew Bible ascribes to God Himself. In addition, "God" or "Lord" is often substituted with the "Memra."

46. In John 1:1–3, the λογος (*Logos* "Word") was *with* God in the beginning, and *was* God, and was the *agent* through which God created all things. Further, the λογος (Word) is identified as Jesus, who "became flesh and dwelt among us" (cf. 1:14–18).

47. Elgvin, "The Genesis Section of 4Q422," 195.

48. Ibid., 184.

Genesis 2:2.[49] The inclusion of the phrase ורוח קודשו (and His Holy Spirit) at the end of line 7 appears to indicate some sort of role for God's Holy Spirit in the act of creating. It is difficult to determine anything more specific concerning the author's presentation of the Holy Spirit's role(s) in creation, due to the fragmentary nature of this text.

In 4Q422, עשה בדברו (He made by His word) is used in line 6 and ורוח קודשו (and His Holy Spirit) is used in line 7. In Psalm 33:6, the terms דבר and רוח are used together in reference to the manner in which God created: בדבר יהוה שמים נעשו וברוח פיו כל־צבאם. However, in the case of Psalm 33:6, רוח is understood as "breath" as the phrase וברוח פיו (and by the breath of His mouth) parallels the previous phrase, בדבר יהוה (by the word of the Lord). Accordingly, Elgvin concluded, "4Q422 assigns more importance to the role of God's holy spirit in the act of creation than Genesis 1 and Ps. 33:6–9."[50] This is indeed the case regarding Psalm 33:6–9, which depicts the manner in which God created by His spoken word. Regarding Genesis 1, however, it is less certain that 4Q422 assigns more importance to the role of the Holy Spirit in creation. First, the fragmentary nature of the text of 4Q422 precludes any definitive conclusion. Second, in the Genesis creation account, the Spirit of God is present at the beginning of creation, "hovering over the face of the waters" (Gen 1:2).

The Creation of Adam with Dominion

The extant text of line 8 reads: [נפ]ש החיה והרמש[ת] (living creature and what moves). This line has been partially reconstructed in different ways. In the DJD edition, Elgvin reconstructed the text as [נתן לאדם לרדות ? בכול הנפ]ש החיה והרמש[ת על הארצ] ([He gave mankind dominion ? over every] living [creat]ure and what move[s on the earth]).[51] This reconstruction was adopted by Parry and Tov in their edition of the text.[52] García Martínez and Tigchelaar, for the most part, reconstructed this line in the same fashion: [כול הנפ]ש החיה והרמש[ת על הארצ].[53] In this case, the beginning part of Elgvin's reconstruction is omitted. If either of these reconstructions is

49. Gen 2:2b: וישבת ביום השביעי מכל־מלאכתו אשר עשה (Then He rested on the seventh day from all His work which He did).

50. Elgvin, "The Genesis Section of 4Q422," 186; see also DJD XIII, 422.

51. Elgvin and Tov, DJD XIII, 421.

52. Parry and Tov, *The Dead Sea Scrolls Reader*, 3:570.

53. García Martínez and Tigchelaar, *The Dead Sea Scrolls Study Edition*, 884.

correct, line 8 would appear to reflect Genesis 1:28b: ורדו בדגת הים ובעוף השמים ובכל־חיה הרמשת על־הארץ (and have dominion over the fish of the sea, over the birds of the air, and over every living creature that moves upon the earth). Elgvin also suggested two other possible reconstructions. For example, line 8 can be reconstructed as [עשה כול נפ]ש החיה והרמש[ת אשר שרצו המים למיניהם] (He made every living creature and what moves, in which the waters abounded, according to their kind). Interestingly, Elgvin adopted this reconstruction in his article, "The Genesis Section of 4Q422."[54] If this reconstruction is correct, line 8 may reflect Genesis 1:21: ויברא אלהים את התנינם הגדלים ואת כל־נפש החיה הרמשת אשר שרצו המים למינהם (Then God created the great sea creatures and every living creature that moves, in which the waters abounded, according to their kind). Another possible reconstruction is [עשה כול נפ]ש החיה והרמש[ת על הארצ] (He made every living creature that moves upon the earth).[55] Depending on which of these possible reconstructions is adopted, line 8 could refer to either the creation of the sea creatures (Gen 1:21) or the dominion of man over the animals (Gen 1:28). It seems more likely that line 8 reflects man's dominion over the animals in light of line 9, which refers to God giving man dominion (המשילו).

Line 9 preserves [ ]צ המשילו לאכול פר[י] (He gave him dominion to eat the fruit).[56] Again, more than one reconstruction is possible. Elgvin, reconstructed line 9 as [שם האדם על ? האר]צ המשילו לאכול פר[י האדמה] ([He set man upon the ear]th, He gave him dominion to eat the frui[t of the ground]).[57] Parry and Tov adopted this reconstruction in their edition.[58] García Martínez and Tigchelaar, however, reconstructed the text as [ע]צ המשילו לאכול פר[י] ([tr]ee, He gave him dominion to eat the frui[t of]).[59] The reconstructed עצ (tree) in line 9 is an intriguing possibility in light of line 10, which refers to the prohibition of eating from the tree (מעצ) of the knowledge of good and evil.

54. Elgvin, "The Genesis Section of 4Q422," 184.

55. This was suggested as a possible reconstruction by Elgvin (Cf. Elgvin and Tov, DJD XIII, 423).

56. As elsewhere in 4Q422, line 9 employs the medial form of *tsade* (צ) instead of the final form (ץ).

57. Elgvin and Tov, DJD XIII, 421; cf. Elgvin, "The Genesis Section of 4Q422," 184.

58. Parry and Tov, *The Dead Sea Scrolls Reader*, 3:570.

59. García Martínez and Tigchelaar, *The Dead Sea Scrolls Study Edition*, 884.

According to the extant text of line 9, not only did God give man dominion over the animals (cf. Gen 1:28), He also "gave him dominion to eat of the frui[t of]." The line is broken off at this point, preventing any certainty as to whether man was given dominion "to eat the fruit of the trees of the garden" or "to eat the fruit of the ground." Nonetheless, the author links the giving of dominion to the eating of fruit. This idea is not found in the Genesis creation account. The dominion given to Adam in line 9 is reworked in the language of the prohibition of line 10:

> 9. [. . . tr]ee (עצ), He gave him dominion to eat (לאכול) the fruit (פרי) [of]
> 10. [. . .] not to eat (אכול) from the tree (מעצ) of the kn[owledge of good and evil]

The author retells the giving of dominion to Adam (line 9), seamlessly drawing the reader's attention to the prohibition given to Adam (line 10) and his subsequent rebellion (line 11). In this manner, 4Q422 seems to contrast Adam's dominion (given by God) with his subsequent rebellion against God, by means of eating the prohibited fruit (cf. Gen 2:16–17; 3:6).

The Prohibition in the Garden of Eden

Line 10 appears to preserve the prohibition given to Adam in the garden: [ ]ל[ב]לתי אכול מעצ הד[עת טוב ורע] ([ ]not to eat from the tree of the know[ledge of good and evil]).[60] This line reflects the language of the prohibition in Genesis 2:17: ומעץ הדעת טוב ורע לא תאכל (But from the tree of the knowledge of good and evil you shall not eat). Notably, like 4Q504, the author of 4Q422 employs לבלתי, which is not found in the prohibition in Genesis 2:17.[61] The use of לבלתי foreshadows Adam's disobedience, employing language from God's accusation in Genesis 3:11: המן־העץ אשר צויתיך לבלתי אכל־ממנו אכלת (Have you eaten from the tree which I commanded you not to eat from it?).[62] The context of the accusation in 3:11 is that Adam has disobeyed God by eating from the prohibited fruit of "the tree of the knowledge of good and evil." Both 4Q504 and 4Q422 link the prohibition

60. Employing the medial form of *tsade* (צ) instead of the final form (ץ), line 10 reads מעצ (instead of מעץ).

61. 4Q504 (col I, line 8): ותקם עליו לבלתי ס[ור] (And You charged him not to turn as[ide]).

62. Chazon, "The Creation and Fall of Adam in the Dead Sea Scrolls," 15.

given to Adam (Gen 2:16–17) to his subsequent disobedience (Gen 3:11). However, compared to 4Q504 (col I, line 8), the retelling of the prohibition in 4Q422 (col I, line 10) reflects more directly the language of Genesis 3:11.[63] This presentation of the prohibition in 4Q422 (col I, line 10) then immediately, and aptly, moves to a description of Adam's rebellion (col I, lines 11–12).

Adam's Rebellion and the Sin–Judgment Cycle

Lines 11–12 refer to Adam's rebellion: [ו]יקום עליו וישכחו[חוקיו] . . . ביצר רע ולמעש[י רשעה] ([and] he rose up against Him and they forgot [His statutes] . . . with an evil inclination and for work[s of wickedness]).[64] Notably, line 12 employs the phrase ביצר רע (with an evil inclination) in reference to Adam's rebellion (Genesis 3). This phrase is adopted from Genesis 6:5, which refers to the antediluvian rebellion.[65] In this manner, the author of 4Q422 links the Eden and Flood stories, applying the "evil inclination" to both, Adam's fall and the antediluvian rebellion. Consequently, Chazon suggested, "The implicit interpretation is that the evil inclination caused these sins."[66] This idea that an "evil inclination" was the cause of Adam's rebellion is not found in the Genesis account. In 4Q422, the references to Adam's rebellion and the "evil inclination" (lines 11–12) immediately follow the prohibition given to Adam (line 10), which reflects the language of Genesis 2:17 and 3:11. This suggests that the author of 4Q422 linked the "evil inclination" to Adam's choice regarding the prohibition from "the tree of the knowledge of good and evil" in Genesis 2:17. The language imported from 3:11 into this retelling of the prohibition in line 10 already indicates that Adam would choose to rebel by eating from the prohibited tree. Thus, the context seems to indicate that the author of 4Q422 viewed the "evil inclination" as the cause of Adam's rebellion. Nonetheless, the fragmentary nature of the text precludes any certainty as to how the "evil inclination" is

63. 4Q422 (col I, line 10): [ ]ל[ב]לתי אכול מעצ הד[עת טוב ורע]; Gen 3:11: המן־העץ אשר צויתיך לבלתי אכל־ממנו אכלת. Concerning 4Q504 (col I, line 8), לבלתי is the only direct lexical link to Gen 3:11.

64. For the reconstruction of the latter part of line 11 as וישכחו[חוקיו] (and they forgot His statutes), cf. 4Q166 II:3–4 (וישכחו . . . מצוותיו) and 4Q436 I:5 (בל ישכחו חוקיכה).

65. Gen 6:5: וכל־יצר מחשבת לבו רק רע כל־היום (and every inclination of the thoughts of his heart was only evil continually).

66. Chazon, "The Creation and Fall of Adam in the Dead Sea Scrolls," 17.

applied to Adam's rebellion. Another possibility is that the author viewed the "evil inclination" as a result of Adam's rebellion.

The literary juxtaposition of Adam's sin (column I) with the antediluvian sin and consequent Flood judgment (column II) is part of the sin-judgment cycle in 4Q422. The Flood story in column II is then linked to the plagues story in column III. Both of these narratives: a) describe well known examples of God's judgment of the wicked and deliverance of His people and b) contain statements regarding the purpose of those judgments, introduced by למען (cf. II:8–9; III:7). The sin-judgment cycle continues in column III, where Pharaoh's heart was hardened to sin (line 7), immediately followed by the plague judgments (lines 7–12). Thus, Adam's rebellion is presented in the larger context of a sin-judgment cycle in which a central concern is to make God's glory known to eternal generations.[67]

Interpretation of the Creation Account in 4Q422: Conclusions

Though often labeled a "paraphrase," 4Q422 is another example of rewritten Bible in the Second Temple period. The author selectively reworked biblical passages, juxtaposing the creation, Flood, and plagues narratives for hortatory or homiletic purposes. The retelling of the creation account in the first column is fragmentary. Nonetheless, several aspects of biblical interpretation are brought to light.

First, the text appears to affirm the biblical teaching of the creation of the universe by God's spoken word (line 6). The author summarizes the Genesis 1 description of the manner in which God created by His spoken word, employing language from Psalm 33:6. The phrase עשה בדברו (He made by His word) may also reflect the ancient understanding of the "word" functioning as God's agent in creating the universe (cf. *Tg. Neof.* Gen 1; John 1:1–3). Second, the inclusion of the phrase ורוח קודשו (and His Holy Spirit) appears to indicate some sort of role for the Holy Spirit in

67. The purpose of judgment is noted twice in the extant text. In regard to the Flood judgment, II:8–9 states: [המי]ם גב[רו]על [הארץ . . . למען]טהר חיט ולמען דעת כבוד על[יון [. . . ([the water]s were migh[ty] upon [the earth in order to] cleanse sin and in order to make known the glory of the Most Hi[gh …]). Regarding the plague judgments, III:7 states: [ו]יחזק את לב[ו ל]חטוא למען דעת א[ת כבוד]אל עד דו[רות]עולם ([and] He hardened [his] heart [so that he would] sin in order to make known [the glory of] God for eternal gener[ations]). In column I, the judgment upon Adam, along with a statement regarding the purpose of that judgment, is not found in the extant text. It is possible that it has been lost. It is also possible that the Eden and Flood stories were woven into a single story.

creation week (line 7; cf. Gen 1:2). The text is too fragmentary at this point to determine anything more specific concerning the author's understanding of the Holy Spirit's role(s) in creation. Third, the author retells the giving of dominion to Adam (line 9), linking it to the prohibition given to Adam (line 10) and his subsequent rebellion (lines 11–12). As a result, 4Q422 contrasts Adam's dominion (to eat the fruit) with his subsequent rebellion (eating the prohibited fruit). Fourth, the prohibition given to Adam in line 10 (לבלתי אכול מעצ הד[עת טוב ורע]) reflects Genesis 2:17 and foreshadows his disobedience in lines 11–12 by employing language from God's accusation in Genesis 3:11 (המן־העץ אשר צויתיך לבלתי אכל־ממנו אכלת). Last, the phrase ביוצר רע (with an evil inclination) is employed in reference to Adam's rebellion (line 12), suggesting that the author understood the "evil inclination" as the cause of Adam's rebellion. If this is the case, a further implication is that 4Q422 understands Adam as being created with good and evil inclinations.[68]

68. Elgvin noted, "4Q422 probably contains an early allusion to what later developed into the rabbinical concept of 'the good and evil inclinations'" ("The Genesis Section of 4Q422," 188).

CHAPTER SIX

QUMRAN INTERPRETATION OF THE GENESIS CREATION ACCOUNT

4QINSTRUCTION (4Q416, 4Q417, 4Q423)

Discovery of 4QInstruction

SEVERAL FRAGMENTARY COPIES OF a wisdom text known as *Musar le-Mebin* (4QInstruction)[1] were discovered by Bedouin in Cave 4 in 1952. Fragments from three of these copies (4Q416, 4Q417, and 4Q423) contain material dealing with the Genesis creation account. It should also be noted that another copy of this work (1Q26), consisting of several small fragments, had previously been discovered among the scrolls from Cave 1. Soon after, in 1955, 1Q26 was published by J. T. Milik in volume 1 of the *Discoveries in the Judaean Desert* series. However, the texts from Cave 4 (4Q415–418, 423) would not be published until the 1990s. Preliminary publications of 4QInstruction appeared in 1992 by Ben Wacholder and Martin Abegg Jr. in *A Preliminary Edition of the Unpublished Dead Sea*

1. This composition was formerly called *Sapiential Work A*. The title מוסר למבין (*Musar le-Mebin*), meaning "Instruction for the Understanding One," was later assigned to this composition in the 1990s (see Elgvin, "An Analysis of 4QInstruction," 5; Strugnell and Harrington, DJD XXXIV, 3). Hence, the work is often referred to by the abbreviation 4QInstruction.

Scrolls and by Robert Eisenman and Michael Wise in *The Dead Sea Scrolls Uncovered*. Then in 1999, over forty-five years after the discovery of these texts, the official edition of 4QInstruction was published by John Strugnell, Daniel Harrington, and Torleif Elgvin in volume 34 of the *Discoveries in the Judaean Desert* series. Strugnell and Harrington were responsible for 4Q415–418 and a re-edition of 1Q26, while Elgvin published 4Q423.

Physical Description of 4QInstruction

4QInstruction is the largest and best preserved wisdom text from Qumran.[2] There are several fragmentary copies of this composition: 1Q26, 4Q415, 4Q416, 4Q417, 4Q418, 4Q418a, and 4Q423.[3] In all, these copies are represented by over four hundred fragments. All of the manuscripts are written in Hebrew and are dated to the first century BC or the first half of the first century AD. Among the fragmentary copies, only 4Q416, 4Q417, and 4Q423 preserve material that touches on the interpretation and pedagogical use of the Genesis creation account.

4Q416 consists of 22 fragments. Many of the fragments are quite small. However, two fragments are notable. Fragment 1 likely represents the beginning of the composition based on the wide right margin.[4] Portions of eighteen lines of text from this first column are preserved. Fragment 2 is the longest fragment of 4QInstruction, preserving large portions of text from four columns. The bottom margin is preserved for the first three columns and the top margin is also preserved for the second and third columns (which contain 21 lines of text). The scribal hand is transitional between late Hasmonean and early Herodian, dating the manuscript to the early to mid-first century BC.[5]

2. Goff, *4QInstruction*, 1–2; Lange, "Wisdom Literature from the Qumran Library," 2419. The largest copy of 4QInstruction is 4Q418, which consists of roughly three hundred fragments. It has been proposed that, in its original form, the length of this copy likely rivaled the largest Qumran manuscripts (Strugnell and Harrington, DJD XXXIV, 2; see also Kampen, *Wisdom Literature*, 38).

3. For a discussion on determining the number of copies, see Goff, *4QInstruction*, 3–7.

4. This fragment is generally recognized as representing the beginning of the composition. Cf. Strugnell and Harrington, DJD XXXIV, 73; Goff, *4QInstruction*, 4–8; Kampen, *Wisdom Literature*, 39.

5. For a letter-by-letter paleographical analysis, see Strugnell and Harrington, DJD XXXIV, 74–76. They also conclude that 4Q416 is some twenty-five years older than

4Q417 is represented by 29 fragments. Most of these fragments are small, with a number of these poorly preserved (e.g. damaged surface and letters). Two fragments are larger, preserving a more substantial amount of text. Fragment 1 preserves portions of two columns of text. The bottom margin is clearly preserved for the first column, which contains 27 lines of text. It is uncertain if the small amount of blank space above the first extant line represents the top margin or if there was another line of text that is now lost. This column contains several lines of text addressing creation theology. Fragment 2 is notable in that it preserves a large portion of a column of text. The top, bottom, and right margins are preserved for this column, which contains 28 lines of text.[6] Paleographical analysis indicates that 4Q417 was written in an early Herodian formal hand, dating the manuscript to the latter part of the first century BC.[7]

4Q423 consists of 24 fragments. Many of these fragments are quite small, but a few are more moderate (e.g. frags. 1 and 5). Fragment 1 preserves the top margin and portions of seven lines of text. The extant text of this fragment is significant due to its portrayal of the Garden of Eden, along with dominion and wisdom for the מבין (*mebin* "understanding one"). The scribal hand is middle or late Herodian, dating the manuscript to the first half of the first century AD (AD 1–50).[8]

4QInstruction: A Qumran Composition?

4QInstruction evidently represents a Jewish composition from the Second Temple period. However, this work may not have been composed by the Qumran sectarian community. First, 4QInstruction is generally believed to have been composed sometime in the late third century or first half of the second century BC.[9] If this is the case, then 4QInstruction was composed

4Q415, 4Q417, and 4Q418.

6. The DJD edition included other pieces for fragment 2, which represent a second column.

7. Strugnell and Harrington, DJD XXXIV, 143–47; Goff, *4QInstruction*, 5.

8. Elgvin proposes a range of 10 BC–AD 50. He then concludes, "A date in the early first century CE seems probable" (DJD XXXIV, 506–07). Similarly, Goff places it in the "first half of the first century C.E." (*4QInstruction*, 7).

9. For example, see Elgvin, "An Analysis of 4QInstruction," 183–89; Goff, *4QInstruction*, 28–29; Kampen, *Wisdom Literature*, 43; Lange, "Wisdom Literature from the Qumran Library," 2418–19; Wold, "Genesis 2–3 in Early Christian Tradition and 4QInstruction," 329.

prior to the sectarian settlement at Qumran.[10] Second, this work does not contain distinctly sectarian language or teaching that is found in sectarian texts at Qumran.[11] Nonetheless, as Matthew Goff noted, "there are striking affinities between the core writings of the *yahad* and 4QInstruction."[12]

While 4QInstruction was likely not composed at Qumran, it appears to have been a fairly important work for the sectarian community. First, the numerous copies of 4QInstruction found at Qumran indicate that this composition was likely used by the Essenes.[13] Second, these copies, dated to the first century BC and the first half of the first century AD, indicate that this work was transmitted over a period of time up until a late stage in the history of the Qumran settlement.[14] Third, a copy (1Q26) was found in Cave 1, where some of the most important texts related to the Qumran community were stored.[15] Last, the rest of the copies were found in Cave 4, a dwelling space directly linked to the Qumran site.[16] Thus, 4QInstruction appears to have been an important wisdom composition that was transmitted, studied, and used by the Essenes at Qumran.

10. Benjamin Wold attested, "4QInstruction is commonly viewed as predating the *Yahad* . . ." ("Genesis 2–3 in Early Christian Tradition and 4QInstruction," 329).

11. For example, there are no references to the office of the *maskil*, or to figures such as the "Teacher of Righteousness" or the "Wicked Priest" (see Goff, *4QInstruction*, 27); Cf. Nitzan, "The Ideological and Literary Unity of 4QInstruction and its Authorship," 257. Also, in 4QInstruction, the root יחד (*yahad*) is used adverbially (meaning "together"), not as a noun denoting the "community" as is commonly employed in sectarian texts. For example, while the *Community Rule* (1QS) does employ the root adverbially in places, this sectarian document repeatedly employs the term to denote the community: היחד (the community), אנשי היחד (the men of the community), and יחד אל (the community of God).

12. Goff, *4QInstruction*, 28. For example, רז נהיה (the mystery that is to be) is a repeated key phrase in 4QInstruction that is employed in the *Community Rule* (1QS) XI:3–4.

13. Ibid.

14. Elgvin, "The Reconstruction of Sapiential Work A," 559; "An Analysis of 4QInstruction," 10.

15. For example, the *Community Rule* (1QS), *War Scroll* (1QM), *Hodayot* (1QH[a]), and *Habakkuk Pesher* (1QpHab). Torleif Elgvin suggested, ". . . probably only copies of the most important books were hidden in Cave 1" ("An Analysis of 4QInstruction," 10); see also Kampen, *Wisdom Literature*, 43.

16. Thus, it is likely that 4QInstruction was present in the Qumran community before it was conveniently placed in this nearby cave as the Romans approached Qumran in AD 68.

View of Khirbet Qumran looking south, with Cave 4 in close proximity (Photograph by Jeremy D. Lyon)

History of Research on 4QInstruction

Due to the substantial delay in publishing the numerous fragmentary texts from Cave 4, scholarly research on 4QInstruction would not begin until the 1990s. Since then, this wisdom text has received a significant amount of scholarly attention. Many publications deal with a broad range of issues related to the composition as a whole, while some specifically address interpretation of the creation account in 4QInstruction. This survey of the history of research on 4QInstruction is necessarily select, focusing on some of the works most relevant to the study of Qumran interpretation of the creation account.

Torleif Elgvin

Torleif Elgvin provided substantial contributions to the study of 4QInstruction during the 1990s. At a conference on the Dead Sea Scrolls in 1992,

Elgvin presented an introduction to 4QInstruction, along with its relationship to other Qumran texts. He also addressed some of the theology based on the order of creation. This conference paper was then published in 1994 as a chapter, titled "Admonition Texts from Qumran Cave 4," in *Methods of Investigation of the Dead Sea Scrolls and the Khirbet Qumran Site: Present Realities and Future Prospects.*[17] In 1995, he published a reconstruction of the textual material in an article in *Revue de Qumran*, titled "The Reconstruction of Sapiential Work A."[18] Elgvin's most extensive research on 4QInstruction can be found in his unpublished 1997 doctoral thesis, "An Analysis of 4QInstruction."[19] His purpose was to "provide a systematic analysis of 4QInstruction."[20] This analysis included: 1) a reconstruction of the textual material, 2) an investigation of the composition's literary genres and styles, major themes, and provenance, and 3) a text edition of the major fragments.[21] The text edition provides detailed commentary on the sections of 4QInstruction relating to the Genesis creation account. In 1999, Elgvin published the official edition of 4Q423 in volume 34 of the *Discoveries in the Judaean Desert* series.[22]

John Strugnell and Daniel J. Harrington

John Strugnell and Daniel J. Harrington were responsible for publishing 4Q415–18 and a re-edition of 1Q26 in the DJD edition of 4QInstruction.[23] For each manuscript, the edition included a physical description of the text, paleographical and orthographical notes, a transcription and translation of the text, notes on the readings, line-by-line comments on the text, and plates of the text. Thus, this edition provides detailed observations on the texts relating to the creation account. Harrington has further addressed 4QInstruction through a number of publications.[24]

17. Elgvin, "Admonition Texts from Qumran Cave 4," 179–94.

18. Elgvin, "The Reconstruction of Sapiential Work A," 559–80.

19. Elgvin's research was conducted at the Hebrew University of Jerusalem.

20. Elgvin, "An Analysis of 4QInstruction," 5.

21. Within the discussion of major themes, Elgvin briefly surveys texts that deal with creation, God's ordering of the universe, and man's place on earth (Ibid., 146–50).

22. Strugnell et al., *Qumran Cave 4, XXIV: Sapiential Texts, Part 2.*

23. Ibid.

24. For example, see Harrington, "Wisdom at Qumran," 137–52; *Wisdom Texts from Qumran*, 40–59; "Two Early Jewish Approaches to Wisdom: Sirach and Sapiential

Eibert Tigchelaar

In 1999, Eibert Tigchelaar contributed a chapter, titled "Eden and Paradise: The Garden Motif in Some Early Jewish Texts," in *Paradise Interpreted: Representations of Biblical Paradise in Judaism and Christianity.*[25] He examined interpretation of the Eden motif (the use of the garden and trees) in early Jewish literature, which included texts from Qumran. Tigchelaar's 2001 work, *To Increase Learning for the Understanding Ones*, essentially functioned as a supplement to the DJD edition of 4QInstruction.[26]

Matthew Goff

Several works by Matthew Goff have enhanced the study of 4QInstruction in general and are relevant to the study of Qumran interpretation of the creation account. In 2003, Goff published a revised version of his dissertation, titled *The Worldly and Heavenly Wisdom of 4QInstruction.* He included discussion of the theme of creation and the use of Genesis 1–3 in 4QInstruction. In 2013, Goff published a commentary, titled *4QInstruction*, which contains a critical text, translation, textual notes, and commentary on all the major fragments of 4QInstruction. Particularly helpful is the detailed commentary on the texts (4Q416, 4Q417, 4Q423) dealing with the creation account.[27] In book chapters such as "Genesis 1–3 and Conceptions of Humankind in 4QInstruction, Philo and Paul" (2009) and "Adam, the Angels and Eternal Life: Genesis 1–3 in the Wisdom of Solomon and 4QInstruction" (2010), he has dealt specifically with issues of interpretation concerning the creation account in 4QInstruction. Goff has also published other works on 4QInstruction, including articles in *Dead Sea Discoveries* (2003, 2004) and the *Eerdmans Dictionary of Early Judaism* (2010).

Work A," 263–75; "Creation," 155–57; "Wisdom Texts," 976–80.

25. Tigchelaar, "Eden and Paradise," 37–62.

26. The second part of this volume (chs. 13–18) discusses in more detail matters such as the beginning of the composition, the relationship of 4QInstruction to the *Community Rule* (1QS) and the *Hodayot* (1QH[a]), and certain themes. For another discussion on the beginning of 4QInstruction, see Tigchelaar, "Towards a Reconstruction of the Beginning of 4QInstruction," 99–126.

27. For example, Goff notes that 4Q423, frag 1, 1–3, is "important for understanding the interpretation of Gen 1–3 in early Jewish literature." He observes that the addressee (the *mebin*) is likened to Adam and that the Garden of Eden "functions as a metaphor for the knowledge that the *mebin* can obtain through his elect status" (*4QInstruction*, 290–96).

Benjamin Wold

Benjamin Wold has contributed several works relating to creation in 4QInstruction. In his 2005 publication, *Women, Men and Angels: The Qumran Wisdom Document "Musar leMevin" and Its Allusions to Genesis Creation Traditions*, he systematically identifies and analyzes allusions to Genesis 1–3 traditions in 4QInstruction and its understanding of women, men, and angels. In a 2013 *Revue de Qumran* article, "The Universality of Creation in *4QInstruction*," Wold examined passages concerning the creation and division of humanity.[28] Then in 2016, he published an article, titled "Genesis 2–3 in Early Christian Tradition and 4QInstruction," in *Dead Sea Discoveries*. Notable is the association of the Garden of Eden with human choice in both 4QInstruction and early Christian interpreters.

John Kampen

In 2011, John Kampen published *Wisdom Literature*, which contains commentary on various wisdom texts from Qumran, including 4QInstruction. Kampen introduces 4QInstruction with a general description of the manuscripts and the composition's content, provenance, and literary matters (such as the beginning of the composition and key terms). Most relevant to this study on interpretation of the creation account is his line-by-line commentary on the texts of 4Q416, 4Q417, and 4Q423.

Structure, Genre, and Content of 4QInstruction

The various copies of 4QInstruction are fragmentary in nature, making it difficult to determine the original sequence of texts (hence, the original structure of the composition). However, as noted, 4Q416, frag 1, likely represents the beginning of the composition based on the wide right margin (c. 3 cm). The preserved portion of this first column of text speaks of God's ordering and ruling of the cosmos (lines 1–9) and the eschatological judgment of the righteous and the wicked (lines 10–17). Also, within the context

28. For example, Wold observed, "In *4QInstruction* all of humankind was created in the likeness of God and the angels and they all originally sought mysterious, revealed wisdom as well as the knowledge of good and evil" ("The Universality of Creation in *4QInstruction*," 211). This task is likened to tending and keeping the Garden of Eden and the ones who do not search for knowledge and wisdom are expelled from the garden.

of the eschatological judgment is a reference to the righteous discerning between "good and evil" and to the "inclination of the flesh" (lines 15–17). In this manner, the composition appears to establish a theological framework for the wisdom instruction that follows.[29] Goff noted, "These two themes complement one another and establish a theological framework for the rest of the composition that stresses eschatological recompense as an expression of God's dominion over the natural order."[30] Beyond the placement of 4Q416, frag 1, it is difficult to determine much about the original structure of the rest of the composition.[31] However, general reconstructions of a particular text in relation to another text within the composition can be reasonably determined when there is overlapping text and/or the texts are from the same wad of texts.

The composition is pedagogical in nature and is often addressed to a מבין (*mebin* "understanding one"). Thus, 4QInstruction is generally considered to be a wisdom text. Elgvin has suggested that this composition represents a "conflation of two literary layers."[32] The *sapiential admonitions* (similar to biblical wisdom texts such as Proverbs) concern daily life such as family relationships, farmer responsibilities, work ethics, financial matters, and humble lifestyle.[33] The *theological discourses* deal with eschatology and the revelation of God's mysteries. These longer discourses include a variety of genres such as wisdom instruction, announcements of judgment and salvation, and biblical paraphrase. Elgvin concluded that an author/editor "with a strong interest in divine revelation and eschatology combined a

29. Strugnell and Harrington, DJD XXXIV, 8.

30. Goff, *4QInstruction*, 45.

31. Matthew Goff observed, "Beyond the identification of 4Q416 1 as the beginning of 4QInstruction, relatively little can be plausibly inferred about the original structure of the composition" (*4QInstruction*, 8); John Kampen has gone so far as to state, "A systematic reconstruction of a unified text incorporating all of the fragments is not possible" (*Wisdom Literature*, 39).

32. Elgvin, "An Analysis of 4QInstruction," 53–57; "Wisdom and Apocalypticism in the Early Second Century BCE—The Evidence of 4QInstruction," 226–28; See also, Nitzan, "The Ideological and Literary Unity of 4QInstruction and Its Authorship," 257–79.

33. While similar to admonitions found in Proverbs, there are also some notable differences. For example, Bilha Nitzan observed, ". . . it is noteworthy that its admonitions are not phrased in brief maxims, such as those found in such traditional sapiential books as Proverbs and Sirach, et al., but in composite sayings. . . . many issues in the admonitions of 4QInstruction are structured by several sayings in different styles, creating composite messages" ("The Ideological and Literary Unity of 4QInstruction and Its Authorship," 259).

number of longer discourses with older wisdom admonitions representing traditional sapiential viewpoints, and thus created a larger, composite didactic work."[34] Goff also observed, "4QInstruction does more, however, than repeat teachings found in older wisdom. The text combines traditional wisdom with an apocalyptic worldview."[35] Thus, 4QInstruction can perhaps be understood as "apocalyptic wisdom."

An important and distinctive phrase in the composition is רז נהיה (*raz nihyeh*), meaning "the mystery that is to be" or perhaps "the mystery of existence."[36] The phrase occurs over twenty times in the extant portions of the composition.[37] The word רז (*raz*), often translated "mystery" or "secret," is a Persian loanword that often indicates the revelation of Divine knowledge.[38] The word occurs nine times in the Aramaic section of the book of Daniel (2:18–19, 27–30, 47 [2x]; 4:6).[39] The word is used in reference to God revealing knowledge/wisdom to Daniel concerning the interpretation of Nebuchadnezzar's dream.[40] In this case, the "mystery" revealed by God concerns "the future course of human history."[41] The word

34. Elgvin, "An Analysis of 4QInstruction," 57.

35. Goff, "Reading Wisdom at Qumran," 265.

36. For the translation "the mystery that is to be," see Collins, "Wisdom Reconsidered, in Light of the Scrolls," 272–74; Goff, "The Mystery of Creation in 4QInstruction," 165–69; *4QInstruction*, 9, 14–17; Nitzan, "The Ideological and Literary Unity of 4QInstruction and Its Authorship," 261–62. For similar translations such as "the mystery that is to be/come," see Harrington, "Sapiential Work," 825–26; "the mystery that is to come," see Strugnell and Harrington, DJD XXXIV; "the mystery to come," see Elgvin, "Wisdom and Apocalypticism in the Early Second Century BCE—The Evidence of 4QInstruction," 232–36. For the translation "the mystery of existence," see Wold, *Women, Men, and Angels*, 20–24, 234–35; "Genesis 2–3 in Early Christian Tradition and 4QInstruction," 329; Stuckenbruck, "4QInstruction and the Possible Influence of Early Enochic Traditions," 259–61; Kampen, *Wisdom Literature*, 46–48.

37. Cf. Strugnell and Harrington, DJD XXXIV, 32; Goff, "The Mystery of Creation in 4QInstruction," 163; Wold, *Women, Men, and Angels*, 20, 244; Nitzan, "The Ideological and Literary Unity of 4QInstruction and Its Authorship," 261; Abegg, Bowley, and Cook, *The Dead Sea Scrolls Concordance*, 681.

38. See Goff, "The Mystery of Creation in 4QInstruction," 165.

39. In the Hebrew Bible, רז (*raz*) occurs only in the book of Daniel.

40. For example, see Dan 2:28–30: "But there is a God in heaven who reveals mysteries/secrets (רזין), and He has made known to King Nebuchadnezzar what will be in the last days. . . . and He who reveals mysteries/secrets (רזיא) has made known to you what will be. But as for me, this mystery/secret (רזא) has not been revealed to me because I have more wisdom than anyone living, but for our sakes who make known the interpretation to the king, and that you may know the thoughts of your heart."

41. Kampen, *Wisdom Literature*, 46.

רז (*raz*) is also used in several Hebrew Qumran texts.[42] For example, the *Habakkuk Pesher* employs the term in reference to the hidden meanings of Scripture that have been revealed by God (1QpHab VII:4–5).[43] While the word רז (*raz* "mystery") occurs fairly frequently in Second Temple period literature (including the Dead Sea Scrolls), the phrase רז נהיה (*raz nihyeh* "the mystery that is to be") occurs very rarely.[44] Outside of 4QInstruction, this phrase occurs in only two other compositions, the *Community Rule* (1QS XI:3–4) and the *Book of Mysteries* (1Q27 1 I:3–4; 4Q300 3, 4).[45] The רז נהיה (*raz nihyeh*) denotes revealed knowledge about God in 1QS XI:3–4,[46] and is associated with the eschatological judgment in 1Q27 1 I:3–4.[47] In 4QInstruction, the phrase indicates supernatural revelation that has been disclosed to the *mebin* (מבין) concerning not only future (eschatological) events, but also the Divine plan for the whole of history from creation to judgment.[48] In fact, understanding the future is tied up in understanding the created order, established from the beginning.[49] Wold has observed that the phrase רז נהיה (*raz nihyeh*) often occurs in fragments containing allusions to creation,[50] which presupposes "a link between this mystery and

42. For example, 1QS III:23; IV:6, 18; IX:18; XI:3, 5, 19; 1QpHab VII:5, 8, 14; 1QM III:9; XIV:9, 14; XVI:11, 16; XVII:9; 1QH^{a} V:6, 8, 19; IX:11, 13, 21, 29; XII:27; XIII:25; XV:27; XVII:23; XIX:10; XX:13, 20.

43. 1QpHab VII:4–5: פשרו על מורה הצדק אשר הודיעו אל את כול רזי דברי עבדיו הנבאים (Its interpretation concerns the Teacher of Righteousness, to whom God has made known all the mysteries of the words of His servants, the prophets).

44. Wold, *Women, Men and Angels*, 20; Goff, "The Mystery of Creation in 4QInstruction," 166.

45. Tigchelaar, *To Increase Learning for the Understanding Ones*, 204–05; Wold, *Women, Men and Angels*, 20; Kampen, *Wisdom Literature*, 49; Goff, *4QInstruction*, 14; Abegg, Bowley, and Cook, *The Dead Sea Scrolls Concordance*, 680–81.

46. 1QS XI:3–4: "For from the source of His knowledge He has disclosed His light, and my eyes have observed His wonders, and the light of my heart the mystery that is to be (רז נהיה)."

47. 1Q27 1 I:3–4: "And they do not know the mystery that is to be (רז נהיה), and they do not understand ancient matters. And they do not know what is going to come upon them, and their souls will not escape the mystery that is to be (רז נהיה)."

48. Goff, *4QInstruction*, 9, 15; "The Mystery of Creation in 4QInstruction," 168; Elgvin, "Wisdom and Apocalypticism in the Early Second Century BCE—The Evidence of 4QInstruction," 232; Wold, *Women, Men and Angels*, 234–35, 244–45; Kampen, *Wisdom Literature*, 47–48.

49. Wold noted, "This mystery likely coordinates *Urzeit* with *Endzeit*" (*Women, Men and Angels*, 245); see also Kampen, *Wisdom Literature*, 47–48.

50. For example, 4Q416 frag 2, II:9; II:9, 14, 18, 21; 4Q417 frag 1, I:2, 8, 13, 18, 21,

creation."[51] Thus, the various allusions to Genesis 1–3 are foundational for the wisdom instruction. Further, the *mebin* (מבין) is often exhorted to study and contemplate the רז נהיה (*raz nihyeh*). This divinely revealed knowledge of the created order (from creation to judgment) is the means by which wisdom/knowledge is attained.

The Divinely Ordered Cosmos

4Q416 frag 1 preserves a fragmentary column of text which likely represents the beginning of the composition. The extant text speaks of God's ordering and ruling of the cosmos (lines 1–9), which serves as the framework for the following description of eschatological judgment and exhortations for the righteous to discern between good and evil (lines 10–17). The extant text of 4Q416 frag 1 is primarily on the right-hand side of the column. The missing text of the left-hand side of the column is accentuated in lines 1–9, while lines 10–15 preserve more text. Fortunately, some of the missing text on the left-hand side of the column can be reconstructed based on the overlapping material from 4Q418 (frags 1–2c, 229). Tigchelaar observed that the additional text from the overlapping fragments of 4Q418 ". . . shows that the first lines (4Q416 1 1–10) not only deal with 'God's orderly rule over the cosmos—the heavenly hosts and the luminaries,' but more specifically with the orderly courses of these luminaries and hosts."[52] In addition, there are a number of lexical links between these opening lines of 4QInstruction and Genesis 1–2: רוח "spirit" (4Q416 1 1; Gen 1:2), כוכבי "stars (of)" (4Q416 1 1, cf. 4Q418 229; ככבים Gen 1:16), אור "light" (4Q416 1 1, cf. 4Q418 229; Gen 1:3–5, 15–18), מועד "season/appointed time" (4Q416 1 3, 8; Gen 1:14), צבאם "their host" (4Q416 1 4, 6; Gen 2:1), השמים "the heavens" (4Q416 1 7; Gen 1:1, 14–15, 17; 2:1, 4), מאורות "luminaries/lights" (4Q416 1 7, cf. 4Q418 1–2c; Gen 1:14–16), אתות "signs" (4Q416 1 8; Gen 1:14). It is readily apparent that much of this language reflects the biblical description of the creation of the luminaries on day four (Gen 1:14–19). Thus, this description of the divinely ordered nature of the cosmos in lines 1–9 (along with overlapping fragments from 4Q418) employs language from the Genesis creation account.

25; 4Q418 frag 177, 7.

51. Wold, *Women, Men and Angels*, 244–45.

52. Tigchelaar, *To Increase Learning for the Understanding Ones*, 177.

> 1. every spirit [. . . stars of light,] 2. And to mete out His desire [. . . they run on from time eternal,] 3. season by season and [. . . without ceasing, properly they go] 4. according to their host to have dom[inion with authority and to . . . for kingdom] 5. and kingdom, for pro[vince and province, for man and man . . .] 6. according to the need of their host. [And the regulation of all of them belongs to Him . . .] 7. And the host of the heavens He has established f[orever . . . and luminaries] 8. for their wonders and signs of [their] se[asons . . . they proclaim] 9. one after another. And all their assignments [they] c[omplete and] make known [. . .] (4Q416 frag 1 and 4Q418 frags 1–2c and 229)

Lines 1–3 indicate that the proper order of the cosmos is being described. The end of line 1 preserves a reference to "stars of light" (ככבי אור). The beginning of line 2 preserves the phrase "and to mete out His desire" (ולתכן חפצו), which apparently refers to God's desire.[53] In the context of lines 2–3, this phrase likely depicts the idea that "the structure of the cosmos is an expression of God's desire for order."[54] The following text in lines 2b–3 refers to the continual and orderly course of the luminaries: "they run on from time eternal, season by season and . . . without ceasing, properly they go."

According to line 4, these heavenly objects properly go "according to their host" (לפי צבאם). In the Hebrew Bible, the word צבא (host) can refer to an army (human or angelic) or the heavenly bodies. Genesis 2:1, for example, employs צבאם (their host) in reference to the heavenly bodies.[55] Likewise, in the Qumran literature, צבא (host) can refer to an angelic army (e.g. 1QM XII:1)[56] or to the heavenly bodies (e.g. 4Q422 I:6).[57] Goff has

53. Strugnell and Harrington, DJD XXXIV, 84; Goff, *4QInstruction*, 46; Kampen, *Wisdom Literature* 60–61. It is also possible to read חפצו (His desire) as חפצי, which could be understood as "delights/pleasures of" (e.g. Lange, "Wisdom Literature from the Qumran Library," 2437) or "matters of" (e.g. Wold, *Women, Men and Angels*, 89). Tigchelaar understands חפצי as "tasks of." He further suggests that the two phrases (ככבי אור "stars of light" and ולתכן חפצי "and to mete out the tasks of") "possibly belong to two parallel clauses, for example, 'to establish the paths of the stars of light; and to mete out the tasks of the luminaries of . . .'" (*To Increase Learning for the Understanding Ones*, 178).

54. Goff, *4QInstruction*, 46–47.

55. Gen 2:1: "Thus the heavens and the earth and all their host (צבאם) were finished."

56. 1QM XII:1: "For there is a multitude of holy ones in heaven and hosts of angels (וצבאות מלאכים) in Your holy dwelling to p[raise] Your [truth]."

57. 4Q422 I:6: "[The heavens and the earth and all] their host (צבאם) He made by [His] word."

suggested that in 4Q416 frag 1, "host" refers to angels.[58] This suggestion is likely correct, but it is difficult to conclude with certainty based on the fragmentary nature of the text.

Lines 4–5 appear to further depict God's order and rule of the cosmos. He has made the heavenly objects move in an unceasing and orderly fashion (cf. lines 1–3) according to their host "to have dominion with authority" (למשור במשורה) (line 4). This is a somewhat difficult phrase. The root of the infinitive למשור (to rule/have dominion) may be either שרר or שרה, both meaning "to rule."[59] The term משורה can mean "measure," which coincides with the description of the orderly cosmos in lines 2–3.[60] Alternatively, Tigchelaar has suggested that משורה is a variant spelling of מסורה, which can refer to the "orbit," "station," or "position" of the stars (cf. 1QS X:3–4; 4QEn[c] 1 I:19 [*1 En* 2:1]; 4Q209 28, 2 [*1 En* 82:10]).[61] The extant text picks up again with the phrase "[for kingdom] and kingdom, for province and province, for man and man . . ." (line 5), which may depict God's order and rule over the cosmos as extending over all the affairs of man (kingdoms, provinces, and individuals). Strugnell and Harrington also suggested the possibility that this may depict "the heavenly bodies as giving their chronological signs to all lands and peoples."[62] The rest of the text from line 5 is not preserved.

Line 6 then begins with another difficult phrase: "according to the need of their host" (לפי מחסור צבאם).[63] The reference to "their host" (צבאם)

58. Goff, *4QInstruction*, 47.

59. Strugnell and Harrington, DJD XXXIV, 84; Goff, *4QInstruction*, 47. Cf. HALOT, 1354, 1362–63; BDB 976, 979.

60. HALOT, 640. Cf. Lev 19:35 and 1 Chr 23:29. Lange, for example, translates this phrase "to rule measured" ("Wisdom Literature from the Qumran Library," 2437).

61. Tigchelaar, *To Increase Learning for the Understanding Ones*, 178–79. Cf. Abegg, Bowley, and Cook, *The Dead Sea Scrolls Concordance*, 473, 878. Tigchelaar suggests possible translations for למשור במשורה as "to make an orbit" or "to keep station" (p. 179). Similarly, Wold translates this phrase as "to keep in its keeping" (*Women, Men and Angels*, 89).

62. Strugnell and Harrington, DJD XXXIV, 84.

63. The difficulty of this phrase was noted by Strugnell and Harrington, "The sense of מחסור when combined with צבאם (cf. 4Q415 9 9) is doubtful. 'Poverty,' 'lack,' or 'deficiency' fit ill with 'the angelic host' or 'the stellar host'" (DJD XXXIV, 84). Tigchelaar has suggested the possibility of a scribal error in which the copyist employed מחסור (need, lack) instead of מסחור (circuit, going around) (*To Increase Learning for the Understanding Ones*, 179). If this is the case, the phrase could be understood as "according to the circuit of their host," which would seemingly fit the context. However, the term מחסור (need, lack) occurs over twenty times in 4QInstruction (Abegg, Bowley, and Cook, *The*

likely denotes the angels (cf. line 4). The next phrase, ומשפט כולם לו (And the regulation of all of them belongs to Him), appears to indicate that the regulation of the angels belongs to God.[64] Thus, the divine order of the cosmos includes the heavenly bodies (lines 1–3), the affairs of man (line 5), and the angelic host (lines 4, 6).[65]

Line 7 further establishes God's creating and ordering of the celestial angelic host: "And the host of the heavens He has established f[orever . . .]" (וצבא השמים הכין מ[עת עולם]). In Genesis 2:1, the "host" of the heavens refers to the heavenly bodies. However, here in 4Q416 1 7, there is no reason to understand the phrase צבא השמים (the host of the heavens) as anything other than the angelic host (cf. lines 4, 6).[66] The material from the overlapping 4Q418 fragments further indicates that the term צבא (host) (lines 4, 6, 7) was employed in distinction from the language of the heavenly bodies such as כוכבי אור (stars of light) (line 1) and the מאורות (luminaries) (line 7).

Lines 7–9 further discuss the nature of the orderly structure of the cosmos. An intriguing statement is preserved in lines 7b–8: "and luminaries for their wonders and signs of [their] se[asons . . .] (ומאורות למופתיהמה ואותות מו]עדיהמה . . .]). The antecedent for the phrase "for their wonders and signs of their seasons" (line 8) is the "luminaries" (heavenly bodies) mentioned in line 7. Here in 4QInstruction, the continuous and orderly course of the luminaries (heavenly bodies) is described as "wonders" and "signs." These terms are found in the Hebrew Bible in reference to the plagues of Egypt (cf. Exod 3:20; 4:21; 7:3; Deut 6:22). Observing this, Goff

Dead Sea Scrolls Concordance, 440), which appears to argue against a scribal error in this case. Goff observed, "The term מחסור as written, however, seems to accord with the rest of 4Q416 1 6, which asserts that the 'regulation' (משפט) or orderly arrangement of the angels belongs to God. He controls all aspects of the celestial angels—both in terms of their needs and their movement" (*4QInstruction*, 48). Wold suggested, ". . . the description of the host as 'lacking' may be insightful. For instance, 4Q418 55 and 69 discuss angelic beings, in contrast to the addressee, as pursuing truth without becoming tired. . . . if 'lacking' refers to the imperfect *obtainment* of wisdom (רז נהיה) the hosts here may be described as 'lacking' too" (*Women, Men and Angels*, 89–90n20).

64. The context indicates that משפט likely denotes "regulation" rather than "judgment." See Tigchelaar, *To Increase Learning for the Understanding Ones*, 179; Goff, *4QInstruction*, 48. For the translation of משפט as "judgment," see Elgvin, "An Analysis of 4QInstruction," 238–39; Strugnell and Harrington, DJD XXXIV, 81–85; García Martínez and Tigchelaar, *The Dead Sea Scrolls Study Edition*, 848–49; Parry and Tov, *The Dead Sea Scrolls Reader*, 4:92–93; Kampen, *Wisdom Literature*, 60; Lange, "Wisdom Literature from the Qumran Library," 2437.

65. Lange, "Wisdom Literature from the Qumran Library," 2437.

66. See Strugnell and Harrington, DJD XXXIV, 84.

noted, "The regular, predictable structure of the cosmos is presented as 'wonders and signs,' testimony to God's dominion over the natural world, not unlike the plagues in the Exodus story."[67] In addition, the terms "luminaries" (מאורות), "signs" (אתות), and "seasons" (מועדים) in lines 7b–8 are found together in Genesis 1:14, reinforcing the astronomical function of the luminaries as chronological markers.[68] Accordingly, the "wonders" and "signs" of the luminaries in 4QInstruction may be understood as astronomical, perhaps even calendrical.[69] Tigchelaar has proposed that ". . . the text deals with the tasks of the luminaries, i.e., following their proper courses at the proper times . . . in order that men may know the set times of the festivals."[70]

Lines 8b–9 continue, "[. . . they proclaim] one after another. And all their assignments [they] c[omplete and] make known" (. . . יגידו] זה לזה וכל פקודתמה י[שלימו וי]ספרו). The first word, "they proclaim" (יגידו), is largely reconstructed. It is possible to understand the phrase "they proclaim one after another" as referring to the luminaries. For example, the *Community Rule* (1QS X:4, 7) describes the rotation of the heavenly bodies in conjunction with the days and seasons of the calendar as being in order, "one after another" (זה לזה).[71] The next phrase in line 9, וכל פקודתמה י[שלימו וי]ספרו (and all their assignments they complete and make known), seemingly points to "the adherence of the heavenly phenomena to the structure God provided for them."[72]

67. Goff, *4QInstruction*, 49.

68. Gen 1:14: "Then God said, 'Let there be luminaries (מארת) in the firmament of the heavens to divide the day from the night; and let them be for signs (אתת) and seasons (מועדים), and for days and years."

69. See Strugnell and Harrington, DJD XXXIV, 85; Goff, *4QInstruction*, 49.

70. Tigchelaar, *To Increase Learning for the Understanding Ones*, 179.

71. See Kampen, *Wisdom Literature*, 61–62. In light of the content of 4Q416 1 and the use of the rare phrase זה לזה (one after another) attested in 1QS X:4, 7, Kampen rejects the reconstruction "they proclaim" in favor of "day of his decree."

72. Goff, *4QInstruction*, 48. Note, however, that two issues add caution to this particular understanding: 1) the incomplete and fragmentary nature of these lines of text and 2) the meaning of the term פקודתמה (translated here as "their assignments"). The root of פקודתמה (פקודה) can mean "punishment, visitation" (cf. Abegg, Bowley, and Cook, *The Dead Sea Scrolls Concordance*, 621–22), but can also refer to a "commission, appointment, or office" (see HALOT, 958). Here in 4Q416 1 9, פקודתמה is generally understood as "their assignment(s)" or "the assignment of them." See Tigchelaar, *To Increase Learning for the Understanding Ones*, 179; García Martínez and Tigchelaar, *The Dead Sea Scrolls Study Edition*, 848–49; Goff, *4QInstruction*, 44, 49; Kampen, *Wisdom Literature*, 60. Similarly, the term has been translated as "their order" in Elgvin, "An Analysis of

The fragmentary nature of these opening lines of 4QInstruction (4Q416 1) requires a degree of caution regarding an understanding of certain aspects of the text. Nonetheless, the extant text speaks of God's order and rule of the cosmos, which includes the heavenly bodies, the angelic host, and the affairs of man. The theme of God's creation of the luminaries and their orderly courses goes back to the Genesis creation account and is well attested in Second Temple period literature (*Sir* 16:26–28; 43:1–10; *1 En* 2; 82–83; 1QS X:1–9; 1QH[a] IX:9–25; XX:1–11). The author never directly quotes the Genesis creation account, but draws from the language of the biblical record in depicting this theme of a divinely ordered creation. This description of God's order and rule of the cosmos (lines 1–9) serves as the framework for the following description of eschatological judgment and exhortations for the righteous to discern between good and evil (lines 10–17). Regarding the role of 4Q416 frag 1 within the composition as a whole, Harrington noted that the wisdom instructions that follow "were intended to help the one who is being instructed both to align himself with the correct order of the cosmos (as discerned from Gen 1 and probably on the basis of a solar calendar) and to prepare for the divine judgment."[73] These opening lines of 4QInstruction indicate the significance of creation (that is, the created order) as the theological basis for the sapiential instruction that follows.[74]

The Garden of Eden and Moral Freedom

4Q423 frag 1 is a relatively short fragment[75] containing paraphrase and interpretation of the Garden of Eden narrative of Gen 2–3. The language of the opening lines of text draws directly from the biblical account.

4QInstruction," 239; "their appointments" in Wold, *Women, Men and Angels*, 90. Alternatively, however, this term was translated as "their visitation (?)" in Strugnell and Harrington, DJD XXXIV, 83; "their punishment" in Lange, "Wisdom Literature from the Qumran Library," 2437. Accordingly, Lange views the phrase "and all their punishment they shall finish" in line 9 as moving the attention of the text to God's eschatological judgment.

73. Harrington, *Wisdom Texts from Qumran*, 41.

74. Wold, *Women, Men and Angels*, 91.

75. 4Q423 frag 1 technically consists of two fragments and preserves portions of seven lines of text.

1 [ ]וכל פרי תנובה וכל עץ נעים נחמד להשכיל הלוא גן נ[עים ונחמד]
2 [ ]ל[ה]שכיל מ[או]דה ובו המשילכה לעבדו ולשמרו ג[ן נאות]
3 [והאדמה] קוץ ודרדר תצמיח לכה וכוחה לא תתן לכה [ ]
4 [ ]במועלכה *vacat*

1 [ ] and every fruit of the produce and every delightful tree, desirable to make one wise. Is it not a garden de[lightful and desirable]

2 [ ] to make one v[er]y wise? And He has given you authority over it to work it and to keep it. *vacat* A [lush] gar[den . . .]

3 [. . . but the ground] will cause thorn and thistle to sprout for you and its strength will not yield to you . . .

4 [ ] when you are unfaithful. *vacat*

This column of text begins with an intriguing description of the Garden of Eden. In line 1, the phrase וכל פרי תנובה (and every fruit of the produce) seems to enhance the depiction of Eden as a lush garden. Though this phrase is not found in the Genesis account, the term פרי (fruit) occurs in the context of God's provision of eating from the trees of the garden (Gen 1:29; 3:2; cf. 2:16) and the prohibition of eating from the tree of the knowledge of good and evil (Gen 3:3, 6; cf. 2:17). This line continues by describing *every* tree of the garden as נעים (delightful) and נחמד (desirable) to make one wise. The phrase וכל עץ נעים נחמד להשכיל (and every delightful tree, desirable to make one wise) is a conflation of Gen 2:9, which describes Eden as containing כל־עץ נחמד למראה (every tree that is desirable to the sight), and Gen 3:6, which describes the tree of the knowledge of good and evil as נחמד העץ להשכיל (the tree desirable to make one wise). Both of these verses employ the term נחמד (desirable), but do so in different ways. In Gen 2:9, every tree is נחמד (desirable) *to the sight*, not to make one knowledgeable/wise. In Gen 3:6, only the tree of the knowledge of good and evil is נחמד (desirable) *to make one knowledgeable/wise*. Here in 4QInstruction, *every* tree of the garden is "desirable to make one wise." The end of line 1 then reframes this language in the form of a rhetorical question, "Is it not a garden de[lightful and desirable] [. . .] to make one v[er]y wise?" In other words, it should be evident to the *mebin* that the Garden of Eden is beautiful and can provide knowledge/wisdom.

Line 2 continues: ובו המשילכה לעבדו ולשמרו (And He has given you authority over it to work it and to keep it). This line employs language from Gen 2:15 and asserts that God has given the *mebin* authority over this beautiful garden that produces wisdom "to work it and to keep it." Here, the second person singular pronominal suffix (כה "you") in המשילכה (He has given you authority) indicates that the *mebin* is being likened to Adam in the garden.[76] Also, the same verb form המשילכה (He has given you authority) is used elsewhere in 4QInstruction (4Q418 81 3) in reference to the God-given inheritance of the *mebin* among the "sons of Adam" (בני אדם).[77] Presumably, 4Q423 1 2 is referring to the elect "son of Adam" (that is, the *mebin*), who is likened to Adam and who apparently has access to the knowledge/wisdom that Adam had in the garden.[78] This beautiful garden can produce knowledge/wisdom for the *mebin* who is "to work it and to keep it" (לעבדו ולשמרו; cf. Gen 2:15 לעבדה ולשמרה).[79] Throughout 4QInstruction, the *mebin* has access to the "the mystery that is to be" (that is, divinely revealed knowledge of the created order) and is repeatedly called to study and meditate upon it (e.g. 4Q417 1 I:1–27).[80] Thus, knowledge/wisdom is obtained through study and meditation upon "the mystery that is to be." Here, 4Q423 employs the Garden of Eden as a metaphor for the knowledge/wisdom the *mebin* (who is likened to Adam) can acquire through "tending and keeping" it.[81]

76. Elgvin also observed, "The 2nd sing. form המשילכה (line 2) in a passage which rephrases Genesis 2 points to some kind of relation between Adam and the addressee" (DJD XXXIV, 509).

77. Recognizing this, Elgvin concluded, "Therefore, המשילכה could have a double meaning in the text discussed here; referring both to Adam and the Garden of Eden as well as to the elect 'son of Adam' in his relation to the end-time community and inheritance" (DJD XXXIV, 510).

78. See Goff, *4QInstruction*, 293. He noted, "4Q423 1 2 implies, by metaphorically placing the *mebin* in the garden, that he has the potential to obtain the same knowledge that Adam once possessed in Eden, a restoration of primordial knowledge."

79. Here, in 4Q423 1 2, לעבדו ולשמרו has the meaning "to work it and keep it," in reference to the garden. However, 4Q423 1 2 employs the masculine pronominal suffixes instead of the feminine pronominal suffixes as found in Gen 2:15 (לעבדה ולשמרה). This may be instructive concerning the language of the biblical text. In Gen 2:15, לעבדה ולשמרה is likely better understood as "to worship and to obey," based on the grammatical construction and the literary context. For further discussion, see Sailhamer, *The Pentateuch as Narrative*, 100–01; "Genesis," 45.

80. For example, 4Q417 1 I:6–8 (with overlapping text from 4Q418 43–45 I): ". . . day and night meditate upon the mystery that is to be and seek/study it continually. And then you will know truth and iniquity, wisdom and folly. . . . And then you will know the difference between good and evil according to their deeds, for the God of knowledge is a foundation of truth."

81. Similarly, Prov 3:18 employs the "tree of life" as a metaphor for wisdom: "She [wisdom] is a tree of life (עץ חיים) to those who take hold of her, and happy are all who retain her."

Not only does the garden produce knowledge/wisdom (lines 1–2), but according to lines 3–4, it can also bring forth "thorn and thistle" due to the unfaithfulness of the *mebin*. Note that these lines of text continue to address the *mebin* through the repeated use of second person singular pronominal suffixes (line 3, לכה "to/for you" 2x; line 4, במועלכה "when you are unfaithful"). In line 3, the phrase קוץ ודרדר תצמיח לכה ([the ground] will cause thorn and thistle to sprout for you) directly reflects Gen 3:18: וקוץ ודרדר תצמיח לך (and it will cause thorn and thistle to sprout for you). The following phrase, וכוחה לא תתן לכה (and its strength will not yield to you), is drawn from Gen 4:12: לא־תסף תת־כחה לך (it [the ground] will no longer yield its strength to you). Goff observed, "In both Gen 3:18 and 4:12 the harshness of the soil is emphasized in the context of expulsion—Adam from the garden and Cain from his family."[82] Here in 4QInstruction, however, there is no prohibition from the garden. Rather, the *mebin* has been given authority over the garden. This garden can produce both knowledge/wisdom (lines 1–2) and "thorn and thistle" (line 3) for the *mebin*.[83]

4QInstruction employs the Garden of Eden metaphorically for pedagogical purposes. This beautiful garden can produce knowledge/wisdom for the *mebin* who is to "work it and keep it" *or* this same garden can sprout thorns and thistles for the *mebin* due to being unfaithful in this task of pursuing knowledge/wisdom. The author, utilizing material from Genesis 2–3, metaphorically places the *mebin* in the Garden of Eden with the exhortation to choose wisdom. Consequently, Wold proposed, "In 4QInstruction, tending wisdom producing trees in Eden relates to humanity's freedom of choice either to pursue and practice wisdom or not."[84] It seems likely that the author assumed the theme of moral freedom in Genesis 2–3 in this metaphorical depiction of Eden. The view that Genesis 2–3 teaches moral freedom (that is, every person, like Adam, is responsible for making decisions) is found elsewhere in Second Temple period literature (e.g. *Sir* 15:14–17)[85] and is attested by a number of Christian interpreters from the

82. Goff, *4QInstruction*, 295.

83. The understanding that the garden in 4Q423 1 3 can bring forth "thorn and thistle" is supported in *Hodayot* (cf. 1QH^a XVI:4–25). Concerning 4Q423 1 3, Wold likewise concluded that "wisdom trees, thorns and thistles grow together in the same garden" ("Genesis 2–3 in Early Christian Tradition and 4QInstruction," 333).

84. Wold, "Genesis 2–3 in Early Christian Tradition and 4QInstruction," 333. Goff also appears to approach this idea, stating, "The garden can symbolize either the right or the wrong path" (*4QInstruction*, 295).

85. *Sirach* 15:14–17: "It was He who created humankind in the beginning, and He

second and third centuries AD (e.g. Irenaeus, *Against Heresies*, IV.37.1).[86] While questions remain, 4Q423 frag 1 provides an intriguing example of how the Eden narrative of Genesis 2–3 was understood and employed in the context of wisdom instruction.

left them in the power of their own free choice. If you choose, you can keep the commandments, and to act faithfully is a matter of your own choice. He has placed before you fire and water; stretch out your hand for whichever you choose. Before each person are life and death, and whichever one chooses will be given." Translation from Wright III, "Wisdom of Ben Sira," 2250.

86. Pagels, *Adam, Eve, and the Serpent*, xxiii, xxvi, 73–74, 76, 108. Elaine Pagels noted, for example, "Clement of Alexandria (c. 180 C.E.) . . . agreed with most of his Jewish and Christian contemporaries that the real theme of the story of Adam and Eve is moral freedom and moral responsibility. Its point is to show that we are responsible for the choices we freely make—good or evil—just as Adam was" (p. xxiii). She further noted, "The whole point of the story of Adam, most Christians assumed, was to warn everyone who heard it not to misuse that divinely given capacity for free choice" (p. 108).

CHAPTER SEVEN

QUMRAN INTERPRETATION OF THE GENESIS CREATION ACCOUNT

MEDITATION ON CREATION (4Q303–305)

Discovery of 4Q303–305

A FEW SMALL FRAGMENTS, representing three copies of a composition titled *Meditation on Creation* (4Q303–305), were found in 1952 among the large cache of fragmentary texts from Cave 4. Though small, these fragments contain a number of allusions to the Genesis creation account. Like many of the other scrolls from Cave 4, the publication of 4Q303–305 would be delayed for decades. A preliminary edition was published in 1992 by Ben Zion Wacholder and Martin Abegg Jr. in *A Preliminary Edition of the Unpublished Dead Sea Scrolls.*[1] In 1997, the official edition of 4Q303–305 was published by Timothy Lim in volume 20 of the *Discoveries in the Judaean Desert* series.[2]

1. Wacholder and Abegg Jr., *A Preliminary Edition of the Unpublished Dead Sea Scrolls.*

2. Lim, "303. 4QMeditation on Creation A," 151–53; "304. 4QMeditation on Creation B," 155; "305. 4QMeditation on Creation C," 157–58 (hereafter, collectively referred to as DJD XX).

Physical Description of 4Q303–305

4Q303 consists of a couple small fragments of dark brown skin that are joined together. Portions of fourteen lines of text are preserved. The top margin is also preserved, but not the bottom, left, or right margins of this column. Thus, the extant lines of text represent the interior of the column, with the beginning and end of each line missing. Lines 1–11 generally preserve a few words of text, while lines 12–14 preserve only a few letters. The Hebrew text is written in a late Hasmonean or early Herodian formal script, dating the manuscript to c. 50–1 BC.[3]

4Q304 consists of only a single, tiny fragment, measuring 2.8 cm high and 2.9 cm wide.[4] This fragment preserves small portions of three lines of Hebrew text. The right margin of this column of text is preserved. It is possible that the top margin is also preserved, but the point in which the manuscript is damaged equally allows for the possibility that there was originally another line of text above the first extant line of text. The text is written in a Hasmonean script, dating the manuscript to the first century BC.

4Q305 is another relatively small fragment preserving small portions of four lines of Hebrew text. The top and right margins are preserved for this column of text. Only a few words (or portions of words) from the beginning of each line are extant. On the other side of the right margin is a badly damaged column of text with only a few extant letters. Doubts have been raised as to whether this illegible column on the right side belongs to the same composition as the column on the left.[5]

Combined, these copies of *Meditation on Creation* (4Q303–305) consist of only a few small fragments, each containing only portions of a few lines of text.[6] One particular caution seems warranted at this point. Though all three of these texts contain the theme of creation, manuscripts 4Q304 and 4Q305 are too fragmentary to conclude with any certainty whether or not they are copies of 4Q303.[7]

3. Lim, DJD XX, 151.

4. Ibid., 155.

5. For example, Lim views the two columns as more likely representing two different compositions based on the top margins not being aligned for these two adjacent columns. He noted, "So far as I am aware, there is no example of a Qumran text that has different top margins for adjacent columns of the same text" (DJD XX, 157).

6. 4Q303 (14 lines), 4Q304 (3 lines); 4Q305 (4 lines).

7. Giere, "A New Glimpse of Day One," 138n237.

History of Research on 4Q303–305

Since its publication in the 1990s, *Meditation on Creation* (4Q303–305) has not received as much scholarly attention as the other Qumran texts in this study. Generally speaking, the few scholarly treatments on this text are brief and, in some cases, serve only as ancillary components of broader studies. Nonetheless, several works are notable concerning this current study on interpretation of the creation account in 4Q303–305.

As noted, the official edition of *Meditation on Creation* (4Q303–305) was published in 1997 by Timothy Lim in volume 20 of the DJD series. This publication represents perhaps the most extensive treatment of 4Q303–305.[8] The publication of the primary text, 4Q303, includes a physical description, summary of contents, paleographical notes, transcription and translation of the text, notes on textual readings, and line-by-line comments on the text. The publication of both 4Q304 and 4Q305, however, includes only a brief physical and paleographical description, followed by a transcription and translation of the text.

Then, in 1999, Howard Jacobson made a substantial contribution in a very brief article (3 pages), titled "Notes on 4Q303," in *Dead Sea Discoveries*. Jacobson noted that the DJD edition of *Meditation on Creation* required "supplementation and correction." Thus, he sought to "clarify the text and its interpretation."[9] Jacobson addressed both the textual readings and interpretation of the text in line-by-line fashion and then proposed a new translation of 4Q303. Further, he suggested that this text represents wisdom literature based on his reading of the injunction or command ("you who understand, pay heed") in line 1 and the presence of the theme of creation.[10]

In a 2005 monograph, *Women, Men and Angels*, Benjamin Wold addressed Genesis creation traditions in *Musar le-Mebin* (4QInstruction). Woven into his discussion on the knowledge-bearing trees of Eden in 4Q423, he provided a brief, but helpful treatment of *Meditation on Creation*, which he understood as also representing a "positive conception of gaining the knowledge of good and evil."[11]

8. Nonetheless, the DJD publication devotes only three pages to 4Q303, one page to 4Q304, and two pages to 4Q305.

9. Jacobson, "Notes on 4Q303," 78.

10. Ibid., 80.

11. Wold, *Women, Men, and Angels*, 113–20. For the discussion on *Mediation on Creation*, see 117–18.

In 2009, Samuel D. Giere published a monograph, titled *A New Glimpse of Day One: Intertextuality, History of Interpretation, and Genesis 1.1–5*, in which he examined the intertextuality of Genesis 1:1–5 in Hebrew and Greek texts up to AD 200.[12] Included in his survey of the non-biblical Hebrew texts in chapter four is a short discussion on 4Q303 and its intertextual links to Genesis 1–3.[13]

Jean-Sébastien Rey provided a substantive discussion on the interpretation of the "knowledge of good and evil" in several Second Temple period texts, including 4Q303, in a 2017 chapter, "In the Garden of Good and Evil: Reimagining a Tradition (Sir 17:1–14, 4Q303, 4QInstruction, 1QS 4:25–26, and 1QSa 1:10–11)."[14] He did not seek here to answer the question of the meaning of that repeated phrase in Genesis 2–3, but rather "to evaluate the way ancient writers have read, rewritten, and reimagined it in late antiquity and, especially, how the vetitive related to knowledge of good and evil has been transformed and reimagined as a gift or a revelation to human beings."[15]

Content and Genre of 4Q303–305

Preserved only in fragmentary form, 4Q303 is the primary copy of the composition known as *Meditation on Creation*. Lim observed that the title of the composition ". . . appropriately describes what appears to be a reflection on God's creation."[16] While the fragmentary nature of 4Q303 makes it difficult to conclude too much about the composition as a whole, the extant portion of text focuses, at least in part, on creation. The fact that both the beginning and the end of each line of text is missing makes some of the readings more difficult to ascertain.

An Exhortation/Command for the Understanding Ones

The first line of 4Q303 reads: [ ].מבינים שמעו ו[ ]. In the DJD edition, Lim views מבינים as a plural participle ("having understood") and שמעו as a 3cp

12. This is a revision of his 2006 doctoral thesis at the University of St. Andrews.

13. Giere, *A New Glimpse of Day One*, 189–92.

14. Rey, "In the Garden of Good and Evil," 473–92.

15. Ibid., 473.

16. Lim, DJD XX, 151.

Qal *qatal* verb ("they listened"). Thus, he reads the first line as "having understood, they listened and [. . .]."[17] However, the plural participle, מבינים, can also be understood as the "understanding ones." Further, while it is possible to understand the verb form שמעו as a 3cp Qal *qatal* verb ("they listened"), it can also be understood as a masculine plural imperative ("listen/take heed"). Thus, the text can be read, perhaps more likely, as "[. . .] understanding ones listen/take heed and [. . .]." This understanding of line 1 as an injunction or imperative has generally been adopted.[18] Jacobson has noted that such a reading is "more likely," adding, "Such exhortations are commonplace (especially in wisdom texts)."[19]

The extant text of line 2 appears to continue the opening appeal: [ ]מים וישביתו מעל נ[ ] ([ ]*mym* and cause them to cease treachery *n*[ ]).[20] Lim reads this line "[ ]*mym* and they caused treachery to cease *n*[ ]."[21] However, in light of the imperative verb שמעו (listen/take heed) in the preceding phrase in line 1, וישביתו in line 2 is better understood as a 3mp Hiphil *yiqtol* verb with a regular *waw* conjunction (and cause them to cease).[22] Another intriguing reading has been proposed for line 2. The beginning of the line is broken off with only part of the initial מ (*mem*) preserved in מים. It is possible to reconstruct this word as [חכ]מים ("the wise ones") in parallel fashion to מבינים ("the understanding ones") mentioned

17. Ibid., 153.

18. The understanding of line 1 as an injunction or command is generally adopted: "[. . .] understanding ones listen, and [. . .]" (García Martínez and Tigchelaar, *The Dead Sea Scrolls Study Edition*, 668–69); "you who understand, pay heed and . . ." (Jacobson, "Notes on 4Q303," 78, 80); "those of understanding pay heed and . . ." (Nitzan, "The Idea of Creation and Its Implications in Qumran Literature," 253); "[. . .] those of understanding listen and [. . .]" (Giere, *A New Glimpse of Day One*, 189–90); "[. . . All] you who possess understanding, listen and [. . .]" (Wise et al., *The Dead Sea Scrolls: A New Translation*, 378). Lim acknowledged that שמעו can alternatively be read as "listen" or "hear" and also noted, "Qimron suggests that the plural participle may refer to 'sages,' namely those of understanding . . ." (DJD XX, 153).

19. Jacobson, "Notes on 4Q303," 78. See also, Nitzan, "The Idea of Creation and Its Implications in Qumran Literature," 253n47.

20. For this translation, see Nitzan, "The Idea of Creation and Its Implications in Qumran Literature," 253; Giere, *A New Glimpse of Day One*, 189–90.

21. Lim, DJD XX, 153.

22. Nitzan noted, "The verbs שמעו and וישביתו need not necessarily refer to the same subject. In reading שמעו in the imperative form, and וישביתו in the imperfect form, the combination of the phrases מבינים שמעו and וישביתו מעל may refer to those of understanding that they will cause other people to cease treachery" ("The Idea of Creation and Its Implications in Qumran Literature," 253n47).

in the previous line.[23] It is also possible that the preserved מים is not part of a larger word and can thus be read as "water(s)."[24] In addition, the word מעל could be read as מֵעַל (above/upon), instead of מַעַל (treachery). Thus, Jacobson has suggested the reading "[ ] water (?) and will stop above (?) [ ]" which recalls Gen 1:7.[25] Nitzan, however, observed that such a reading "cannot be supported according to this context, because the details of the 'wonderful acts of God,' namely the wonders of creation that the author intends to tell . . . as suggested correctly by Jacobson for line 3, do not precede this declaration (summoning) but follow it (see lines 4–11)."[26] Giere adds that Jacobson's reading is "tenuous and impossible to verify."[27] It should be noted that *any* reading of this particular line is difficult to verify at this point due to the incomplete nature of the text in question. In light of its placement immediately after the exhortation of line 1 and prior to the recounting of God's wonderful acts in creation in lines 3–11, the most likely reading of line 2 appears to be "([ ]*mym* and cause them to cease treachery *n*[ ]." Thus, the opening two lines of 4Q303 appear to preserve some sort of exhortation for those who have understanding to: 1) listen/take heed and 2) cause them (others) to cease treachery.

A Retelling of God's Wondrous Acts in Creation

Line 3 represents a transition in the text from the author's exhortation in lines 1–2 to a recounting of God's wonderful acts in creation: {.ר.ס}א[ ] [ר]נפלאות אל אש. Lim reads this line as "[ ] . . . . . wonderful acts of God whi[ch]," but does not reconstruct the partially damaged first word.[28] Though the first word is partially damaged, it is apparent that there are at least five letters.[29] Based on an examination of an enlarged digital image of

23. For example, Qimron reconstructed this word in this manner as noted by Lim (DJD XX, 153).

24. For the reading of מים[ ] as "water(s)," see Jacobson, "Notes on 4Q303," 78–80; Wise et al., *The Dead Sea Scrolls: A New Translation*, 378.

25. Jacobson, "Notes on 4Q303," 78–80; Similarly, Wise reads this line as "[. . .] the waters and they caused to cease from upon a[ll . . .]" (Wise et al., *The Dead Sea Scrolls: A New Translation*, 378).

26. Nitzan, "The Idea of Creation and Its Implications in Qumran Literature," 253n47.

27. Giere, *A New Glimpse of Day One*, 190n234.

28. Lim, DJD XX, 153.

29. Ibid., 152.

this line, it is reasonable to read the first four letters as {א{ספר.. The rest of the damaged portion is more difficult to discern and may represent one or two letters. Jacobson has suggested several possible readings here: אספר את or אספר כל or אספרה.[30] Meanwhile, Rey has expressed more certainty in reading this first word as אספרה.[31] Thus, this line can be read: "I {will tell/ recount} the wonderful acts of God whi[ch]."[32]

Lines 4–11 then appear to recount the wonderful acts of God in the heavens and in man, reworking material from the opening chapters of Genesis. Lines 4–6 recount God's work in the heavens:

4 [ ]לאור עולם ושמי טוה[ר . . .]
5 [או]ר במקום תהו וב[הו . . .][33]
6 [ ]כולמעשיהם עד ק.[. . .]

4 [ ]for eternal light and cle[ar] heavens [ ]
5 [ligh]t in place of formlessness and vo[id]
6 [ ]all their works/activities until *q*.[ ]

While language from line 4 (אור and שמי; MT שמים) is found in the opening verses of the Genesis creation account, it is not certain whether this line is taken from Gen 1:1–5. For example, in the Hebrew Bible the exact phrase לאור עולם (for eternal light) occurs only in Isa 60:19–20 (in both verses), where the eternal light is God Himself. Thus, "eternal light" in line 4 may refer back to God (mentioned in line 3). Another possibility according to Rey is that the "eternal light" here is a reference to "the creation of light in Gen 1:3, distinguishing this light from the lights of the fourth day

30. Jacobson, "Notes on 4Q303," 79.

31. Rey expressed, "In line 3, the first traces of letters have to be read without doubt as אספרה" ("In the Garden of Good and Evil," 483n29). He based this conclusion on the digital image B-295764 (which in my estimation certainly allows for this reading, but is not conclusive) and the use of אספרה in Ps 9:2 (MT) and 4Q511 63–64 II:2 (which employs the same language).

32. Cf. "[ ] I will tell (?) the wonders of God who (?)[ ]" (Jacobson, "Notes on 4Q303," 80); "[ ] I {will tell} the wonderful acts of God whi[ch]" (Nitzan, "The Idea of Creation and Its Implications in Qumran Literature," 253); "[ ] I will tell the marvels of God wh[ich . . .] (Rey, "In the Garden of Good and Evil," 483).

33. While Lim transcribed תהווב[הו] without a space (DJD XX, 152), the photograph (plate XIII) does appear to show a space between the words. An examination of an enlarged electronic image of this line seems to confirm this. The "smudge" appears to be the remnant of the letter ו (*waw*). Perhaps the scribe initially, by accident, started to write these words without a space and then corrected this, moving the initial ו of וב[הו].

by qualifying it as 'eternal.'"[34] The language of line 5 (תהו ובהו "formlessness and void"), appears to be a clear reference to Gen 1:2.[35] The mention of "[ligh]t in place of formlessness and vo[id]" appears to parallel the creation of light (אור) in Gen 1:3–5, following the reference to the heavens and the earth as תהו ובהו in Gen 1:2.[36] The extant text continues in line 6 with "[ ] all their works/activities until *q*.[ ]," which may refer to the works/activities of the cosmos.

Lines 7–11 then recount the creation of man and woman, reworking material primarily from Gen 2:

7 [. . .]ר בם מלך לכולם[. . .]
8 [. . .]ר ושכל טוב ורע ל[. . .]
9 [. . .]לוקח ממנה אדם כיא[. . .]
10 [. . . ו]עשה לו עזר כ[נגדו . . .]
11 [. . .]לו לאשה כיא ממנו[לקחה זאת . . .]

7 [. . .] . . . among them a king for all of them [. . .]
8 [. . .] . . . and knowledge of good and evil [. . .]
9 [. . .] Adam was taken from it because [. . .]
10 [. . . and]He made for him a helper co[mparable to him]
11 [. . .]to him as a wife, because from him[she was taken . . .]

Line 7 reads [. . .]ר בם מלך לכולם[. . .] ([. . .] . . . among them a king for all of them [. . .]), which may be a retelling or paraphrase of Gen 1:26, 28 (cf. 4Q381 1 7), which refers to the creation of man and the dominion given to humanity over every living creature and all the earth.[37] Alternatively, this fragmentary line has been read by Wise as "[. . . ove]r whom he

34. Rey, "The Garden of Good and Evil," 484.

35. In the Hebrew Bible, the exact phrase תהו ובהו occurs only in Gen 1:2 and Jer 4:23, while the words תהו and בהו also appear in Isa 34:11 in parallel construction (though not directly together). Giere sees in line 5 a "strong intertextual link to MT Gen 1:2," but also sees the possibility that this line resembles Jer 4:23 more closely (*A New Glimpse of Day One*, 191–92). Looking strictly at line 5, Giere's observations are notable. However, given the context of 4Q303, it appears more likely that the phrase תהו ובהו in line 5 is a reference to Gen 1:2.

36. Nitzan, for example, understood line 5 as referring to Gen 1:2–5 ("The Idea of Creation and Its Implications in Qumran Literature," 254).

37. See Jacobson, "Notes on 4Q303," 79. Cf. Gen 1:26: "Then God said, 'Let Us make man in Our image, according to Our likeness; let them have dominion over the fish of the sea, over the birds of the air, and over the cattle, over all the earth and over every creeping thing that creeps on the earth"; cf. also 4Q381 frag 1, line 7: ". . . And by His Spirit He appointed them to rule over all these on the earth and over all [. . .]."

reigned, and for all of them [. . .]," perhaps as a reference to God's rule over the cosmic order described in the previous lines.[38] Thus, the transition from the retelling of the wondrous works of God in the heavens (ending in line 6 or 7?) to the retelling of the creation of man and woman (beginning in line 7 or 8?) is not exactly clear-cut. The reading of line 7 as "[. . .] . . . among them a king for all of them [. . .]," though not certain, is generally adopted and seems preferable.[39] The extant text of line 8, [. . .]ר ושכל טוב ורע ל[. . .] ([. . .] . . . and knowledge of good and evil [. . .]), recalls Gen 2:9, 17 (cf. 3:5, 22). Line 9 then preserves [. . .]לוקח ממנה אדם כיא[. . .], which Lim read as " [ ]a man takes from it because [ ]."[40] The fragmentary nature of this line of text equally allows for other readings. For example, Wold proposed the reading "Adam taking from her because," in reference to Adam taking the fruit from Eve (cf. Gen 3:6).[41] Jacobson, on the other hand, proposed reading line 9 as "[ ] man was taken from it, for [ ]," which recalls the creation of Adam from the ground in Gen 2:7 (cf. 3:19, 23).[42] The next two lines deal with the creation of Eve. Line 10 reads [. . . ו]עשה לו עזר כ[נגדו] [. . . ([. . . and]He made for him a helper co[mparable to him]), which directly recalls Gen 2:18.[43] Line 11, [. . . לו לאשה כיא ממנו] לקחה זאת[. . .] ([. . .]to him as a wife, because from him [she was taken . . .]), recalls Gen 2:23.[44] The *vacat* in the following line appears to demarcate the end of this retelling of the creation of Adam and Eve.

38. Wise et al., *The Dead Sea Scrolls: A New Translation*, 378. In his translation, line 7 is grouped with the previous verses which he categorized as "Creation of the waters, the heavenly lights, and their realms." Lines 8–11 are then grouped together in the category "Creation of Adam and Eve" (378–79).

39. See Lim, DJD XX, 153; Jacobson, "Notes on 4Q303," 80; Nitzan, "The Idea of Creation and Its Implications in Qumran Literature," 253; García Martínez and Tigchelaar, *The Dead Sea Scrolls Study Edition*, 669; Parry and Tov, *The Dead Sea Scrolls Reader*, 4:295; Giere, *A New Glimpse of Day One*, 190; Rey, "In the Garden of Good and Evil," 483.

40. Lim, DJD XX, 153.

41. Wold, *Women, Men, and Angels*, 118.

42. Jacobson, "Notes on 4Q303," 79–80.

43. Gen 2:18: ויאמר יהוה אלהים לא־טוב היות האדם לבדו אעשה לו עזר כנגדו (Then the Lord God said, 'It is not good that man should be alone; I will make him a helper comparable to him.')

44. Gen 2:23b: לזאת יקרא אשה כי מאיש לקחה־זאת ('She shall be called woman, because she was taken out of man').

Content and Genre: Concluding Remarks

Though uncertainties remain regarding such a fragmentary text, the extant portions of 4Q303 appear to begin with an exhortation to the understanding ones to listen and to cause others to cease from treachery (lines 1–2), followed by some sort of retelling of God's wondrous works (line 3) in the heavens (lines 4–6) and in the creation of man and woman (lines 7–11). This reflection on the created order reworks material from the Genesis creation narrative(s). If this fragmentary text is properly understood, then it seems that lessons are being drawn from the created order to illustrate an exhortation or command rooted in moral/ethical implications.[45] Based on the opening injunction or command ("understanding ones take heed") and the presence of the creation theme (common in wisdom texts),[46] Jacobson suggested that 4Q303 is an example of wisdom literature.[47]

Adam and the Knowledge of Good and Evil

Concerning biblical interpretation, the fragmentary remains of 4Q303, along with 4Q305, may reflect a positive understanding of Adam's possession of the knowledge of good and evil in the Garden of Eden. In 4Q303, lines 8–11, the preserved text appears to be a reworking of material from Genesis 2. Notably, line 8 preserves [. . .]ר ושכל טוב ורע ל[. . .] ([. . .] . . . and knowledge of good and evil [. . .]) which recalls the language of Gen 2:9, 17 (cf. 3:5–6, 22).[48] In Genesis 2, "the tree of the knowledge of good and evil" is located in the midst of the garden (Gen 2:9) and is the tree which Adam is prohibited to eat from (Gen 2:17). It is uncertain, however, as to how the phrase "and knowledge/insight of good and evil" was utilized in line 8 due to the missing text at the beginning and end of this line (also, the missing text at the end of the previous line and the beginning of the

45. See Lim, DJD XX, 151; Nitzan, "The Idea of Creation and Its Implications in Qumran Literature," 254. Unfortunately, the incomplete nature of these lines of text precludes any certainty as to what exact lessons are being drawn from God's wondrous works in creation.

46. For the creation theme in wisdom literature, see e.g. Job 36–39; Prov 8:22–31; 30:4; 4Q381, frag 1; 4QInstruction (4Q416, frag 1; 4Q417, frag 1; 4Q423, frag 1); *Sir* 16:17–17:10; 24:1–9; 43:1–33.

47. Jacobson, "Notes on 4Q303," 80.

48. Note, however, Gen 2:9, 17 both utilize the term דעת for "knowledge" rather than שכל in reference to "the tree of the knowledge of good and evil."

subsequent line). In other words, there is enough missing text surrounding this extant phrase in line 8 to warrant caution. Nonetheless, the use of the term שכל (insight or knowledge) in reference to "good and evil" in line 8 may shed some light. Interestingly, the same root is employed in Gen 3:6, which records that Adam and Eve ate from the tree of the knowledge of good and evil after she observed "the tree was good for food, that it was pleasant to the eyes, and a tree desirable to make wise/insightful (להשכיל – root שכל)." Thus, it is reasonable to suggest that the phrase in line 8 (ושכל טוב ורע) may refer to Adam's possession of this insight/knowledge of good and evil as a result of taking the fruit from Eve (Gen 3:6). This is intriguing in light of the immediately following text in line 9, לוקח ממנה [אדם]כוא, which Wold reads as "Adam taking from her because," in reference to Adam taking the fruit from Eve in Gen 3:6.[49] It is at this point that the text of 4Q303 then refers to the creation of Eve. Line 10 preserves "[. . . and]He made for him a helper co[mparable to him . . .]" (cf. Gen 2:18), while line 11 reads "[. . .]to him as wife, because from him[she was taken . . .]" (cf. Gen 2:23). If the reading for line 9 ("Adam taking from her because") is correct (this is debatable), then 4Q303 appears to reverse the order of events recorded in Genesis, where the creation of Eve (Gen 2:18, 21–23) precedes the eating from the prohibited tree of the knowledge of good and evil (Gen 3:6). Consequently, Wold concluded, "If it is the fruit that man takes in 4Q303 line 9, and woman is described as a 'helper' in the following line 10, the woman's act of giving from the fruit of the tree would be seen as a positive (thus a 'helper')."[50] It should also be noted at this point that Jacobson's proposed reading for line 9 as "man was taken from it," in reference to the creation of Adam from the ground (Gen 2:7; cf. 3:19), is a viable option.[51] If Jacobson's reading is correct, then line 9 may simply preserve a reference to the creation of man, followed by the creation of woman in lines 10–11. In this case, a positive conception of Adam's possession of the knowledge of good and evil may still be present in the text (based on line 8), indicating perhaps that Adam possessed this knowledge when he was created,[52] rather than as

49. Wold, *Women, Men, and Angels*, 118. לוקח (root לקח), which employs the plene/full spelling, is read here as a participle.

50. Ibid.

51. Jacobson, "Notes on 4Q303," 79–80. While לוקח (root לקח), can be read as a participle, it can just as easily be read as a passive verb. Jacobson opted for the latter, noting, "It is much more likely that לוקח is passive (plene spelling) and refers to Adam's being created from the earth" (79). Cf. Rey, "In the Garden of Good and Evil," 485.

52. Due to the fact that portions of text are missing, the possibility still remains that

a result of taking the fruit from Eve. Either way, given the context, the idea that 4Q303 presents a positive understanding of Adam's possession of the knowledge of good and evil in Eden is plausible, perhaps even probable, but is by no means certain due to the missing portions of text.

Adding to this discussion, the legible portion of 4Q305 preserves a fragmentary reference to knowledge being given to Adam.

1 ויברא בו חיות [. . .]
2 נתן לאדם דע[ת . . .]
3 ורע לדעת [. . .]
4 ל[. . .]

1 Then He created in it living creatures [. . .]
2 He gave to Adam knowled[ge . . .]
3 and evil, to know [. . .]
4 . . . [. . .]

The beginning of line 1 preserves a description of God creating life. Unfortunately, the rest of the line has been lost. The extant text then picks up again at the beginning of line 2 with the statement that God has given to Adam knowledge. The rest of this line is missing as well. The next line opens with "and evil, to know [. . .]," which may indicate more particularly that Adam was given the knowledge of good and evil. Once again, the rest of this line is also missing. While this fragment may represent a positive understanding of Adam gaining the knowledge of good and evil (see Wold),[53] the lacunae prevent any certainty regarding this. At the least, however, 4Q305 does provide an explicit reference to God actively providing Adam with knowledge (cf. 4Q504 8 4–5).[54]

Though uncertainties remain, *Meditation on Creation* appears to present a positive understanding of Adam's possession of the knowledge of good and evil in Eden, which is attested in other wisdom literature from the Second Temple period (e.g. *Sir* 17:7).[55] Though 4Q303 begins

line 8 could simply be a reference to the prohibition of eating from the tree (cf. Gen 2:9, 17) rather than a reference to Adam's possession of the knowledge of good and evil (cf. Gen 3:6). Line 8, however, employs the term שכל (insight/knowledge) which is used in Gen 3:6, instead of דעת (knowledge) which is found in Gen 2:9, 17.

53. Wold, *Women, Men, and Angels*, 117–18.

54. 4Q504 8 4–5: "[Adam] our [fa]ther You formed in the likeness of [Your] glory . . . [the breath of life] You [br]eathed into his nostrils, and understanding and knowledge [. . .]."

55. *Sirach* 17:7: "He filled them with knowledge and understanding, and showed

with an apparent exhortation/command (lines 1–2), the fragmentary nature of the text precludes any certainty as to exactly what lessons are being drawn here regarding the creation of man and woman (lines 8–11). In any case, concerning biblical interpretation, the phrase "and insight/ wisdom of good and evil" (ושכל טוב ורע) in line 8 recalls the tree of the knowledge of good and evil (Gen 2:9, 17) which Eve saw in Gen 3:6 as able "to make wise" (להשכיל), apparently linking the knowledge of good and evil to wisdom.[56] Rey concluded, "While the text is fragmentary, it seems clear that knowledge of good and evil is not forbidden but is a gift of God to humanity."[57] If understood correctly, *Meditation on Creation* (4Q303 8–11, 4Q305 1–3) diverges from Gen 2–3, which depicts Adam's knowledge of "good and evil" as a result of disobeying God's command (cf. Gen 2:16–17; 3:6, 22–24).

---

them good and evil." Translation from Wright III, "Wisdom of Ben Sira," 2254.

56. See Wold, "Genesis 2–3 in Early Christian Tradition and 4QInstruction," 334.

57. Rey, "In the Garden of Good and Evil," 485.

CHAPTER EIGHT

QUMRAN INTERPRETATION OF THE GENESIS CREATION ACCOUNT

MISCELLANEOUS RULES (4Q265)

Discovery of 4Q265

ANOTHER INTRIGUING TEXT KNOWN as *Miscellaneous Rules* (4Q265) was among the large cache of fragmentary manuscripts recovered from Cave 4 in 1952. As early as 1959, scholars were made aware of this text in tantalizing fashion through J. T. Milik's brief description of some of its contents.[1] It was not until the 1990s that several preliminary editions and translations of 4Q265 were made available to scholars.[2] Then, in 1999, Joseph Baumgarten published the official edition of 4Q265 in volume 35 of the *Discoveries in the Judaean Desert* series.[3]

1. Milik, *Ten Years of Discovery in the Wilderness of Judaea*, 96.

2. Preliminary editions of the Hebrew text of 4Q265 include: Wacholder and Abegg, *A Preliminary Edition of the Unpublished Dead Sea Scrolls: The Hebrew and Aramaic Texts from Cave Four III* (1995); García Martínez and Tigchelaar, *The Dead Sea Scrolls Study Edition* (1997). The early English translations include: García Martínez, *The Dead Sea Scrolls Translated* (1994); Wise et al., *The Dead Sea Scrolls: A New Translation* (1996); Vermes, *The Complete Dead Sea Scrolls in English* (1997).

3. Baumgarten, "265. 4QMiscellaneous Rules" (hereafter, DJD XXXV), 57–78, Pl. V–VIII.

Physical Description of 4Q265

Typical of manuscripts from Cave 4, *Miscellaneous Rules* is also quite fragmentary. The surviving text of 4Q265 consists of seven identified fragments (labelled 1–7) and twelve unidentified fragments (labelled a–l). While the unidentified fragments are very small, the identified fragments are, for the most part, relatively moderate in size. The Hebrew text is written in a late Herodian hand, dating the manuscript to the first half of the first century AD (c. AD 25–50).[4]

Fragment 1 is relatively small (c. 6.2 cm wide and c. 4.1 cm high), preserving portions of six lines of text.[5] Some lines preserve a few words, while other lines preserve only a few partial letters. Fragment 2 is the smallest of the identified fragments (c. 1.9 cm wide by c. 1.7 cm high), with only partial remains of a few words. Fragment 3 consists of two relatively smaller fragments. The first fragment measures approximately 4.6 cm wide and 3 cm high, with partial remains of three lines of text. The second fragment measures only about 1.7 cm wide by 2.7 cm high, with partial remains of two lines of text. Both fragments preserve the bottom margin. Fragment 4 consists of several fragments and actually preserves portions of two columns of text. Frag 4 i consists of two fragments. The first, suffering some shrinkage, measures about 2.6 cm in width and 7.25 cm in height. This fragment preserves the beginning of eight lines of text along with the bottom and right margins. The second fragment is rather large, measuring around 6.25 cm in width and 12 cm in height. This fragment preserves both the top and bottom margins along with portions of twelve lines of text (the first two lines have incurred surface damage and are illegible).[6] Frag 4 ii (technically consisting of two fragments) is moderate in size (c. 7.3 cm by c. 8.1 cm), preserving portions of nine lines of text and the top margin. Fragment 5 consists of several very small fragments, each preserving the top margin. The largest of these fragments is roughly 3 cm wide by 4.3

4. See Milik, *Ten Years of Discovery in the Wilderness of Judaea*, 96; Baumgarten, "The Cave 4 Versions of the Qumran Penal Code," 271; Schiffman, "Serekh-Damascus," 868; Hempel, *The Damascus Texts*, 93; "Cutting the Cord with the Familiar," 510. Vermes, in contrast to all of the aforementioned, viewed 4Q265 as "dating probably to the end of the first century BCE" (*The Complete Dead Sea Scrolls in English*, rev. ed., 155). García Martínez also viewd 4Q265 as "a manuscript from the end of the first century BCE" ("The History of the Qumran Community in the Light of Recently Available Texts," 214).

5. Fragment measurements in this section are from Baumgarten, DJD XXXV, 57.

6. See the PAM 43.304 image (cf. B-360525).

cm high, with remains of four lines of text. Fragment 6 is a nice fragment, measuring roughly 12.5 cm in width and 6.5 cm in height. A substantial amount of seven lines of text is preserved along with the right margin. Fragment 7 constitutes another sizable fragment (c. 9.7 cm wide by c. 14.5 cm high), preserving fairly substantial portions of seventeen lines of text as well as the bottom margin. The right margin is partially preserved at lines 9–10 and 16, with only the first letter(s) of the first word in most other lines missing due to the long vertical break in the fragment. The left hand side of the column, however, is broken off. This fragment is of particular interest as it preserves language from the Garden of Eden narrative.

History of Research on 4Q265

There are several notable studies pertaining to 4Q265 in general, and to its interpretation of the Garden of Eden in particular. In a 1994 book chapter, "Purification after Childbirth and the Sacred Garden in 4Q265 and Jubilees," Joseph Baumgarten examined the reworked biblical material (preserved in fragment 7) pertaining to the creation of Adam and Eve and their entrance into the Garden of Eden.[7] He deduced that the use of this material in order to explain the etiology of certain purification laws conveyed a particular understanding of "Eden as a sanctuary."[8]

Subsequent studies have echoed Baumgarten's observations. For example, in 1997, Esther Eshel published a chapter, "Hermeneutical Approaches to Genesis in the Dead Sea Scrolls," in which she addressed various modes of interpretation identified in Qumran texts. In her discussion of "Halakhic-Aetiological Exegesis," she also saw in 4Q265, frag 7, the concept of the Garden of Eden as a prototype of the sanctuary.[9] Then in 2000, Charlotte Hempel surveyed the contents of 4Q265 in a work titled, *The Damascus Texts*. In her discussion of fragment 7, this concept of the Garden of Eden as a prototype of the sanctuary was recognized once again.[10]

7. This chapter, published in *New Qumran Texts and Studies*, was first presented in 1992 at the "First Meeting of the International Organization for Qumran Studies" in Paris. Then in 1999, Baumgarten included another discussion regarding this in DJD XXXV, 60–61.

8. See Baumgarten, "Purification after Childbirth and the Sacred Garden in 4Q265 and Jubilees," 6, 9–10.

9. Eshel, "Hermeneutical Approaches to Genesis in the Dead Sea Scrolls," 10–11.

10. Hempel, *The Damascus Texts*, 100–101.

Content of 4Q265

4Q265 was originally designated *Serekh Damascus*, reflecting the idea that this text represents a combination of the *Serekh ha-Yahad* (*Community Rule*) and the *Damascus Document*.[11] This provisional title for 4Q265 was problematic for two reasons. First, as Hempel has observed, neither the term "*serekh*" (rule), commonly employed in sectarian rule texts (e.g. *Community Rule*, *Damascus Document*, and *War Scroll*), nor "Damascus" is found in the extant text of 4Q265.[12] Second, while 4Q265 contains significant parallel material to both the *Community Rule* and *Damascus Document*, the various contents and genres represented in these fragments indicate that this text is quite diverse. For this reason, in the official DJD edition, Baumgarten aptly renamed this text with the more descriptive title *Miscellaneous Rules*.[13]

Fragment 1 partially preserves a citation of Isa 54:1–2.[14] The extant text is broken off in the middle of verse 2, and thus, does not preserve an interpretation.[15] It is possible that 4Q265 was here reading Isa 54 in

11. For example, García Martínez noted, "In spite of the small amount of material preserved, it is clear that the composition is a combination of the *Serek* and the *Damascus Document*" ("The History of the Qumran Community in the Light of Recently Available Texts," 214). Schiffman observed that *Serekh-Damascus* (4Q265) "takes its name from the assumption of the initial editors that it represents a combination of the Serek ha-Yahad (Rule of the Community) and the Damascus Document" ("Serekh-Damascus (4Q265)," 868). Collins referred to 4Q265 as "a text that combines elements of the *Serek* and the *Damascus Rule*" (*Beyond the Qumran Community*, 54). Vermes noted that this fragmentary manuscript "preserved remains of a writing dependent both on the Community Rule and on the Damascus Document but also including material which is in neither of these sources" (*The Complete Dead Sea Scrolls in English*, rev. ed., 155).

12. Hempel, *The Damascus Texts*, 91; "Cutting the Cord with the Familiar," 509. See also the discussion in Alexander, "Rules," 799–803.

13. Baumgarten concluded, "The provisional title formerly employed, *Serekh Damascus*, suggesting a blend of excerpts from the Community Rule and the Damascus Document does not adequately reflect the diverse contents of this text. *Miscellaneous Rules* is a more accurate description of the variety of its subject matter" (DJD XXXV, 58).

14. 4Q265, frag 1: "1. [. . .]*m* [. . .] 2. [. . .] which is written [. . .] 3. [. . .] written in the boo[k] of Isaiah the prophet, 4. ['Sing, O barren one who has not borne; break forth into song and] cry aloud you who have not labored with child! For more will be the sons of 5. [the desolate than the sons of the married one,' says the LORD.] 'Enlar[ge] the place of [your] ten[t]' 6. [. . .]*l*[. . .]"

15. Baumgarten reconstructed line 6 with more text from Isa 54:2. Also, from the likely partial remains of a single letter (ל), he reconstructed [. . .]ל[פשרו ע] "[its interpretation conce]rns" (DJD XXXV, 62).

connection to the eschatological hope of the council of the community. Notably, another sectarian text known as the *Isaiah Pesher* (4QpIsa^{d}) interprets Isa 54:11–12 as referring to the council of the community (עצת היחד) in an eschatological context.[16] 4Q265, frag 7, 7–8 also makes reference to the prophets in the description of the establishment of the council of the community (עצת היחד).

Fragment 2 is extremely small and preserves only partial remains of a few words (one word is complete). Thus, not too much can be drawn from this fragment concerning the content.

Fragment 3, line 2, partially preserves a citation of Mal 2:10, which in its context (Mal 2:10–17) concerns interpersonal unfaithfulness and profaning the Temple. Line 3 then preserves a prohibition concerning young boys and women partaking in the Passover sacrifice.[17]

Fragment 4 I–II:2 contains portions of the penal code, reflecting material from both the *Community Rule* (cf. 1QS VI:24–VII:25; 4QS^{e} I:4–15; II:3–9; 4QS^{g} 3 2–4; 5 2–9; 6 1–5) and *Damascus Document* (cf. 4QD^{a} 10 I:11–II:15; 4QD^{b} 9 VI:1–5; 4QD^{e} 7 I:1–15). The material in 4Q265 does not appear to represent mere excerpts from these texts, but an independent version of the penal code.[18]

Fragment 4 II:3–9 then addresses the admission of new members into the community (יחד). Here, 4Q265 more closely parallels the material in the *Community Rule* (cf. 1QS VI:13–23) than the *Damascus Document* (cf. CD XV:5–17).[19] Once again, 4Q265 appears to preserve an independent tradition rather than mere excerpts from these texts.

16. 4QpIsa^{d}: "1. [He will mak]e all Israel like eye-paint around the eye. *Isa 54:11* And I will lay your foundations in sapphi[res. Its interpretation:] 2. they will found the council of the community, [the] priests, and the peo[ple . . .] 3. the assembly of His elect like a sapphire stone in the midst of the stones. [*Isa 54:12* I will make] 4. all your battlements [of rubies]. Its interpretation concerns the twelve [chiefs of the priests who] 5. illuminate with the judgment of the Urim and the Thummim [. . . without] 6. any from among them missing, like the sun in all its light. *Isa 54:12* And al[l your gates of precious stones.] 7 Its interpretation concerns the chiefs of the tribes of Israel in the l[ast days . . .] 8. its lot, the posts of [. . .]"

17. For further discussion on the relationship between the citation of Mal 2:10 and the prohibition here in fragment 3, see Baumgarten, DJD XXXV, 63–64; Hempel, *The Damascus Texts*, 96.

18. For further discussion, see Baumgarten, "The Cave 4 Versions of the Qumran Penal Code," 268–76; DJD XXXV, 64–67; Hempel, *The Damascus Texts*, 93–95; Schiffman, "Serekh-Damascus (4Q265)," 868.

19. Hempel has observed that 4Q265 4 II:3–9 more closely relates to 1QS both in terminology and the procedure for admittance (*The Damascus Texts*, 95).

Fragment 5 preserves only a few words (in some cases, partial words) from four lines of text. This rather small amount of text preserves מכול זרועי האד[מה] (from all that is sown in the grou[nd]) in line 1 and והפריח (and causing to sprout) in line 2, suggesting that this section may have dealt with laws or regulations concerning agriculture.[20]

Fragment 6, along with the first six lines of fragment 7, contains a fairly well preserved section concerning Sabbath prohibitions, which are also dealt with in the *Damascus Document* (CD X:14–XI:18; 4QD[e] 6 V:1–21; 4QD[f] 5 I:1–12). Some of the eight prohibitions partially preserved in 4Q265 parallel those mentioned in the *Damascus Document*. However, there are also some notable differences in the Sabbath legislation of these texts,[21] which according to Hempel "leave no doubt that 4Q265 preserves independent traditions of sabbath halakhah."[22]

Fragment 7, lines 7–10, parallels the *Community Rule* concerning the establishment of the council of the community (עצת היחד) with fifteen men (lines 7–8; 1QS VIII:1–2) and the depiction of this sect as "a pleasant aroma to atone for the earth" (line 9; 1QS VIII:6–10).[23] Other parallels include the reference to the end of injustice/iniquity (עולה) by judgment (במשפט) of the wicked (line 10; 1QS VIII:10).

Fragment 7, line 11, opens with a sufficiently large blank space (indentation), indicating the beginning of a new distinct section within in the composition.[24] 4Q265 7 11–17 closely parallels *Jubilees* 3, both of which employ material from the Eden narrative in order to explain the purification laws in Lev 12:1–5.

It is evident that 4Q265 is a diverse text containing parallel material to other texts such as the *Community Rule*, *Damascus Document*, and

20. Schiffman, "Serekh-Damascus (4Q265)," 868–69. Schiffman additionally suggested, "It is also possible that this is a metaphoric reference to the Dead Sea sect" (869). Hempel, *The Damascus Texts*, 96.

21. For example, when a man falls into water, both 4Q265 frag 6 6b–8a and CD XI:16–17 prohibit another person from pulling him out with an implement. However, 4Q265 frag 6 7, adds the allowance, "let him cast his garment to him to raise him up."

22. Hempel, *The Damascus Texts*, 98.

23. According to Hempel, the reference to the sect as a "pleasant aroma" appears to represent the "underlying idea that the new community serves as a substitute for the temple" (*The Damascus Texts*, 99). Similarly, Schiffman viewed this language as reflecting an understanding of the sect as "a substitute for the sacrificial ritual from which the sect abstained" (Serekh-Damascus (4Q265)," 869).

24. The length of the indentation from the right-hand margin appears to be roughly 14 to 18 letter spaces.

Jubilees.[25] However, the fact that 4Q265 is preserved here only in fragmentary form presents challenges to understanding the literary shaping and purpose of the composition. For example, no introduction or conclusion material appears to be preserved (*if* such were originally included in the composition). Further, the portions of texts denoting the transitions from one apparently disparate section to another are generally not preserved (an exception is frag 7, line 11).[26] Nonetheless, the extant text does appear to provide significant clues as to how these fragmented and diverse sections within the composition are related to one another. Proposing a holistic reading of these fragments, Hempel has convincingly argued that "the fundamental concern for holiness underpinned by both pentateuchal and prophetic texts ties together the various loose ends that were left for us of this fascinating text."[27]

The Garden of Eden as an Archetype of the Sanctuary

4Q265 7 11–17 employs material concerning Adam and Eve and their entrance into the Garden of Eden in order to explain the postpartum purification laws found in Lev 12:1–5, which prohibit women from entering the sanctuary for 40 days after the birth of a male child and 80 days after the birth of a female child. The text of 4Q265 7 11–17 reads:

11 בשבוע הראיש[ון נברא האדם וקודש לא היה לו עד]
12 אשר לא הובא אל גן עדן ועצם [מעצמיו לוקחה לאשה וקודש לא]
13 [ה]יה לה עד אשר לא הובאה אצ[לו בשבוע השני . . .][28]
14 [כי] קדוש גן עדן וכול האב אשר בתוכו קודש [לכן אשה אשר ילדה זכר]
15 וטמאה שבעת ימים כימי נדת דותה תטמא ושל[שים ושלשת ימים תשב בדם]
16 טהרה ואם נקבה תלד וטמאה [שבעים כנדתה וששים יום וששת ימים]
17 [תש]ב בדם טוהרה בכול קודש [לא תגע ואל המקדש לא תבוא עד מלאת]

25. Another text relevant to the study of 4Q265 is 4QOrdinances (4Q159).

26. Hempel, *The Damascus Texts*, 91.

27. Hempel, "Cutting the Cord with the Familiar," 516.

28. For this reconstruction of line 13, see Baumgarten, "Purification after Childbirth and the Sacred Garden in 4Q265 and Jubilees," 3–4; Eshel, "Hermeneutical Approaches to Genesis in the Dead Sea Scrolls," 10; García Martínez and Tigchelaar, *The Dead Sea Scrolls Study Edition*, 550–51. Baumgarten also provided an alternative reconstruction for the end of line 13: [ה]יה לה עד אשר לא הובאה אצ[לו אל גן עדן אחר שמונים יום] (did she [ha]ve until she was brought to h[im in the Garden of Eden after eighty days]) (DJD XXXV, 70).

11 *vacat* In the firs[t] week [Adam was created, but there was nothing holy to him until]
12 he was brought to the Garden of Eden. And a bone [of his bones was taken for the woman, but nothing holy]
13 [w]as to her until she was brought to [his] side [in the second week . . .]
14 [for] the Garden of Eden is holy and every young shoot which is in the midst of it is holy. [Therefore, a woman who begets a male]
15 shall be impure seven days, as in the days of her menstruation shall she be impure, and th[irty-three days shall she remain in the blood]
16 of her purity. *vacat* And if she begets a female, she shall be impure [two weeks as in her menstruation, and sixty-six days]
17 [shall she rem]ain in the blood of her purity. [No] holy thing [shall she touch, and she shall not enter into the sanctuary until the completion of]

The narrative opens in lines 11–14a with a reworked depiction of the creation of Adam and Eve that diverges from the biblical record in one important respect. The Genesis narrative indicates that on the day Adam was created, he was immediately placed in the Garden of Eden, where he was then given a prohibition, named the animals, and Eve was formed to be his helpmate (cf. Gen 1:26–31; 2:7–22). 4Q265, on the other hand, indicates a period of purification in which neither Adam nor Eve was given immediate access to the Garden of Eden due to its holiness. The respective periods of impurity for Adam (seven days) and Eve (fourteen days) before entering the Garden of Eden parallel the respective periods of impurity for the mother who begets a male child (seven days, plus 33 days remaining in her purity) or female child (fourteen days, plus remaining 66 days in her purity) before entering the sanctuary as required in Lev 12:1–5. In this manner, lines 11–14a supply an etiological explanation for the purification laws of Lev 12:1–5 which are explicitly referred to in lines 14b–17. This explanation reflects the understanding of the Garden of Eden as a sanctuary (מקדש), which is further supported by the explicit statement in line 14: "the Garden of Eden is holy" (קדוש גן עדן). Notably, 4Q265 7 11–17 closely parallels *Jubilees* 3, which perhaps represents the earliest example of such an explanation.

4Q265, frag 7, lines 11–17	*Jubilees* 3:8–14[29]
11. *vacat* In the firs[t] week [Adam was created, but there was nothing holy to him until] 12. he was brought to the Garden of Eden. And a bone [of his bones was taken for the woman, but nothing holy] 13. [w]as to her until she was brought to [his] side [in the second week . . .] 14. [for] the Garden of Eden is holy and every young shoot which is in the midst of it is holy. [Therefore, a woman who begets a male] 15. shall be impure seven days, as in the days of her menstruation shall she be impure, and th[irty-three days shall she remain in the blood] 16. of her purity. *vacat* And if she begets a female, she shall be impure [two weeks as in her menstruation, and sixty-six days] 17. [shall she rem]ain in the blood of her purity. [No] holy thing [shall she touch, and she shall not enter into the sanctuary until the completion of]	8. In the first week Adam was created and also the rib, his wife. And in the second week He showed her to him. And therefore the commandment was given to observe seven days for a male, but for a female twice seven days in their impurity. 9. And after forty days were completed for Adam in the land where he was created, we brought him into the Garden of Eden so that he might work it and guard it. And on the 80th day his wife was also brought in. And after this she entered the Garden of Eden. 10. And therefore the command was written in the heavenly tablets for one who bears, "If she bears a male, she shall remain seven days in her impurity like the first seven days. And thirty-three days she shall remain in the blood of her purity. And she shall not touch anything holy. And she shall not enter the sanctuary until she has completed these days which are in accord with (the rule for) a male (child). 11. And that which is in accord with (the rule for) a female is two weeks—like the first two weeks—in her impurity. And sixty-six days she shall remain in the blood of her purity. And their total will be eighty days." 12. And when she finished those eighty days, we brought her into the Garden of Eden because it is more holy than any land. And every tree which is planted in it is holy. 13. Therefore the ordinances of these days were ordained for anyone who bears a male or female that she might not touch anything holy and she might not enter the sanctuary until these days are completed for a male or female. 14. This is the law and testimony which is written for Israel so that they might keep it always.

29. Translation from Kugel, "Jubilees," 296–97.

Both 4Q265 and *Jubilees* 3 explicitly refer to the postpartum purification requirements in Lev 12:1–5 (4Q265 7 14b–17; *Jub* 3:10–11). Both texts offer an etiological explanation in which the purification periods required for the woman who gives birth to a male or female child before entering the sanctuary are patterned after the respective purification periods of Adam and Eve before entering the Garden of Eden (4Q265 7 11–14a; *Jub* 3:8–9).[30] This explanation, attested in both 4Q265 and *Jubilees* 3, is based on the understanding of the Garden of Eden as an archetype of the sanctuary.[31] These texts provide another fascinating example of how the Genesis narrative was both understood and employed during the Second Temple period.

30. See Baumgarten, "Purification After Childbirth and the Sacred Garden in 4Q265 and Jubilees," 9–10; Eshel, "Hermeneutical Approaches to Genesis in the Dead Sea Scrolls," 11; Hempel, *The Damascus Texts*, 100.

31. For this conclusion, see Baumgarten, "Purification After Childbirth and the Sacred Garden in 4Q265 and Jubilees," 10; DJD XXXV, 61; Eshel, "Hermeneutical Approaches to Genesis in the Dead Sea Scrolls," 10–11; Hempel, *The Damascus Texts*, 100; Schiffman, "Serekh-Damascus (4Q265)," 869.

CHAPTER NINE

QUMRAN INTERPRETATION OF THE GENESIS CREATION ACCOUNT

JUBILEES (4QJub[a])

Discovery of 4QJub[a]

A NUMBER OF FRAGMENTARY copies of a pseudepigraphal work known as *Jubilees* were uncovered from Cave 4 in 1952. Among these copies, 4QJub[a] (4Q216) preserves portions of a retelling of creation. Almost 40 years passed before a preliminary edition of 4QJub[a] was published by James C. VanderKam and Jozef T. Milik in a 1991 article, "The First *Jubilees* Manuscript from Qumran Cave 4: A Preliminary Edition."[1] Then in 1994, the official edition of 4QJub[a], along with the other copies of *Jubilees* from Cave 4, was published by VanderKam and Milik in volume 13 of the *Discoveries in the Judaean Desert* series.[2]

1. VanderKam and Milik, "The First Jubilees Manuscript from Qumran Cave 4," 243–70.

2. VanderKam and Milik, "4QJubilees[a]" (hereafter, DJD XIII), 1–22, Pl. I–II.

Qumran Cave 4 (Photograph by Jeremy D. Lyon)

Physical Description of 4QJub[a]

4QJub[a] consists of 18 fragments preserving portions of six columns of Hebrew text. Fragments 3, 12, 13, and 18 are larger while the rest of the fragments range from smaller to more moderate in size. Several fragments preserve text from the beginnings and/or ends of lines and columns (e.g. frags 3i–ii, 5, 10, 12i–ii, 18). Consequently, the number, length, and width of columns can be determined.[3] Fragment 18 is helpful in determining the height of the scroll as it preserves portions of seventeen lines of text along with the top and bottom margins. The size of the writing block (seventeen lines measuring c. 12 cm) and height of the extant leather (c. 14.5 cm) indicates that 4QJub[a] was among the category of medium sized scrolls in antiquity.[4]

3. Ibid., 1.

4. Tov categorized scrolls from the Judean Desert with writing blocks of 15–24 lines as medium sized compared to large (25–34 lines) and very large (35–60 lines) (*Scribal Practices and Approaches Reflected in the Texts Found in the Judean Desert*, 84–89).

Fragment 12 is notable in that it preserves portions of two columns of text (and the margin between these columns) along with the thread stitching two sheets of leather together in this manuscript. The scripts of these two columns of text (cols. IV and V) are different, indicating that they were written by two different scribes. Thus, as VanderKam and Milik suggested, it appears that the outer sheet of the original scroll (containing the first four columns) was worn out or damaged and had to be replaced. A later scribe then recopied the text (in a different style) on a new sheet of leather and sewed it to the original (older) scroll.[5]

This later scribe copied columns I–IV in a late Hasmonean script, dating to the mid-first century BC (c. 50 BC), while the original scribe penned columns V–VII in a semicursive script, dating to c. 125–100 BC.[6] Thus, 4QJub[a] represents the oldest extant copy of the book, dating relatively close to the time *Jubilees* was written (c. 160–150 BC).[7]

The Book of *Jubilees* at Qumran

The fact that 4QJub[a] is a Hebrew text is notable. *Jubilees* was originally composed in Hebrew, translated into Greek, and subsequently translated from Greek into Latin and Ethiopic (Geʿez). The book is preserved in its entirety only in the Ethiopic texts. It appears that the Hebrew text of *Jubilees* passed out of use sometime in antiquity, after the destruction of the Second

5. VanderKam and Milik, "The First *Jubilees* Manuscript from Qumran Cave 4," 246; DJD XIII, 1.

6. VanderKam and Milik, DJD XIII, 2; VanderKam, "Book of Jubilees," 434; Segal, "Book of Jubilees," 844; Flint, *The Dead Sea Scrolls*, 85.

7. Prior to the discovery of the Qumran copies of *Jubilees*, R. H. Charles proposed a late-second century date for the composition of the book. However, the evidence from Qumran makes an earlier date more likely. While various dates are assigned by scholars, the book of *Jubilees* is generally dated early to mid-second century BC. For example, VanderKam has concluded, "A date of composition somewhere between 160 and 150 BCE seems highly likely for the complete book" ("Book of Jubilees," 434). Nickelsburg suggested a slightly earlier date in which "Jubilees was written in the early 160s rather than later . . ." (*Jewish Literature between the Bible and the Mishnah*, 73). Kugel observed, "Most scholars believe that it was written sometime early in the 2nd century BCE," but he also recognized that "a still earlier date is not to be ruled out." Kugel further noted that Nickelsburg "probably speaks for the majority of scholars in assigning the book to 'the early 160s,' although I feel there is no justification for not dating it at least two or three decades earlier" ("Jubilees," 272, 451n2). Stegemann, in fact, has argued for dating the composition of *Jubilees* to the third century BC (*The Library of Qumran*, 92).

Temple in AD 70.[8] Nothing from the Hebrew text of *Jubilees* was thought to have survived until the discoveries at Qumran.[9] In fact, all of the copies of *Jubilees* found at Qumran are Hebrew texts. These earlier Hebrew copies show that the later Ethiopic and Latin versions accurately preserved the text.[10] Though fragmentary, 4QJub[a] (cols. V–VII) represents the only extant Hebrew text of the retelling of creation in *Jubilees* (2:1–24).

4QJub[a] is among the fourteen (or fifteen) copies of *Jubilees* found in the Qumran caves (two from Cave 1; two from Cave 2; one from Cave 3; eight or nine from Cave 4; one from Cave 11).[11] The number of copies is significant when compared to the biblical texts found at Qumran. Only Genesis, Exodus, Deuteronomy, Isaiah, and Psalms were represented by more copies than *Jubilees*. The large number of copies of *Jubilees*, coupled with its citation as an authority in the *Damascus Document* (CD XVI:I:2–4), indicates that this work was viewed as authoritative, perhaps even canonical, at Qumran.[12]

8. For further discussion, see Kugel, "Jubilees," 272–73.

9. VanderKam, "Book of Jubilees," 435.

10. VanderKam observed, ". . . the Qumran copies of Jubilees reveal a text that is close to the wording in the Ethiopic and Latin versions. In many cases entire passages agree word for word, while the deviations that exist tend to be minor" (*The Dead Sea Scrolls Today*, 58). Elsewhere, he noted, ". . . the *Jubilees* manuscripts show that the Ethiopic version has preserved the text of the book in an accurate fashion" ("Book of Jubilees," 435). In similar fashion, Flint noted, "Comparison with the Ethiopic and Latin versions show that the ancient translators carried out their task with great care and literalness, with some exceptions of course" (*The Dead Sea Scrolls*, 85–86).

11. If 4Q217 indeed represents another copy of *Jubilees*, then the total number of copies is fifteen.

12. VanderKam cited both as providing "strong reason for believing that *Jubilees* was considered authoritative at Qumran" ("Book of Jubilees," 437). Flint noted, "The large number of copies and several related works show that *Jubilees* was much used by the Essene movement and very popular at Qumran . . . *Jubilees* was most likely viewed as Scripture by the *Yahad*" (*The Dead Sea Scrolls*, 86). Similarly, Schiffman stated that ". . . the work had an influence on the life of the Qumran sect and may even have had canonical status for its members" (*Reclaiming the Dead Sea Scrolls*, 186). According to Stegemann, ". . . the Qumran settlers considered *Jubilees* one of the most important works of their traditional literature" (*The Library of Qumran*, 92). Likewise, according to Segal, "This high number of copies indicates the special status of the book within the Qumran community" ("Book of Jubilees," 844). Kugel also noted, "*Jubilees* was prized by the Dead Sea Scrolls community" ("Jubilees," 272). For further discussion, see also Wise et al., *The Dead Sea Scrolls: A New Translation*, 317.

Content of *Jubilees*

The book of *Jubilees* reworks biblical stories from Genesis 1 to Exodus 19 in the context of a Divine revelation to Moses while on Mt. Sinai. God Himself speaks to Moses in chapter 1 concerning Israel's future rebellion and subsequent punishment, repentance, and restoration. In chapters 2–50, an Angel of the Presence then dictates the contents of the book to him from the heavenly tablets, covering events from creation to Israel's future entry into the Promised Land (see *Jub* 50:4).[13] The title *Jubilees* is derived from the book's division of history into fifty units of forty-nine years.[14] The book can be outlined as follows:

An Outline of the Book of *Jubilees*	
1:1–29	Introduction: Israel's rebellion and future restoration
2:1–4:32	Narratives about Creation and Adam
4:33–10:26	Narratives about Noah, the Flood, and Babel
11:1–23:8	Narratives about Abraham
23:9–32	Thoughts on Abraham's death and Israel's future restoration
24:1–45:16	Narratives about Jacob and his sons
46:1–49:23	Narratives about bondage in Egypt, Moses, and the Exodus
50:1–13	Conclusion: Israel's future restoration, observance of laws, the Sabbath

This retelling generally follows the order of the biblical narrative, but also includes various additions, omissions, and other changes in order to explain perceived difficulties in the biblical text and to express the author's own interests and ideas. The author sought to communicate a message of hope for the people of Israel in his day and to instruct and admonish them to live according to God's laws.[15] Several notable features emerge from this retelling.

First, the biblical stories are retold within a chronological framework dividing time into jubilees (periods of forty-nine years) and weeks (periods of seven years). The book covers exactly fifty jubilees (50 x 49 years), that

13. In *Jubilees*, the setting for the Divine revelation given to Moses is Mt. Sinai. Thus, entry into the Promised Land is presented as still future.

14. Another title, *The Book of the Division of the Times*, is found in the prologue and *Jub* 1:4. VanderKam suggested that this is likely the original title of the work ("Book of Jubilees," 434).

15. See Kugel, "Jubilees," 272.

is, 2,450 years of history.[16] In this manner, all of the events from creation to the future entry into the Promised Land are dated. For example, according to *Jubilees*, Adam and Eve remained in the Garden of Eden for "the first week of the first jubilee," that is, seven years, before their disobedience and subsequent expulsion (*Jub* 3:15–35; cf. Gen 3).[17] The death of Adam is dated to "the end of the nineteenth jubilee in the seventh week, in the sixth year," that is, 930 years from creation (*Jub* 4:29–30; cf. Gen 5:5). Notably, the Ethiopic version dates the death of Abraham incorrectly to "the first week of this forty-fourth jubilee in the second year" (*Jub* 22:1) while a Hebrew copy from Qumran, 4QJub[d] (II:35–36), dates it to "the first week of the for[ty-]third jubilee, [in its second year]."[18] Israel's future entry into the Promised Land is dated to fifty jubilees, that is, 2,450 years from creation (*Jub* 50:4).[19] According to Michael Segal, "The bounding of the entire composition in a complete cycle of jubilees reflects an attempt to periodize history, a common practice in Second Temple texts."[20] In addition to this distinct chronological framework, the author of *Jubilees* utilized the 364 day solar calendar (e.g. *Jub* 2:8–9; 6:32–38).[21]

Second, Torah observance is a major focus in *Jubilees*. Throughout the work, the author's retelling of these pre-Sinai narratives often include additional material concerning various laws based on the Torah.[22] These expansions of the biblical narratives depict the patriarchs as faithfully observing the laws *before* they were revealed at Sinai.[23]

16. VanderKam, "Book of Jubilees," 435–36; Segal, "Book of Jubilees," 845.

17. Genesis 3 does not state exactly how long Adam and Eve dwelt in Eden before their expulsion.

18. VanderKam and Milik, DJD XIII, 39–54, Pl. IV; Vermes, *The Complete Dead Sea Scrolls in English*, rev. ed., 539; Kugel, "Jubilees," 370.

19. *Jub* 50:4: "On account of this I ordained for you the weeks of years, and the years, and the jubilees (as) forty-nine jubilees from the days of Adam until this day and one week and two years. And they are still forty further years to learn the commands of the Lord until they cross over the shore of the land of Canaan, crossing over the Jordan to its western side."

20. Segal, "Book of Jubilees," 845.

21. The 364 day solar calendar is divisible by seven, equaling exactly fifty-two weeks.

22. Segal, "Book of Jubilees," 844.

23. Nickelsburg, *Jewish Literature between the Bible and the Mishnah*, 69; VanderKam, "Book of Jubilees," 435. Similarly, VanderKam suggested, "The writer may have been combating a current opinion that there had once been a time when the laws that came to separate Jewish people from others were not in existence. His point is that there was never such a time; the chosen race had always been distinguished from other

Third, there is also a focus on the priesthood in which the author presents the patriarchs as priests from the earliest times. The priestly line of Levi goes all the way back to Adam, who offered a sacrifice on the day he went out from the Garden of Eden (*Jub* 3:27). Adam, Enoch, Noah, Abraham, Isaac, Jacob, and Levi represent a continuous line of priests offering sacrifices and observing holy days in the same manner as their successors (the Levitical priests) after Sinai.[24] According to Kugel, the author's purpose is clear: "Things really didn't begin at Sinai, but with Israel's ancestors . . . We were God's people long before the Sinai covenant, we worshiped Him back then in the same way that we worship Him now, and we will remain His people forever."[25]

Fourth, an eschatological outlook is also evident from the outset of the book. The author recalls, in the form of a prediction to Moses, Israel's rebellion and failure to keep the covenant which resulted in judgment/exile (*Jub* 1:7–14), and also relays a message of hope concerning Israel's future repentance and restoration (*Jub* 1:15–18; cf. 23:22–32; 50:5).[26]

A Retelling of the Creation Account

Within this fascinating composition is a retelling of the Genesis creation account (*Jub* 2:1–24). The author reproduces the biblical text in some cases, but generally rewords, abbreviates, or provides additional information in this reworked narrative. Though fragmentary, 4QJub[a] represents the only Hebrew copy of *Jubilees* preserving portions of this reworked creation account. The missing portions of the Hebrew text have been reconstructed by VanderKam and Milik based on the later Ethiopic version (which,

---

nations by special laws that they observed from the earliest days."

24. The offering of sacrifices and/or incense by the patriarchs include: Adam (*Jub* 3:27), Enoch (*Jub* 4:25), Noah (*Jub* 6:1–3), Abraham (*Jub* 13:4–9; 14:6–19; 15:1–4; 16:20–31; 21:1–17), Isaac (*Jub* 22:3–7; 24:22–23), Jacob/Levi (*Jub* 31:26–32:9). Levi was given the "garments of the priesthood" and served as priest (*Jub* 32:1–9). Observance of various holy days by the patriarchs include: the Feast of Weeks by Noah (*Jub* 6:17–19), the Feast of Firstfruits by Abraham, Isaac, and Jacob (*Jub* 15:1–2; 22:1–9), the Feast of Tabernacles by Abraham (*Jub* 16:20–31), Jacob and Levi (Jub 32:1–9), and the Day of Atonement by Jacob (*Jub* 34:12–19). Special instructions are also given concerning the Passover (*Jub* 49:1–23) and the Sabbath (*Jub* 50:1–13).

25. Kugel, "Jubilees," 276.

26. For further discussion, see Kugel, "Jubilees," 275–77; Nickelsburg, *Jewish Literature between the Bible and the Mishnah*, 71–73.

according to the textual evidence of the numerous Hebrew copies from Qumran, appears to accurately preserve the text of *Jubilees*).[27]

Day One: Creation of the Heavens, Earth, Waters, Angels, Abysses, Darkness, and Light

4QJub[a] V:4–11 (= *Jub* 2:2–3) mentions a total of seven great works of creation on day one: the heavens, earth, waters, angels, abysses/depths, darkness, and light. While the biblical base text (Gen 1:1–5) is discernable, this retelling of God's creative acts on day one freely reformulates, omits, and adds material.

> 4. [*vacat* [2:2]For on the first day He created the heave]ns that are above, and the ear[th, 5. and the waters, and all the spirits who serve before Him: the angels] of the Presence, and the angels of holi[ness], 6. and the an[gels of the spirits of fire, and the angels of the spirits of the winds that blo]w, [and] the angels of the spirits of the [clouds,] 7. of dark[ness, ice, hoar-frost, dew, snow, hail, and fro]st, and the angels of sound[s], 8. and the angels of the [storm] winds, [and the angels of the spirits of cold and] heat, and of winter and of summer, [and of all] 9. the spirits of His creatures [which He made in the heavens and which He made on the ear]th, and in every (place); the dept[hs], 10. darkness, dawn, and [light and evening which He prepared through] His [know]ledge. [2:3]Then we saw His works and we [blessed Him] 11. concerning all His [wo]rks and [we offered praise before Him because] He ma[de seven] great works [on the first day].

Line 4 refers to the creation of "[the heave]ns that are above, and the ear[th]" on the first day (cf. *Jub* 2:2), reflecting Gen 1:1. Line 5 likely began with a reference to "the waters" (cf. *Jub* 2:2), drawing from Gen 1:2, which describes the earth as being covered by water when it was created on day one.

Lines 5–9 then refer to the creation of the various angels on day one of creation week.[28] The Genesis account, however, makes no mention

27. VanderKam and Milik noted that the Hebrew reconstructions in the DJD edition "merely retrovert the Ethiopic into Hebrew and are therefore tentative" (DJD XII, 5n1).

28. R. H. Charles classified the angels of the presence and the angels of holiness as "the two chief orders of angels," while the various types of angels that follow constitute "the third or lowest order" (*The Book of Jubilees or the Little Genesis*, 41). See also

of *when* the angels were created.[29] The text of *Jubilees*, before listing the various types of angels (lines 5b–9), introduces all of them as "the spirits (הרוחות) who serve before Him" (line 5; cf. *Jub* 2:2). Angels are referred to as "spirits" in the Hebrew Bible (e.g. Ps 104:4) and in Second Temple period texts (e.g. 1QM X:11–12). Thus, the author may have understood the phrase ורוח אלהים (typically translated as the wind *or* Spirit of God) in Gen 1:2 as alluding to an angel, who "was hovering over the face of the waters."[30] According to lines 6–8, certain angels were in charge of various elements and natural phenomena such as fire, winds that blow, clouds, darkness, ice, snow, hail, frost, sounds (thunder), storm winds, cold, and heat (cf. *1 En* 60:12–22).

The list of God's works of creation on day one continues at the end of line 9 with "the dept[hs]" ([התהו]מות), which is likely taken from the phrase "and darkness was on the face of the deep (תהום)" in Gen 1:2. The beginning of line 10 also includes "darkness" (מאפלה) as being created on day one (Gen 1:2, 4–5 employs the term חשך for "darkness"). Last, *Jubilees* includes "light" among God's works of creation on the first day (line 10; cf. *Jub* 2:2). The biblical account, however, provides more detail concerning the manner in which God created light through His spoken word (Gen 1:3), divided the light from the darkness (Gen 1:4), and called the light "day" (Gen 1:5).

Lines 10b–11 conclude this retelling of the first day of creation week with additional material concerning the angels blessing God for all His works and praising Him "[because He] ma[de seven] great works [on the first day]" (cf. *Jub* 2:3). These works include: the heavens, earth, waters, angels, depths, darkness, and light. Notably, the author of *Jubilees* included the creation of the heavens and the earth (Gen 1:1–2) *as part of* day one.

VanderKam, *The Book of Jubilees*, 126.

29. The idea that angels were present during creation week is attested elsewhere in the Hebrew Bible (e.g. Job 38:4–7). Kugel, however, has suggested that the existence of angels during creation week is implied in Gen 2:1: "And the heavens and the earth and all their hosts were completed." He understands "their hosts" (צבאם) as referring to "the hosts (armies) of heaven" ("Jubilees," 289). While this is certainly possible, צבאם (their hosts) in Gen 2:1 may be a reference to the heavenly bodies, considering the Genesis creation account contains prior discussion on the creation of the luminaries (Gen 1:14–19), but contains no prior discussion on the creation of angels (of which 2:1 would be referring back to). It is also possible that צבאם (their hosts) in Gen 2:1 refers to all the works found in the heavens and the earth.

30. See Kugel, "Jubilees," 289–90.

Consequently, the first five verses (Gen 1:1–5) were understood as constituting the literary boundary of day one.

Day Two: Creation of the Firmament

4QJub[a] V:12–14 (= *Jub* 2:4) preserves only a few words, or partial words, from the retelling of day two of creation week (Gen 1:6–8). All that remains of line 14 are portions of a few letters of the first word.

> 12. [2:4]On the [second] da[y He made the firmament in the mid]st of the [wate]rs, [and the waters were divided on that day. Half of them] 13. went up abo[ve the firmament, and half of them went down beneath the firmament which is in the middle, above the surface of] 14. the earth[. . .]

The text of *Jubilees* generally reflects the biblical base text of Gen 1:7, but omits the phrase, "and it was so."[31] While the preceding Divine speech of Gen 1:6 is omitted, some of the language ("the firmament in the midst of the waters") is folded into this retelling. The text of *Jubilees* then omits Gen 1:8 completely, but adds a concluding remark. The missing text of line 14 likely contained this addition: "This was the only work that He made on the second day."

Day Three: Creation of Dry Land, Gathered Waters, Plants, and the Garden of Eden

According to *Jubilees*, God made four great kinds on day three: gathered waters, dry land, plants, and the Garden of Eden. 4QJub[a] VI:2–4 (= *Jub* 2:7) partially preserves the latter part of this retelling of the third day of creation week (Gen 1:9–13):

> 2. [. . . [2:7]and the reser]voirs and all the de[w of the earth 3. and the seed which brings forth seed in its seed, and all that sprouts, and the tree that produces fruit, and the] forests, and the Garden of E[de]n [in Eden 4. for pleasure and for eating. These four great kinds] He made {He made} on the thi[rd] day.

31. Gen 1:7: "Thus God made the firmament, and divided the waters which were under the firmament from the waters which were above the firmament; and it was so." *Jub* 2:4 reverses the order, mentioning the waters above the firmament and then the waters beneath the firmament.

The preceding lines of text containing the beginning of this day three narrative (4QJub^{a} V:15–VI:1 = *Jub* 2:5–6) have been lost due to scroll damage. Though not extant here, *Jub* 2:5–6 reworks Gen 1:9–10, which speaks of God gathering the waters together into one place and the dry land appearing.[32] The extant text picks up in 4QJub^{a} VI:2 (= *Jub* 2:7), which adds that God's creation of gatherings of water included not only the seas, but also the rivers, the gatherings of waters in the mountains and in all the earth, the reservoirs, and all the dew of the earth. Lines 3–4 continue this list of God's created works, mentioning the various types of plants (Gen 1:11–12) [33] and the Garden of Eden. Gen 1:9–13, however, makes no mention of the Garden of Eden being created on day three. Genesis 2 includes discussion on the creation of Eden, but never explicitly states *when* it was created. The physical description of the Garden of Eden includes the ground (Gen 2:9), every tree good for food (Gen 2:9, 16), the tree of life (Gen 2:9), the tree of the knowledge of good and evil (Gen 2:9, 17), and a river (Gen 2:10). Thus, the author of *Jubilees* deduced that the Garden of Eden was created on day three, that is, the same day as the gatherings of water and the creation of the dry land and plants (Gen 1:9–13).[34]

Day Four: Creation of the Sun, Moon, and Stars

4QJub^{a} VI:5–10 (= *Jub* 2:8–10) discusses the creation of three works on day four: the sun, moon, and stars. The biblical base text (Gen 1:14–19) is discernable, but this retelling of God's creative acts on day four also freely reformulates, omits, and adds material.

> [5. *vacat* [2:8]On the fourth day the LORD made the s]un and the moon and the stars. [Then He placed 6. them in the firmament of the heavens to give light upon all the earth and] to rule over the day and the night, and to div[ide between 7. light and darkness. [2:9]Then He placed the sun as a gr]eat [sign above the earth] for day[s], and for [sa]bbaths, and for [months, 8. and for seasons, and for years, and for the weeks of years, and for jubi]lees, and for

32. The biblical material omitted here includes God naming the gathered waters (seas) and dry land (earth), along with the phrase "And God saw that it was good."

33. Much of the material from Gen 1:11–12 is omitted here, including the Divine speech and the phrase "And God saw that it was good." The concluding statement of 1:13, "And it was evening and it was morning, day three," is also omitted.

34. The idea that the Garden of Eden was created on day three is also found in *Genesis Rabbah* 11.9; 15.3 and 2 *Enoch* 30.1.

> all cyc[les of the years. 9. [2:10]And it separates between the light and the darkness and serves for healing in order that everything that] sprouts and grows in the ea[rth may be well. 10. These three kinds He made on the fourth day. *vac*]*at*

This section opens in line 5 with a summary statement that on the fourth day God made the sun, moon, and stars. The end of line 5 through the beginning of line 7 then reproduces Gen 1:17–18.[35] Lines 7–8 (= *Jub* 2:9) then rework Gen 1:14, endorsing the solar-based calendar: "Then He placed the sun as a great sign above the earth for days, and for Sabbaths, and for months, and for seasons, and for years, and for the weeks of years, and for jubilees, and for all cycles of the years." While Gen 1:14 (cf. 1:16–18) indicates that the sun *and moon* were to be "for signs and seasons, and for days and years,"[36] the author of *Jubilees* excludes the moon from having any calendrical function.[37] This rejection of the lunar calendar in favor of the solar calendar (consisting of 364 days) is discussed in more detail in *Jubilees* 6.[38]

Day Five: Creation of the Great Sea Creatures, Fish, and Flying Creatures

4QJub[a] VI:11–15 (= *Jub* 2:11–12) preserves only a few words, or partial words, from the retelling of day five of creation week (Gen 1:20–23). According to *Jubilees*, God created three great kinds on this day: the great sea creatures, fish, and birds.

> [11. [2:11]And on the fifth day He created] the gre[at sea creatures] in the mid[st of the depth]s of the wa[ters, for these 12. were the first works of flesh by His hands, and everything that moves in the] waters, the fis[h and] all {and al[l]} the birds 13. that fly, and all their kinds. [2:12]And the sun shone upon them for] well-being and up[on everything] that was on the ea[rth, all 14. that sprouted

35. Only the final phrase of 1:18 ("And God saw that it was good") is omitted.

36. Gen 1:14: "Then God said, 'Let there be *lights* (מארת) in the firmament of the heavens to divide the day from the night; *and let them be* (והיו) for signs and seasons, and for days and years." Emphasis added, denoting the use of the plural.

37. In addition to the omission of the moon, 4QJub[a] VI:7–8 (= *Jub* 2:9) asserts that God "placed the sun as a great *sign* (singular) above the earth," replacing the plural "and let them be for signs" in Gen 1:14.

38. *Jubilees* and *1 Enoch* (popular books at Qumran), along with other texts found at Qumran (e.g. 4Q252), endorse the 364 day solar calendar.

> from the earth and every tree that produces fruit and all flesh. These] thr[ee] gr[eat kind]s 15. [He made on the fifth day.] *vacat*

The text of *Jubilees* omits the Divine speech of Gen 1:20. Instead, lines 11–12 (= *Jub* 2:11) begin by reworking Gen 1:21, adding that the great sea creatures "were the first works of flesh by His hands." Also, the phrase "and everything that moves in the waters" is followed by a reference to "fish" (דגים), which is not explicitly stated in Gen 1:21. The refrain, "according to their kind" is also not included here. The end of line 12 and the beginning of line 13 then partially preserves the reading, "and all the birds that fly, and all their kinds," which diverges slightly from the biblical reading, "and every winged bird according to its kind." Lines 13–14 (= *Jub* 2:12) omit Gen 1:22–23, instead supplying new material. Only a few letters are preserved from lines 14–15 (= *Jub* 2:12b) in which the author concludes that three great kinds of living creatures were made on day five.

Day Six: Creation of the Beasts of the Earth, Cattle, Creeping Creatures, and Mankind

4QJub[a] VII:1–5 (= *Jub* 2:13–16) partially preserves the retelling of day six of creation week (Gen 1:24–31).[39] According to *Jubilees*, God created four kinds on this day: the beasts of the earth, cattle, creeping creatures, and mankind. Once again the biblical base text is discernable, but the omissions and additions of material are of particular interest.

> 1. [[2:13]And on] the sixth [da]y {He made} all the anima[ls of the earth, and all the cattle, and everything that creeps upon the earth. [2:14]After all these] 2. He made man, male and fem[ale He made them. Then He caused him to rule over everything that is upon the earth and in the seas and over everything that flies,] 3. and over the animals, and over every creeping thing that [creeps upon the earth, and over the cattle, and over all the earth. Over all these He caused him to rule.] These [four] 4. kinds He made on [the sixth day. [2:15]And in all there were twenty-two kinds. [2:16]And He finished all His works on the sixth day—all] 5. that is in the heavens, and on the earth, [and in the seas, and in the depths, and in the light, and in the darkness, and in every (place).]

39. The first few words of each line are extant in this fragmentary text.

The text of *Jubilees* omits the Divine speech of Gen 1:24. The first line (= *Jub* 2:13) mentions the three kinds of land animals that God made, in keeping with Gen 1:25. The phrase "And God saw that it was good" is not included here. The end of line 1 and the beginning of line 2 (= *Jub* 2:14) echo the latter part of Gen 1:27 in a summary statement about the creation of mankind: "After all these, He made man, male and female He made them." Instead of reproducing the Divine speech in Gen 1:26 (cf. 1:28), lines 2–3 simply present the fact that God caused man to rule over the various animals. Perhaps most notable is the omission of the creation of man "in/by the image of God" (Gen 1:26–27).[40] Kugel has suggested that "this was apparently too anthropomorphic for the author." However, it is also possible that this material was not included because it was not necessary for the author's purposes at this point. The idea that man was created in God's image is, in fact, noted later on in *Jubilees*.[41] The end of line 3 and beginning of line 4 then partially preserve the summary statement: "These four kinds He made on the sixth day." Lines 4–5 (= *Jub* 2:15–16) omit the remainder of the biblical account of day six (Gen 1:28–31),[42] providing new material instead. Having already noted the number of created kinds on day six, *Jubilees* then provides the total number of things created in the first six days: "And in all there were twenty-two kinds." The text of *Jub* 2:16, partially preserved in lines 4b–5, concludes: "And He finished all His works on the sixth day—all that is in the heavens, and on the earth, and in the seas, and in the depths, and in the light, and in the darkness, and in every (place)." This statement echoes the earlier introductory statement to this retelling of creation week in *Jub* 2:1.[43] The author of *Jubilees* removes any possibility that God's creative work may have continued into the seventh day, which could be implied in Gen 2:2: "And on the seventh day God com-

40. Kugel, "Jubilees," 291.

41. *Jub* 6:7b–8: "From the hand of every man, from the hand of every (creature), I will seek the blood of a man. Whoever pours out the blood of a man, by man his blood shall be poured out, because in the image of the Lord He made Adam." Translation from Wintermute, "Jubilees," 66.

42. This includes: God's blessing and mandate for mankind to "be fruitful and multiply" and to "have dominion" over all the animals (Gen 1:28); God's giving a diet for mankind and the animals (Gen 1:29–30); God's seeing that it was "very good" and the concluding remark, "And the evening and the morning were the sixth day" (Gen 1:31).

43. *Jub* 2:1: "And the angel of the presence spoke to Moses by the word of the Lord, saying, 'Write all the words of the creation, *that in six days the Lord God completed all His works and everything that He created*. And He observed a Sabbath on the seventh day and He sanctified it for all ages. And He gave it as a sign for all His works.'" (emphasis added)

pleted His work which He had done, and He rested on the seventh day from all His work which He had done."[44] The author's understanding that God's creative work took place in the span of six days and did not continue into the seventh day is attested in Exod 20:11: "For in six days the LORD made the heavens and the earth, the sea, and all that is in them, and rested the seventh day. Therefore the LORD blessed the Sabbath day and hallowed it."

Day Seven: God's Election of Israel on the Sabbath

4QJub[a] VII:5b–17 (= *Jub* 2:17–24) partially preserves this unique retelling of day seven, linking the Sabbath with God's election of Israel. While the Genesis creation account covers the seventh day in relatively few words (Gen 2:2–3),[45] *Jubilees* devotes a rather significant amount of attention to the Sabbath. Much of this retelling consists of new material.

> [5b. [2:17]He gave to us a great sign—the day] 6. of the Sabbath, which He rested on [it . . .] 7. they were made in six days. [. . .] 8. and we keep the Sabbath on the se[venth] day [(refraining) from all work. [2:18]For we, all the angels of the presence and all the angels of holiness—] 9. these [two] kinds—He sai[d to us to keep Sabbath with Him in heaven and on earth. [2:19]Then He said to us, "Behold, I will separate to Me] 10. a people from among My nations. And [they will keep the Sabbath and I will sanctify them as My people and I will bless them. They will be My people and I will be their God."] 11. [2:20]And He chose the descendants of Jacob from among [all those whom I saw. "I have recorded them to Me as the first-born son and I have sanctified them to Me] 12. forever and ever." And the [seventh] day [I will teach to them in order that they may keep Sabbath on it from everything, [2:21]according to which He blessed them and sanctified them for Himself as a special people] 13.from all the nations and to be [keeping Sabbath] together [with us. [2:22]And He lifted up His commandments like a pleasant fragrance which is acceptable in His presence] 14. every day. *vac*[*at* [2:23]There were twenty-two heads of men] 15. from Adam until him and twenty-two k[inds of work were made until the seventh day. The one is blessed and holy and the other is blessed] 16. and holy. And this one with this one

44. Other Jewish sources address this exegetical question (e.g. *Genesis Rabbah* 10.9).

45. Gen 2:2–3: "And on the seventh day God completed His work which He had done, and He rested on the seventh day from all His work which He had done. Then God blessed the seventh day and sanctified it, because in it He rested from all His work which God had created and made."

> were made together for holiness [and for blessing. 2:24And it was given to this one to be for all days the blessed and holy ones.] 17. And this is the testimony and the fir[st] law [. . .]

According to lines 5b–9a (= *Jub* 2:17–18), a great sign—the Sabbath—was given to the angels of the presence and the angels of holiness, the two chief classes, who were to observe the Sabbath with God in heaven and on the earth. Lines 9b–13a (= *Jub* 2:19–21) then speak of God's election of the descendants of Jacob (= Israel), who would also observe the Sabbath.[46] Just as God had blessed and sanctified the Sabbath and set it apart from the other six days (Gen 2:2–3), so also He would bless and sanctify the descendants of Jacob and set them apart from the nations (cf. *Jub* 2:19–21; Deut 7:6, 14). Thus, according to *Jubilees*, God had already planned the existence (and election) of Israel during creation week (day seven), and it is within this particular context that Israel is called God's "first-born son" (cf. *Jub* 2:20; Exod 4:22).[47] Then, in lines 14–16a (= *Jub* 2:23), the author's attention to the number of created works throughout the retelling of the first six days comes into focus as he provides further rationale for God's election of Israel: "14. [. . . There were twenty-two heads of men] 15. from Adam until him (Jacob) and twenty-two k[inds of work were made before the seventh day. The one is blessed and holy and the other is blessed] 16. and holy. And this one with this one were made together for holiness [and for blessing]." The author's previous assertion that God elected Israel on the first Sabbath (*Jub* 2:19–21) is now shown to be bound up in the created order; there were twenty-two generations from Adam until Jacob, who is "blessed" and "sanctified," just as there were twenty-two created works until the seventh day, which is "blessed" and "sanctified" (*Jub* 2:23). VanderKam noted, ". . . as if to answer the question, 'Why Israel?', the author tells us that the structure of creation is parallel to the structure of sacred history."[48]

According to *Jubilees*, not only is the six days of work and seventh day of rest for Israel patterned after creation week (*Jub* 2:1, 16–17; cf. Exod 20:8–11; 31:17), but also God's election of Israel is rooted in the created order (*Jub* 2:19–23).[49] The purpose of this retelling of day seven (*Jub* 2:17–24),

46. Charles observed that those who observe the Sabbath include God, the two chief orders of angels, and Israel. Those denied this privilege include the third order of angels and the Gentiles (*The Book of Jubilees or the Little Genesis*, 44).

47. For further discussion, see Kugel, "Jubilees," 292.

48. VanderKam, *The Book of Jubilees*, 29.

49. Ibid., 30

perhaps even the entire retelling of creation, is to show that God's election of Israel goes back not to the period of the Sinai covenant, but all the way back to creation week.[50] This idea dovetails nicely with the author's overall purposes of the book and reflects the general structure of this retelling of creation week (*Jub* 2:1–24).

The Retelling of the Creation Account in *Jub* 2:1–24		
Introduction	2:1	a) "... *in six days the* Lord *God completed all His works and everything that He created.* b) *And He observed a Sabbath on the seventh day and He sanctified it for all ages. And He gave it as a sign for all His works.*'"
First Six Days of Creation Week	2:2–3	"For on the first day ..." ... "He made seven great works"
	2:4	"And on the second day ..." ... "This was the only work He made"
	2:5–7	"And on the third day ..." ... "These four great kinds He made"
	2:8–10	"And on the fourth day ..." ... "These three kinds He made"
	2:11–12	"And on the fifth day ..." ... "These three great kinds He made"
	2:13–16	"And on the sixth day ..." ... "These four kinds He made"
		"And in all there were twenty-two kinds"
Conclusion to Day Six	2:16	a) *"And He finished all His works on the sixth day—all that is in the heavens, and on the earth, and in the seas, and in the depths, and in the light, and in the darkness, and in every (place)."*
Introduction to the Sabbath	2:17	b) *"And He gave us a great sign, the Sabbath day, so that we might work six days and observe a Sabbath from all work on the seventh day."*

50. Kugel, "Jubilees," 292–93.

Israel and the Sabbath	2:18–24	". . . And He said to us, 'Behold I shall separate for Myself a people from among all the nations. And they will also keep the Sabbath. And I will sanctify them for Myself, and I will bless them. Just as I have sanctified and shall sanctify the Sabbath day for Myself thus shall I bless them. And they will be My people and I will be their God. And I have chosen the seed of Jacob . . . and I have recorded him as My firstborn son . . .' *"There were twenty-two chief men from Adam until Jacob, and twenty-two kinds of works were made before the seventh day. The former is blessed and sanctified, and the latter is also blessed and sanctified. One was like the other with respect to sanctification and blessing.* And it was granted to the former that they should always be the blessed and sanctified ones of the testimony and the first law just as He had sanctified and blessed Sabbath day on the seventh day."

CHAPTER TEN

CONCLUSIONS

Among the large cache of ancient manuscripts found in the Qumran caves are: 1) copies of Genesis containing portions of the creation account and 2) non-biblical texts containing interpretation of the creation account. As observed in this study, these fragmentary texts have provided priceless insights concerning the *text* and *interpretation* of the Genesis creation account during the Second Temple period.

The Text of the Genesis Creation Account at Qumran

At least nineteen, possibly twenty, fragmentary copies of Genesis were found in the Qumran caves.[1] All of the manuscripts containing enough material for analysis reflect the Masoretic Text tradition, though most contain some orthographical differences and minor textual variants.[2]

1. The majority of the copies of Genesis were found in Cave 4, while individual copies were also found in Caves 1, 2, 6, and 8. At least nineteen copies of Genesis have been identified, but there is question, for example, about 4QGen$^{h\text{-}title}$, which consists of only a single small fragment containing the title (ברשית, spelled without the א) on the recto side of the skin. If 4QGen$^{h\text{-}title}$ represents a distinct manuscript, then there would be twenty copies of Genesis attested at Qumran. For further discussion, see Davila, DJD XII, 63–64. In addition to the Qumran scrolls, four other fragmentary copies of Genesis were found in other sites in the Judean Desert (two from Wadi Murabbaʿat; one from Wadi Sdeir; one from Masada).

2. Davila observed, "All the Qumran manuscripts that contain enough material for analysis belong to the same text type as the Masoretic Text (4QGen^{b} is virtually identical), but most have some orthographic differences from it and contain minor textual variations" ("Book of Genesis," 299). Crawford simply noted, "All of these manuscripts conform to the proto-Masoretic text-type in Genesis" ("Genesis in the Dead Sea Scrolls,"

Six of the Qumran Genesis manuscripts contain text from the creation account: 1QGen, 4QGen[b], 4QGen[d], 4QGen[g], 4QGen[h1], and 4QGen[k]. These fragmentary texts represent the oldest extant copies of the Genesis creation account, dating from the first century BC to the mid-first century AD.[3] These ancient copies of Genesis have provided an unprecedented glimpse into the condition of the biblical text during the Second Temple period and have also proven valuable for textual studies. First, the text tradition preserved in the medieval Masoretic Text is attested in these Qumran Genesis manuscripts containing the creation account. 4QGen[b] and 4QGen[d], for example, are virtually identical to MT, demonstrating the faithful scribal transmission of this text tradition over the centuries.[4] Consequently, when we read the text of the creation account today, which is based on MT, we are reading the same text that people were reading during the Second Temple period. Second, some of the variant readings preserved in these Qumran Genesis scrolls reveal the existence of a Hebrew *Vorlage* (base text) for readings found in the Septuagint. The variant readings in 4QGen[h1] and 4QGen[k], for example, indicate that the Septuagint translator(s) carefully copied from a Hebrew text tradition that differed from MT.[5]

---

354). VanderKam and Flint acknowledged, "It appears that the text of Genesis had become generally stable by the Qumran period, since these manuscripts reveal a text generally close to the traditional Masoretic Text and the Samaritan Pentateuch" (*The Meaning of the Dead Sea Scrolls*, 104). Ulrich similarly observed, "It appears that the text of Genesis had become basically stable by the late Second Temple period. All our manuscripts exhibit basically the same text type; most of the variants are only minor or unintentional" (*The Dead Sea Scrolls and the Origins of the Bible*, 25).

3. 1QGen (100–1 BC); 4QGen[b] (AD 50–68+); 4QGen[d] (50–25 BC); 4QGen[g] (50–25 BC); 4QGen[h1] (50–25 BC); 4QGen[k] (AD 1–30).

4. 4QGen[b] preserves the most material of the creation account (1:1–28) among the Qumran scrolls and is essentially identical to MT, with only one spelling difference. 4QGen[d] preserves a good portion of Gen 1:18–27 and is also essentially identical to MT, containing only a few spelling differences.

5. Gen 1:9a of MT reads: ויאמר אלהים יקוו המים מתחת השמים אל־מקום אחד (Then God said, "Let the waters beneath the heavens be gathered into one place"). The MT reading of מקום (place) is attested in the SP and 4QGen[b], whereas the LXX reads συναγωγην (gathering). 4QGen[h1] reads מקוה (gathering) instead of מקום (place), which provides us with a Hebrew *Vorlage* for the LXX reading of συναγωγην (gathering).

Gen 1:9b of MT reads: ותראה היבשה ויהי־כן (and let the dry land appear. And it was so). The LXX contains additional text describing the accomplishment of the dry land appearing: και συνηχθη το υδωρ το υποκατω του ουρανου εις τας συναγωγας αυτων και ωφθη η ξηρα (And the water beneath the heaven was collected into its gatherings, and the dry land appeared). 4QGen[k] preserves ותרא היב[שה] (and the dry land appeared). ותרא (and it appeared) in 4QGen[k] is a niphal *wayyiqtol* verb, whereas ותראה (and let it

These Qumran Genesis scrolls have also provided us a unique window into certain scribal practices which appear to represent an ancient understanding of the structure of the creation account. Several texts (4QGen^{b}, 4QGen^{d}, 4QGen^{g}, 4QGen^{h1}, and 4QGen^{k}) exhibit the ancient scribal practice of denoting units in a text by means of spacing. A major division was placed after each day of creation week, dividing the text according to days. These major divisions in the creation account may represent: a) scribal transmission of a structure already present in the text or b) an element of interpretation by the scribes of the Qumran texts.[6] Either way, the sense divisions in these Qumran texts reflect an ancient understanding of the creation account and determine a certain structure for the reader of the text.

Qumran Interpretation of the Genesis Creation Account

Several non-biblical texts from Qumran contain the most ancient surviving interpretations of the Genesis creation account, dating from the mid-second century BC to the first century AD.[7] These fragmentary texts contain a wealth of information, revealing various aspects of how the Genesis creation account was *understood* and *employed* during the Second Temple period.

A liturgical text known as *Words of the Luminaries* (4Q504) reworks the biblical account of the creation of Adam within the historical section of the prayer for the first day of the week. This recollection of the creation, fall, and subsequent punishment of Adam provides a historical basis for the petition to God in the prayer. The *Paraphrase of Genesis and Exodus* (4Q422) selectively reworks biblical passages, juxtaposing the creation, Flood, and plagues narratives for hortatory or homiletical purposes. Several copies of a wisdom text known as *Musar le-Mebin* or 4QInstruction (4Q416, 4Q417,

appear) in MT is a niphal jussive verb, indicating that 4QGen^{k} included the additional text in 1:9 that is found in the LXX.

6. The origin of these sense divisions in the creation account remains uncertain due to the fact that there are no known extant Genesis texts dating earlier than the Qumran texts with which we can compare. Whether the sense divisions were part of the original structure intended at the compositional level by the author/editor of the text *or* were inserted by later scribes (prior to Qumran) or the scribes of the Qumran texts, they represent an early understanding of the text.

7. 4Q504 (c. 150 BC), 4Q422 (c. 100–50 BC), 4QInstruction (4Q416 mid-first century BC; 4Q417 late first century BC; 4Q423 AD 1–50), 4Q303 (50–1 BC), 4Q265 (c. AD 25–50), and 4QJub^{a}=4Q216 (c. 125–100 BC).

and 4Q423) employ material from the creation account in the context of instruction. *Meditation on Creation* (4Q303–305) is a fragmentary wisdom text that employs language and themes from the creation account in the context of what appears to be an admonition. A diverse text known as *Miscellaneous Rules* (4Q265) employs the Garden of Eden narrative in order to explain the etiology of certain purification laws in Leviticus. A pseudepigraphal text known as *Jubilees* (4QJub[a]) reworks biblical stories from Genesis 1 to Exodus 19, communicating a message of hope for Israel and exhorting them to live according to God's laws. The retelling of the creation narrative freely reformulates, omits, and adds material in order to express the author's own interests and ideas. It is within these various literary contexts and purposes that these texts reveal various aspects of interpretation of the Genesis creation account. The following will synthesize, in summary form, the findings from these texts.

The Creation of the Universe by the Word of God

The first column of 4Q422 selectively recounts creation and humanity's rebellion (Genesis 1–3). The extant text begins in line 6 with what appears to be an affirmation of the creation of the universe by God's spoken word: צבאם עשה בדבר[ו] (their hosts He made by [His] word).[8] The author summarizes the Genesis 1 description of the manner in which God created by His spoken word,[9] employing language found in Psalm 33:6.[10] The phrase עשה בדברו (He made by His word) may also reflect the ancient understanding of the "word" functioning as God's agent in creating the universe (cf.

8. This fragmentary line has been partially reconstructed as [השמים והארץ וכול] צבאם עשה בדבר[ו] ([the heavens and the earth and all] their hosts He made by [His] word) (see Elgvin, "The Genesis Section of 4Q422," 184). This line likely reworks Gen 2:1: ויכלו השמים והארץ וכל צבאם (And the heavens and the earth and all their hosts were finished). This language is also likely attested in 4Q304 (*Meditation on Creation B*): ואת הארץ וכ[ול צבאם] (and the earth and a[ll their hosts]).

9. The more lengthy biblical creation narrative (Gen 1:1–2:3) employs the phrase ויאמר אלהים (Then God said) ten times in depicting God's creation of the universe and life itself. In 4Q422, the author was highly selective in reworking the biblical text. The extant text of column I (lines 6–13) indicates that there was not a lot of space devoted to this retelling of the creation account, which would help to explain the summary-type use of the phrase עשה בדברו (He made by His word).

10. 4Q422 I:6: "[the heavens and the earth and all] their hosts (צבאם) He made (עשה) by [His] word (בדבר[ו])." Cf. Ps 33:6: "By the word (בדבר) of the Lord the heavens were made (נעשו), and all their hosts (צבאם) by the breath of His mouth."

Tg. Neof. Gen 1; John 1:1–3),[11] though this is difficult to conclude with any certainty due to the fragmentary nature of the text.

The Role of the Holy Spirit in Creation

The extant text of the first column of 4Q422 picks up again in line 7: [אש]ר עשה ורוח קודש[ו] ([whi]ch He did. And [His] Holy Spirit).[12] The inclusion of the phrase ורוח קודשו (And His Holy Spirit) in the context of this summary-type recounting of creation appears to indicate some sort of role for the Holy Spirit in creation week (cf. Gen 1:2). Unfortunately, the text is too fragmentary at this point to determine anything more specific concerning the author's understanding of the Holy Spirit's role(s) in creation.

The Creation of the Heavens and Earth on Day One

4QJub[a] V:4–11 (= *Jub* 2:2–3) retells God's creative acts on day one. Though the biblical base text (Gen 1:1–5) is discernable, this retelling freely reformulates, omits, and adds material. The author mentions a total of seven works of creation on day one: the heavens, earth, waters, angels, depths, darkness, and light. One particular matter of interpretation in this retelling concerns the nature and relationship of the opening verses of the creation narrative. The author of *Jubilees* included the creation of the heavens and the earth (Gen 1:1–2) *as part of* day one.[13] Consequently, the first five verses (Gen 1:1–5) were understood as constituting the literary boundary of day one.[14]

11. See Elgvin, "The Genesis Section of 4Q422," 195.

12. The missing portion of the beginning of this line has been partially reconstructed as [וישבת ביום השבעי מכול מלאכתו אש]ר עשה ורוח קודש[ו] ([Then He rested on the seventh day from all His work whi]ch He did. And [His] Holy Spirit). If this reconstruction is correct, then the first part of this line recalls Gen 2:2: וישבת ביום השביעי מכל־מלאכתו אשר עשה (Then He rested on the seventh day from all His work which He did). This reconstruction makes good sense when considering the previous line (4Q422 I:6) appears to rework Gen 2:1.

13. The author of *Jubilees* apparently understood Gen 1:1 as describing God's initial creative acts on day one, as opposed to representing: a) a description of the creation of everything (earth, plants, sun, moon, stars, animals, man, etc.) or b) an introductory heading, summarizing the content of the creation account.

14. Other Jewish sources understood Gen 1:1–5 as constituting the creative acts of day one. For example, see *b. Hag.* 12a.

The Creation of Angels on Day One

The Genesis creation narrative makes no mention of *when* the angels were created. However, the idea that angels were present during creation week is attested elsewhere in the Hebrew Bible (e.g. Job 38:4–7).[15] This particular question of when the angels were created was addressed by Jews in antiquity. For example, in *Genesis Rabbah* the angels were created on day two of creation week (*Gen. Rab.* 11.9).[16] However, 4QJub[a] V:5–9 (= *Jub* 2:2) refers to the creation of the various angels on day one of creation week.[17] Before listing the various types of angels, the text of *Jubilees* introduces them as "the spirits (הרוחות) who serve before Him" (cf. line 5; *Jub* 2:2). Sometimes angels are referred to as "spirits" in the Hebrew Bible (e.g. Ps 104:4) and in Second Temple period literature (e.g. 1QM X:11–12). Thus, the author may have understood the phrase ורוח אלהים (typically translated as the wind *or* Spirit of God) in Gen 1:2 as alluding to an angel, who "was hovering over the face of the waters."[18] According to lines 6–8, certain angels were in charge of various elements and natural phenomena (cf. 1 *En* 60:12–22).

The Creation of the Garden of Eden on Day Three

Gen 1:9–13 records the gathering of the waters into one place, the appearance of dry land, and the creation of plants on day three of creation week. According to *Jub* 2:5–7, which reworks the biblical narrative, God made four great kinds on day three: the gathered waters, dry land, plants, and the Garden of Eden (*Jub* 2:7 is partially preserved in 4QJub[a] VI:2–4). Gen 1:9–13, however, makes no mention of the Garden of Eden being created on day three. Genesis 2 includes discussion on the creation of Eden, along with a physical description of the garden (e.g. the ground, waters, and trees), but never explicitly states *when* it was created. Thus, the author of *Jubilees* deduced that the Garden of Eden was created on day three, that is,

15. Some have suggested that the existence of angels during creation week is implied in Gen 2:1 (e.g. Kugel, "Jubilees," 289).

16. According to *Gen. Rab.* 1.3 none of the angels were created on day one, lest someone say that they assisted God in the creation of the world.

17. *Jub* 2:2 lists the "angels of the presence" and the "angels of holiness," which are generally understood to represent the two chief classes of angels, followed by the various angels thought to constitute the lowest or third class of angels (see Charles, *The Book of Jubilees or the Little Genesis*, 41; VanderKam, *The Book of Jubilees*, 126).

18. See Kugel, "Jubilees," 289–90.

on the same day as the gatherings of waters and the creation of dry land and plants (Gen 1:9–13). In other words, when God created the trees and plants on day three, He created the trees of the Garden of Eden as well.[19]

The Divinely Ordered Cosmos

The extant text of the opening lines of 4QInstruction (4Q416 1 1–9; cf. 4Q418)[20] speaks of God's order and rule of the cosmos, which apparently includes the heavenly bodies, the angelic host, and the affairs of man. The theme of God's creation of the luminaries and their orderly courses goes back to the Genesis creation account and is well attested in Second Temple period literature.[21] The author of 4QInstruction never directly quotes the Genesis text, but draws extensively from the language of the biblical record (cf. Gen 1:14–19) in depicting this theme of a divinely ordered creation. The continuous and orderly course of the luminaries (heavenly bodies) is described as "wonders" and "signs," which testify to God's dominion over the natural world and serve as chronological markers for calendrical purposes.[22] This description of God's order and rule of the cosmos (4Q416 1 1–9; cf. 4Q418) serves not only as the framework for the following description of eschatological judgment and exhortations for the righteous to discern between good and evil (4Q416 1 10–17), but also for the wisdom instructions that follow.

The Creation of Adam in the Likeness of God's Glory

The *Words of the Luminaries* (4Q504) recalls the creation of Adam: [אדם א]בינו יצרתה בדמות כבוד[כה] ([Adam] our [fa]ther You formed in the likeness of [Your] glory) (frag. 8, line 4). This line combines elements from Gen 1:26 and 2:7. The identification of Adam as "our father" is not explicitly stated in Genesis 1–3 (though it is presumed, for example, in Gen 3:20).

19. The idea that God created the Garden of Eden on day three is also found in *Genesis Rabbah* 11.9; 15.3 and 2 *Enoch* 30.1.

20. Cf. the overlapping fragments from 4Q418.

21. E.g. *Sir* 16:26–28; 43:1–10; 1 *En* 2; 82–83; 1QS X:1–9; 1QH^a IX:9–25; XX:1–11.

22. The proper observance of the festivals at their appointed times is directly linked to the orderly courses of the luminaries at their proper times as understood from Genesis 1 and likely on the basis of the solar calendar. See Tigchelaar, *To Increase Learning for the Understanding Ones*, 179; Harrington, *Wisdom Texts from Qumran*, 41.

In this manner, the prayer of 4Q504 acknowledges that the Jewish people are descendants of Adam, the first human. This idea is also found in other Second Temple period texts (e.g. *Jub* 2:23; *Wis* 10:1). The second part of line 4, בדמות כבוד[כה] (in the likeness of [Your] glory), alludes to Gen 1:26 and also echoes Gen 5:1.[23] Like the biblical account, this prayer in 4Q504 presents Adam as made from dust (frag. 8, line 1), yet elevated to a privileged status in God's creation. This idea that Adam shared in, or reflected, God's glory is not explicitly stated in the Genesis account, but is attested in antiquity (1QS IV:23; CD III:20; *3 Apoc Bar* 4:16).[24]

The Creation of Adam with Dominion

In 4Q504 (frag 8, line 6), the author reworked the giving of Adam's dominion (Gen 1:26–28) into the Eden narrative (Gen 2:8, 15): [בג]ן עדן אשר נטעתה המשלת[ה אותו] ([In the Gar]den of Eden which You planted, Yo[u] gave [him] dominion). While Gen 1:26, 28 uses the verb רדה, 4Q504 employs the verb משל, which is also used in the context of creation in Psalm 8:7 and a number of other Qumran texts (e.g. 4Q287 4 2; 4Q381 1 7; 4Q422 I:9; 4Q423 2 2). In addition, 4Q504 appears to limit the focus of Adam's dominion to the Garden of Eden, whereas the biblical account states that God gave Adam dominion "over all the earth" (Gen 1:26, 28).

4Q422 I:9–10 also appears to focus on Adam's dominion within the context of the Eden narrative: [ע]צ המשילו לאכול פר[י . . .] [. . .] ל[ב]לתי אכול מעצ הד[עת טוב ורע] ([...tr]ee, He gave him dominion to eat the frui[t ...] [...] not to eat from the tree of the know[ledge of good and evil]).[25] The author retells the giving of dominion to Adam (line 9), linking it to the prohibition given to Adam (line 10; cf. Gen 2:16–17) and his subsequent rebellion (lines 11–12). As a result, 4Q422 appears to contrast Adam's

23. Gen 1:26: "Then God said, 'Let Us make man in Our image, according to our likeness (כדמותנו).'" Gen 5:1 reiterates that God made Adam "in the likeness (בדמות) of God."

24. Though the Genesis account refers the creation of Adam in the "image" and "likeness" of God (Gen 1:26–27), there is no explicit reference to the creation of Adam in the likeness of God's *glory*. Both Qumran texts, the *Community Rule* (1QS IV:23) and *Damascus Document* (CD III:20), refer to the "glory of Adam" (כבוד אדם). *3 Apoc Bar* 4:16 refers to Adam's sin and subsequent loss of the "glory of God."

25. Employing the medial form of *tsade* (צ) instead of the final form (ץ), line 9 reads [ע]צ (instead of [ע]ץ) and line 10 reads מעצ (instead of מעץ).

dominion (to eat the fruit) with his subsequent rebellion against God (eating the prohibited fruit).

God's Election of Israel on the Seventh Day

The Genesis creation narrative discusses the seventh day in relatively brief fashion, while the book of *Jubilees* reworks the narrative, devoting a rather significant amount of attention to the Sabbath (adding much new material).[26] It is also instructive to note (concerning the days of creation week) that the Genesis narrative devotes the most attention to day six and the creation of man, whereas *Jubilees* devotes the most attention to day seven, linking the Sabbath with God's election of Israel. 4QJub[a] VII:5b–17 (= *Jub* 2:17–24) partially preserves this unique retelling of day seven. According to lines 9b–13 (= *Jub* 2:19–21) God elected the descendants of Jacob (= Israel) to observe the Sabbath. Just as God had blessed and sanctified the Sabbath and set it apart from the other six days, He would also bless and sanctify the descendants of Jacob and set them apart from the nations.[27] Thus, according to *Jubilees*, God had already planned both the existence and election of Israel during creation week (on the very first Sabbath), and it is within this context that Israel is referred to as God's "first-born son" (*Jub* 2:20). Lines 14–16a (= *Jub* 2:23) then provide the rationale that God's election of Israel on the first Sabbath is bound up in the created order; there were twenty-two generations from Adam until Jacob, who is "blessed" and "sanctified," just as there were twenty-two created works until the seventh day, which is "blessed" and "sanctified."[28] According to *Jubilees*, not only is the six days of work and seventh day of rest for Israel patterned after creation week (*Jub* 2:1, 16–17),[29] but also God's election of Israel is rooted in the created order (*Jub* 2:19–23). Consequently, this unique retelling of day seven presents God's election of Israel as going back not to the period of the Sinai covenant, but all the way back to creation week.

26. Cf. Gen 2:2–3; *Jub* 2:17–24.

27. Cf. *Jub* 2:19–21; Deut 7:6, 14.

28. A notable feature of this reworked creation week narrative in *Jubilees* is the number of created entities listed for each of the six days of creation, totaling twenty-two.

29. Cf. Exod 20:8–11; 31:17.

Adam's Knowledge in the Garden of Eden

4Q504 introduces the idea of the giving of knowledge to Adam prior to his eating from "the tree of the knowledge of good and evil" (frag. 8, line 5; cf. Gen 2:17; 3:5–7), which is not explicitly stated in the Genesis creation narrative. The extant text of 4Q504, however, makes no mention of this knowledge given to Adam prior to his disobedience as including "evil."[30] Knowledge is a dominant motif in this prayer[31] and the author apparently links the people praying this prayer to Adam their father (frag. 8, lines 4–5). Just as God gave knowledge to Adam who dwelt in Eden, so also He gave knowledge to his descendants dwelling in the Promised Land (cf. frag. 4, lines 14–15).

Meditation on Creation (4Q303–305), however, appears to present a positive understanding of Adam's possession of the knowledge of good and evil in Eden, which is attested in other Second Temple period wisdom literature (e.g. *Sir* 17:7). The phrase "and insight/wisdom of good and evil" (ושכל טוב ורע) in 4Q303, line 8, recalls the tree of the knowledge of good and evil (Gen 2:9, 17) which Eve saw in Gen 3:6 as able "to make wise" (להשכיל), apparently linking the knowledge of good and evil to wisdom. Concerning Adam's acquisition of this knowledge/wisdom in 4Q303, the fragmentary nature of the text seems to allow for two possible options: a) Adam obtained this knowledge as a result of taking (and eating) the fruit from Eve or b) Adam possessed this knowledge when he was created. Either way, given the context, 4Q303 appears to present a positive conception of Adam's knowledge of good and evil in Eden. In addition, 4Q305 (lines 2–3) preserves a fragmentary reference to knowledge being given to Adam: "He gave to Adam knowled[ge . . .] and evil, to know [. . .]" (נתן לאדם דע[ת [. . .] ורע לדעת [. . .).[32] If understood correctly, *Meditation on Creation* (4Q303 8–11; 4Q305 1–3) diverges from Gen 2–3, which depicts Adam's knowledge of "good and evil" as a result of disobeying God's command (cf. Gen 2:16–17; 3:6, 22–24).

30. Another Second Temple period text known as *Ben Sira*, on the other hand, teaches that from the beginning (prior to Adam's disobedience) God "filled them with knowledge and understanding, and showed them good and evil" (*Sir* 17:7).

31. See 4Q504 frag. 8, lines 5, 10; frag. 4, lines 4–5, 14–15.

32. This may have referred to Adam being given the knowledge of good and evil, though the lacunae prevent any certainty. At the least, 4Q305 provides an explicit reference to God actively providing Adam with knowledge (cf. 4Q504 8 4–5).

The Prohibition in the Garden of Eden

In 4Q504 (frag. 8, line 8), the retelling of the prohibition is partially preserved: ותקם עליו לבלתי ס[ור] (And You charged him not to turn as[ide]). The author's use of לבלתי (not found in Gen 2:17) likely foreshadows Adam's disobedience, employing language from God's accusation in Gen 3:11: המן־העץ אשר צויתיך לבלתי אכל־ממנו אכלת (Have you eaten from the tree which I commanded you not to eat from it?). The context in Gen 3:11 is that Adam has disobeyed God by eating from "the tree of the knowledge of good and evil." Not only this, the language of this retelling (לבלתי סור) recalls the later prohibition given to the Israelites in the Promised Land (e.g. Josh 23:6).[33] Thus, the prohibition given to Adam in Eden also appears to be understood as a portent of the prohibitions given to the Israelites in the Promised Land. To "turn aside" from God's commands in either locale would lead to expulsion from the land.[34]

4Q422 I:10 also partially preserves a retelling of the prohibition given to Adam in the garden: ל[ב]לתי אכול מעצ הד[עת טוב ורע] (not to eat from the tree of the know[ledge of good and evil]). Unlike 4Q504, the language of 4Q422 reflects more directly the language of the prohibition in Gen 2:17: ומעץ הדעת טוב ורע לא תאכל (but from the tree of the knowledge of good and evil you shall not eat). Notably, like 4Q504, the text of 4Q422 employs לבלתי, which is not found in Gen 2:17. While both 4Q504 and 4Q422 link the prohibition given to Adam (Gen 2:16–17) to his subsequent disobedience (Gen 3:11), the retelling of the prohibition in 4Q422 reflects more directly the language of Gen 3:11.[35]

Adam's Sin and Punishment

Though Adam's act of disobedience is not preserved in 4Q504 (frag. 8), the extant text of line 9 assumes Adam's disobedience with a description of his punishment: בשר הואה ולעפר ה[ואה ישוב] (he is flesh and to dust h[e returns]). This retelling paraphrases Gen 3:19. In addition, the phrase

33. In Josh 23:6, the Israelites (dwelling in the Promised Land) are addressed: "Therefore be very courageous to keep and to do all that is written in the Book of the Torah of Moses, lest you turn aside from it (לבלתי סור־ממנו) to the right hand or to the left" (cf. Deut 17:14–20; Jer 32:40).

34. Cf. Gen 2–3; Deut 28, 30, 32; Josh 23; 2 Kgs 25; 2 Chr 36.

35. 4Q422 I:10: ל[ב]לתי אכול מעצ הד[עת טוב ורע]; Gen 3:11: המן־העץ אשר צויתיך לבלתי אכל־ממנו אכלת.

בשר הואה (he is flesh) likely alludes to Gen 6:3, 12, perhaps foreshadowing the antediluvian sin and subsequent punishment (Genesis 6–8).[36] The immediately following text, though very fragmentary, appears to recall the Flood account.[37] If this is the case, the author's juxtaposition of the creation and Flood accounts may highlight the theme of human sin and Divine judgment.

4Q422 I:11–12 preserves a unique retelling of Adam's rebellion: [ו]יקום עליו וישכחו[חוקיו] . . . ביצר רע ולמעש]י רשעה] ([and] he rose up against Him and they forgot[His statutes] . . . with an evil inclination and for work[s of wickedness]). The phrase ביצר רע (with an evil inclination), used here in reference to Adam's rebellion, is drawn from Gen 6:5, which refers to the antediluvian rebellion. Thus, 4Q422 links the Eden and Flood narratives, applying the "evil inclination" to both Adam's fall and the antediluvian rebellion. This understanding that an "evil inclination" was the cause of Adam's rebellion (not found in the Genesis account) also implies the understanding that Adam was created with good and evil inclinations. Further, the literary juxtaposition of Adam's sin (column I) with the antediluvian sin and consequent Flood judgment (column II) is part of the larger sin-judgment cycle presented in 4Q422.

The Garden of Eden and Moral Freedom

4QInstruction (4Q423 1 1–4) employs the Garden of Eden metaphorically for pedagogical purposes. This beautiful garden can produce knowledge/wisdom for the *mebin* ("understanding one") who is to "work it and keep it" (lines 1–2) *or* this same garden can produce thorns and thistles for the *mebin* due to being unfaithful in this task of pursuing knowledge/wisdom (lines 3–4). The author of 4QInstruction, utilizing material from Gen 2–3, metaphorically places the *mebin* in the Garden of Eden with the exhortation to choose wisdom. The understanding that Gen 2–3 teaches moral freedom (that is, every person, like Adam, is responsible for making decisions) relates, in this case, to the choice to pursue and cultivate wisdom or not.[38]

36. See Chazon, "The Creation and Fall of Adam in the Dead Sea Scrolls," 15.

37. For example, line 14 likely alludes to Gen 6:11–13.

38. The understanding that Gen 2–3 teaches moral freedom is found elsewhere in Second Temple period literature (e.g. *Sir* 15:14–17) and is attested by a number of Christian interpreters from the second and third centuries AD (e.g. Irenaeus, *Against Heresies*, IV.37.1). See also the discussion in Pagels, *Adam, Eve, and the Serpent*, xxiii, xxvi, 73–74,

The Garden of Eden as a Land of Glory

The reworked account of the creation of Adam in 4Q504 (frag. 8, lines 6–7) preserves an intriguing description of the Garden of Eden.[39] While the phrase "in the Garden of Eden which You planted" (line 6) alludes to Gen 2:8, the phrase "in a land of glory" (בארץ כבוד) (line 7) describes Eden with language not directly found in the Genesis account. The author of 4Q504 may have imported this idea of God's glory dwelling in Eden from traditions outside the Bible[40] or from other biblical texts which speak of God's glory dwelling in the tabernacle/temple.[41] In the Hebrew Bible, there are a number of lexical and thematic links between the descriptions of the sanctuary (Exod 25–31; 35–40; 1 Kgs 7–8; 2 Chr 3–5) and the Eden narrative (Gen 2–3). Consequently, the sanctuary is depicted as a recreation of Eden. Thus, the author of 4Q504 may have retrofitted the idea of God's glory dwelling in the sanctuary into this reworked Eden narrative.

The Garden of Eden as an Archetype of the Sanctuary

4Q265 7 11–17 reworks the biblical material concerning Adam and Eve and their entrance into the Garden of Eden in order to explain the etiology of postpartum purification laws found in Lev 12:1–5, which prohibit women from entering the sanctuary for 40 days after the birth of a male child and 80 days after the birth of a female child. While the Genesis narrative indicates that Adam was immediately placed in the Garden of Eden on the day he was created (cf. Gen 1:26–31; 2:7–22), 4Q265 indicates a period of purification in which neither Adam nor Eve was given immediate access to the garden due to its holiness. The respective periods of impurity for Adam (seven days) and Eve (fourteen days) *before entering the garden* directly parallel the respective periods of impurity for the mother who gives birth to a male child (seven days, plus 33 days remaining in purity) or female child (fourteen days, plus 66 days remaining in purity) *before*

76, 108.

39. 4Q504 8 6–7: [. . . בג]ן עדן אשר נטעתה המשלת[ה אותו] [. . .].ם ולתהלך בארץ כבוד [. . .].א ([. . . in the Gar]den of Eden which You planted, You gave [him] dominion [. . .] .*m* and to walk in a land of glory [. . .]).

40. There is a tradition, for example, preserved in *3 Enoch* 5:1–6 that God's glory dwelt in the Garden of Eden until the generation of Enosh.

41. E.g. Exod 29:42–43; 40:34–35; Lev 9:6, 23; Num 14:10; 16:19; Ps 26:8; 2 Chr 5:14; 7:1–3.

entering the sanctuary as required in Lev 12:1–5. Thus, according to 4Q265, the postpartum purification periods required before entering the sanctuary are patterned after the respective purification periods of Adam and Eve before entering the Garden of Eden.[42] This etiological explanation for the purification laws of Lev 12:1–5 reflects an understanding of the Garden of Eden as an archetype of the sanctuary.[43]

42. Notably, 4Q265 7 11–17 closely parallels *Jub* 3:8–14, which perhaps represents the earliest example of such an explanation.

43. Likewise, *Jub* 3:8–14 presents the Garden of Eden as an archetype of the sanctuary.

APPENDIX A

TEXT AND TRANSLATION OF COLUMN I (FRAG 8) OF WORDS OF THE LUMINARIES (4Q504)[1]

1. Text and translation is adapted from Baillet, DJD VII; García Martínez and Tigchelaar, *The Dead Sea Scrolls Study Edition*.

Column I (frag 8)

1 [... זכו]ר אד[ו]נ[י]כיא מעפ[ר יצרתנו]

2 [...]קתנו ואתה חי עול[מים]

3 [...] נפלאות מקדם ונוראות [...]

4 [... אדם א]בינו יצרתה בדמות כבוד[כה]

5 [... נשמת חיים נ]פחתה באפו ובינה ודעת [...]

6 [... בג]ן עדן אשר נטעתה המשלת[ה אותו]

7 [...].ם ולתהלך בארץ כבוד א.[...]

8 [...]א שמר ותקם עליו לבלתי ס[ור]

9 [...] בשר הואה ולעפר ה[ואה ישוב]

10 [...]תו ואתה ידעתה [...]

11 [...] לדורות עולם [...]

12 [...] אל חי וידכה [...]

13 [...] האדם בדרכי[...]

14 [... למלוא את ה]ארץ ח]מס ולשפו[ך דם נקי ...]

15 [...] ... [...]

1 [. . . Remem]ber Lord that from dus[t You formed us]

2 [. . .]*qtnw* but You live forev[er]

3 [. . .] wonders from of old and awesome deeds [. . .]

4 [. . . Adam] our [fa]ther You formed in the likeness of [Your] glory

5 [. . . the breath of life] You [br]eathed into his nostrils, and understanding and knowledge [. . .]

6 [. . . in the Gar]den of Eden which You planted, Yo[u] gave [him] dominion

7 [. . .].*m* and to walk in a land of glory [. . .]

8 [. . .] he kept. And You charged him not to turn as[ide]

9 [. . .] he is flesh and to dust h[e returns]

10 [. . .]*tw vacat* And you, you know [. . .]

11 [. . .] for everlasting generations [. . .]

12 [. . .] the living God, and your hand [. . .]

13 [. . .] the man in the paths of [. . .]

14 [. . . to fill the] earth with [vi]olence and to pour out [innocent blood]

15 [. . .] . . . [. . .]

APPENDIX B

TEXT AND TRANSLATION OF PARAPHRASE OF GENESIS AND EXODUS

(4Q422)[1]

Column I

1–5 [...]

6 [...] השמים והארץ וכול] צבאם עשה בדבר[ו]

7 [...] מלאכתו אש]ר עשה ורוח קודש[ו ...]

8 [...] כול הנפ]ש החיה והרמש[ת על הארץ ...]

9 [... ע]ץ המשילו לאכול פר[י האדמה]

10 [...] [...]ל[ב]לתי אכול מעץ הד[עת טוב ורע]

11 [... ו]יקום עליו וישכחו[חוקיו]

12 [...]ביוצר רע ולמעש[י רשעה]

13 [...]שלום[...]

1. Text and translation is adapted from Elgvin, DJD XIII; "The Genesis Section of 4Q422 (4QParaGenExod)"; García Martínez and Tigchelaar, *The Dead Sea Scrolls Study Edition*; Feldman, "The Story of the Flood in 4Q422."

1–5 [. . .]

6 [. . . the heavens and the earth and all] their host He made by [His] word

7 [. . . His work whi]ch He had done. And [His] Holy Spirit [. . .]

8 [. . . every] living [creat]ure and what moves [on the earth . . .]

9 [...tr]ee, He gave him dominion to eat the frui[t of the ground]

10 [. . .] not to eat from the tree of the know[ledge of good and evil]

11 [. . . and] he rose up against Him and they forgot [His statutes]

12 [. . .] with an evil inclination and for work[s of wickedness]

13 [. . .] peace [. . .]

Column II

1 [...וירא אל כיא] רבה ו.[...]

2 [...]ב את ה[...]

2a [...צדיק ב]דורו ע[ל הארץ ... א]תו אל חיה

3 [...] נצלו על [הארץ ... ע]ל הארץ כיא[...]

4 [... את נוח]ואת בניו א[שתו ונשי בניו מפני]מי המבול ומ[...]

5 והע[וף ויס]גור אל בעדם [... צו]העליו את כ[ו]ל [...] [... כול]

6 אשר בחרבה [כל] א[שר]ארובות השמי[ם]נפ[ת]חו ח.[... גשם הרי]קו על הארץ

7 תחת כול השמ[ים ... ל]עלות מים על האר[ץ ... ארבעים] יום וארב[עים]

8 לילה היה ה[גשם]ע[ל הארץ ... המי]ם גב[רו] על [הארץ ... למען]טהר חיט ולמען

9 דעת כבוד על[יון ...]את[...] הגיש לפניו

10 ויאר על [ה]שמ[ים ... הא]רץ וא[...]ימה אות לדור[ות]

11 עולם לחרא[... ולוא עוד] היות מבול[לשחת הארץ ...]

12 [מו]עדי יום ולילה [... מאורות להאיר ע]ל שמים ואר[ץ ...]

13 [הארץ ומ]ל[ו]אה [... הכו]ל נתן[לאדם]

1 [. . . and God saw that] great, and [. . .]
2 [. . .] . . . the [. . .]
2a [. . . righteous in] his generation up[on the earth . . . with]him God kept alive

3 [. . .] were saved on [the earth . . . o]n the earth for [. . .]

4 [. . . Noah] and his sons, [his] w[ife and the wives of his sons from] the waters of the Flood and [. . .]

5 and the bir[ds . . . and] God [sh]ut behind them [. . . commanded] him a[l]l [. . .] [all]

6 which was on dry ground all [. . .] the windows of heaven were opened . . . [and] they [pou]red out [rain] on the earth

7 under all the heaven[s . . . to] raise water upon the ear[th . . . forty] days and for[ty]

8 nights there was [rain] up[on the earth . . . the water]s were migh[ty] upon [the earth in order to] cleanse sin and in order to

9 make known the glory of the Mo[st High . . .] . . . [. . .] He placed before him

10 and it illuminated [the] heav[ens . . . the ea]rth and [. . .] . . . a sign for the generation[s of]

11 eternity, to . . . [. . . and no more] will there be a Flood [to destroy the earth . . .]

12 [the fixed ti]mes of day and night [. . . luminaries to illuminate] heaven and ear[th . . .]

13 [the earth and] its [fu]ll[ne]ss [. . . everythi]ng He gave [to mankind]

Column III

1 [...]ת ולוא [...]

2 [ש]תי המיל[דות ... וישליכו את]

3 [ב]ניהם ליוא[ר ...]...[... א]ותם

4 [ו]ישלח להמה את מו[שה ...]במראת[...]

5 באותות ומופתים [...]תמכו וע[...]אחי חבר עמי

6 וישלחם אל פרעוה[...].ות נגועים [...]נפ[ל]אות למצרים[...] ויביאו דברו

7 אל פרעוה לשלח א[ת עמם ו]יחזק את לב[ו ל]חטוא למען דעת א[ת כבד]אל
עד דו[רות]עולם ויפך לדם[מים]יהמה

8 הצפרדעים בכול אר[צם] וכנים בכול גבול[ם ו]ערוב [בב]תיהסה ו[היה נג]ע
בכול פ[...]הסה ויגוף בדב[ר את]

9 מקניהסה ובהמתם ל[מו]ת הסגיר ישי[ת חו]שך בארצם ואפלה ב[בתי]הסה בל
ירא[ה] איש את אחיו [ויד]

10 בברד ארצם ואדמת[ם ב]חנמל לה[אביד כו]ל פרי אוכ[ל]ם ויבא ארבה
לכסות עין הא[רץ] חסל כבד בכול גבולם

11 לאכול כול ירוק בא[רצם] ל[...]ם ויח[זק]אל את לב [פרעו]ה לבלתי [ש]
לח[ם]ולמען הרבות מופתים

12 [ויק בכורם] רשית לכו[ל אונם ...]...[...]

1 [. . .] and not [. . .]

2 the two mid[wives . . . and they threw]

3 their sons into the Nil[e . . .] . . . [. . . t]hem

4 [and] He sent Moses to them [. . .] in the vision of [. . .]

5 with signs and wonders [. . .] . . . and . . . [. . .] my brother, as a companion with me.

6 And He sent them to Pharaoh [. . .] . . . plagues [. . .] wo[nd]ers to Egypt [. . .] and they reported His word

7 to Pharaoh, to let [their people] go. [And] He hardened [his] heart [so that he would] sin in order to make known [the glory of] God for eternal gener[ations] and He turned their [water] into blood.

8 Frogs were in all [their] lan[d], and lice in all [their] territory, [and] gnats (?) [in] their hou[ses], and [there was afflict]tion in all their [. . .] and He struck with pestil[ence]

9 their livestock, and their animals He delivered to [dea]th. He pla[ced dark]ness in their land, and dimness in their [houses] so that no-one could see his brother. [And He struck]

10 their land with hail, and their ground [with] frost to de[story al]l the fruit which they ea[t]. And He brought locusts to cover the face of the ea[rth], heavy locust in all their territory

11 to eat all the vegetables in [their] l[and . . .] and God har[dened] the heart of [Pharao]h so that he would not [let them] go, and in order to multiply wonders.

12 [And He struck their firstborn,] the firstfruits of al[l their manhood . . .] . . . [. . .]

APPENDIX C

TEXT AND TRANSLATION OF 4QINSTRUCTION (4Q416, 4Q417, 4Q423)[1]

4Q416 frag 1, column I

(overlapping frags 4Q418 1–2c, 229 underlined)

1 כל רוח[... כוכבי אור]

2 ולתכן חפצו [... ירוצו מעת עולם]

3 מועד במועד ו[... ואין להדמות בכול עת ילכו]

4 לפי צבאם למש[ור במשורה ול... ... לממלכה]

5 וממלכה למד[ינה ומדינה לאיש ואיש ...]

6 לפי מחסור צבאם [ומשפט כולם לו ...]

7 וצבא השמים הכין מ[עת עולם ... ומאורות]

8 למופתיהמה ואתות מו[עדיהמה ... יגידו]

9 זה לזה וכל פקודתמה י[שלימו וי]ספרו[...]

10 בשמים ישפוט על עבודת רשעה וכל בני אמתו ירצו ל[פניו ...]

11 קצה ויפחדו ויריעו כל אשר התגללו בה כי שמים יראו[תרעש ממקומה ארץ]

12 [י]מים ותהמות פחדו ויתערערו כל רוח בשר ובני השמי[ם ... ביום]

13 [מש]פטה וכל עולה תתם עוד ושלם קץ האמ[ת לעולם ...]

14 בכל קצי עד כי אל אמת הוא ומקדם שני[עולם ... ל]

15 להבין צדק בין טוב לרע ל[ ]ר כל משפ[ט ... א]

16 [י]צר בשר הואה ומביני[ם ... ל ... ל ...]

17 בראתיו כי ה.[...]

18 [...]וד.[...]

1. Text and translation is adapted from Strugnell, Harrington, and Elgvin, DJD XXXIV; Goff, *4QInstruction*; García Martínez and Tigchelaar, *The Dead Sea Scrolls Study Edition*; Kampen, *Wisdom Literature*.

1 every spirit[. . . stars of light]

2 And to mete out His desire [. . . they run on from time eternal]

3 season by season and [. . . without ceasing, properly they go]

4 according to their host to have dom[inion with authority and to . . . for kingdom]

5 and kingdom, for pro[vince and province, for man and man . . .]

6 according to the need of their host. [And the regulation of all of them belongs to Him . . .]

7 And the host of the heavens He has established f[orever . . . and luminaries]

8 for their wonders and signs of [their] se[asons . . . they proclaim]

9 one after another. And all their assignments [they] c[omplete and] make known [. . .]

10 in heaven He will judge over the work of wickedness, but all the sons of His truth will be favorably accepted be[fore Him]

11 its end. And all who have defiled themselves in it will be terrified and cry out, for heaven will fear. [Earth will shake from its place]

12 [s]eas and the depths are terrified, and every spirit of flesh will be laid bare, but the sons of heave[n . . . on the day of]

13 its judgment. And all iniquity will end again and the time of tru[th] will be completed [forever]

14 in all the times of eternity, for He is the God of truth and from of old, years of [eternity]

15 to cause the righteous one to understand between good and evil to . . . every judgme[nt]

16 it is an [in]clination of flesh and understanding [ones . . .]

17 His creatures, for . . . [. . .]

18 [ ]*wd* . . . [. . .]

4Q417 frag 1, column I

(overlapping frags 4Q418 43–45 i underlined)

1 [... ו]אתה מב[י]ן[...]

2 [...].. וה.. [ו]ברזי פל[אי אל הנוראים תשכיל ראש ...]

3 [...].ו בפ...[ ]כה ... והבט[ברז נהיה ומעשי קדם למה נהיה ומה נהיה]

4 [במה ...]ל.. [עו]לם לתש[... למה הויא]

5 [ולמה נהיה במה ...]ש בכול[...]מעשה ומ[עשה]

6 [... יומם ולילה הגה ברז נ]היה ודורש תמיד ואז תדע אמת ועול חכמה

7 [ואול]ת ת[ ].. מעש[יהם]בכול דרכיהם עם פקודתם לכול קצי עולם ופקודת

8 עד ואז תדע בין [טו]ב ל[רע כמ]עשי[הם כ]יא אל הדעות סוד אמת וברז נהיה

9 פרש את אושה ועשה ע[שה בחכ]מה ולכל[בער]מה יצרה וממשלת מעשיה

10 לכ[ו]ל[ ]..למה וכול [א]ת כ[ו]ל ..בא[פ]רש למ[ב]ינתם לכול מ[עשי]ה להתהלך

11 ב[יצר] מבינתו ויפרש לא[נוש]..כי[ ]...ריה ובכושר מבינות נוד[עו נס]תרי

12 מחשבתו עם התהלכו[כי ת]מי[ם בכול מ]עשיו אלה שחר תמיד והתבונן [בכו]ל

13 תוצאותמה ואז תדע בכבוד ע[וזו ע]ם רזי פלאו וגבורות מעשיו ואתה

14 מבין רוש פעלתכה בזכרון הע[ת כי]בא חרות החוק{כה} וחקוק כול הפקודה

15 כי חרות מחוקק לאל על כול ע[ו]נ[ו]ת בני שית וספר זכרון כתוב לפניו

16 לשמרי דברו והואה חזון ההגות ספר זכרון וינחילה לאנוש עם עם רוח כ[י]א

17 כתבנית קדושים יצרו ועוד לוא נתן הגוי לרוח בשר כי לא ידע בין

18 [טו]ב לרע כמשפט[ר]וחו ואתה בן מבין הבט ברז נהיה ודע

19 [נתיבו]ת כול חי והתהלכו הפקוד על מעש[יו]ל[...] ועו[ל ...] ל[ ]

20 [הב]ין בין רוב למעט ובסודכמה[...]

21 [...]ציכה ברז נהיה[ל ...]

22 [...]י כול חזון דע ובכול[ל ...]

23 ות[ת]חזק תמיד אל תוגע בעולה[... כיא כול הנוגע]

24 בה לא ינקה כפי נחלתו בה יר[שע ... ואתה]

25 בן משכיל התבונן ברזיכה ובאוש[י עולם דע ...]

26 [י]וסדו בכה כ[ול מע]שיהן עם פעולת[...]

27 לוא תתרו אחר[י] לבבכ[מה] ואחרי {ו}עי[נ]יכמה[...]

1 [. . .] you, under[stan]ding one [. . .]

2 [. . .] . . . the mysteries of the wond[ers of the God of awesome deeds you shall understand. The beginning of . . .]

3 [. . .] . . . and consider [the mystery that is to be and the works of] old, upon what is to be and what is to be

4 [in what . . .] . . . [for]ever to . . . [. . . for what is]

5 [and for what is to be with them . . .] . . . in every . . . work and w[ork . . .]

6 [. . . day and night meditate upon the myṣtery that] is to be and study it continually. And then you will know truth and iniquity, wisdom

7 [and foll]y. You . . . [their] work[s] in all their ways together with their punishment for all eternal periods, and the punishment

8 of eternity. And then you will know the difference between [go]od and [evil according to their] works, [f]or the God of knowledge is a foundation of truth. And with the mystery that is to be

9 He spread out its foundation and indeed He ma[de it with wi]sdom, and concerning everything, [with clever]ness He formed it. And the dominion of its works

10 for a[l]l . . . and all [wi]th a[l]l . . . He has ex]pounded for their understanding every w[or]k in order to walk

11 in [the inclination of] his understanding, and He expounded for m[an] . . . for . . . and in the correctness of understanding were made kn[own the sec]rets of

12 His plan, with those who walk [bl]amele[ss in all] his [w]orks. These things seek continually and understand [concerning a]ll

13 their consequences. And then you will know about the glory of [His] st[rength wi]th the mysteries of His wonders and the mighty acts of His works. And you,

14 understanding one, inherit your reward in remembrance of the per[iod for] it comes. Engraved is your statute and ordained is all the punishment

15 because engraved is what is ordained by God upon all the iniquities of the sons of Seth. And the book of remembrance is written before him

16 for the ones who keep His word. And it is the vision of meditation of the book of remembrance. And He gave it as an inheritance to man together with a spiritual people, f[o]r

17 according to the likeness of the holy ones He formed him. But He did not give this meditation to the spirit of flesh, for it did not know the difference between

18 [go]od and evil according to the judgment of his [sp]irit. *vacat* And you, understanding son, gaze *vacat* upon the mystery that is to be and know

19 [the . . .] of all life and the manner of his walking that is appointed over [his] work[s] . . . and iniquity . . . .

20 [under]stand between great and small, and in your counsel [. . .]

21 [. . .] . . . in the mystery that is to be . . .

22 [. . .] every vision know, and in every . . .

23 and be strong continually. You shall not be touched by iniquity [. . . for all who touch]

24 it will not be innocent. According to his inheritance in it, he will be con[sidered wicked . . . and you,]

25 son of knowledge/wisdom, understand your mysteries and in the foundation[s . . .]

26 founded upon you a[ll] their [wo]rks, with the reward of . . .

27 Do not follow after your heart and after your e[y]es [. . .]

4Q423 frag 1

1 [...]וכל פרי תנובה וכל עץ נעים נחמד להשכיל הלוא גן נ[עים ונחמד]

2 [...]ל[ה]שכיל מ[או]דה ובו המשילכה לעבדו ולשמרו ג[ן נאות]

3 [... והאדמה] קוץ ודרדר תצמיח לכה וכוחה לא תתן לכה [...]

4 [...] במועלכה

5 [...] ילדה וכל רחמי הור[ות] ל[ ] ...

6 [...] בכל חפציכה כי כל תצמי[ח לכה ...]

7 [...]ובמטע[ ]בם ה...

1 [. . .] and every fruit of the produce and every delightful tree, desirable to make one wise. Is it not a garden de[lightful and desirable]

2 [. . .] to make one v[er]y wise? And He has given you authority over it to work it and to keep it. *vacat* A [lush] gar[den . . .]

3 [. . . but the ground] will cause thorn and thistle to sprout for you and its strength will not yield to you . . .

4 [. . .] when you are unfaithful. *vacat*

5 [. . .] she has given birth and all the wombs of pregnant [women . . .]

6 [. . .] in all your desires because it will make everything sprou[t for you . . .]

7 [. . .] and with the planting [. . .] . . .

APPENDIX D

TEXT AND TRANSLATION OF MEDITATION ON CREATION (4Q303–305)[1]

4Q303

1 [...]מבינים שמעו ו.[...]

2 [...]מים וישביתו מעל נ[...]

3 [...]א{ס.ר..} נפלאות אל אש[ר ...]

4 [...]לאור עולם ושמי טוה[ר ...]

5 [... א]ור במקום תהו וב[הו ...]

6 [...]כולמעשיהם עד ק.[...]

7 [...]ר בם מלך לכולם[...]

8 [...]ר ושכל טוב ורע ל[...]

9 [...]לוקח ממנה [אדם]כיא[...]

10 [... ו]עשה לו עזר כ[נגדו ...]

11 [...]לו לאשה כיא ממנו] לקחה זאת ...]

12 [...]חה [...]

13 [...]ל לפי[...]

14 [...]ל[...]

1. Text and translation is adapted from Lim, DJD XX; Jacobson, "Notes on 4Q303"; Giere, "A New Glimpse of Day One"; García Martínez and Tigchelaar, *The Dead Sea Scrolls Study Edition.*

1 [. . .] understanding ones, listen and [. . .]

2 [. . .] . . . and cause them to cease treachery [. . .]

3 [. . .] . . . the wonderful acts of God whi[ch . . .]

4 [. . .] for eternal light and the pur[e] heavens [. . .]

5 [. . . ligh]t in place of unformed and unfil[led . . .]

6 [. . .]all their works until . . . [. . .]

7 [. . .] . . . among them a king for all of them [. . .]

8 [. . .] . . . and knowledge of good and evil [. . .]

9 [. . .] [Adam] was taken from it because [. . .]

10 [. . . and]He made for him a helper co[mparable to him]

11 [. . .]to him as a wife, because from him[she was taken . . .]

12 [. . .] . . . *vacat*

13 [. . .] . . . according to[. . .]

14 [. . .] . . . [. . .]

4Q304

1 ואת הארץ ו.[...]

2 החשך על כן נ.[...]

3 עשה ...[...]

4Q305, column II

1 ויברא בו חיות[...]

2 נתן לאדם דע[ת ...]

3 ורע לדעת [...]

4 ל[...]

1 and the earth and [. . .]

2 the darkness, therefore . . . [. . .]

3 He made . . . [. . .]

1 Then He created in it living creatures [. . .]

2 He gave to Adam knowle[dge . . .]

3 and evil, to know

4 . . . [. . .]

APPENDIX E

TEXT AND TRANSLATION OF MISCELLANEOUS RULES

(4Q265)[1]

Fragment 7

1 [...]. ביום ה[שבת ...]

2 [... ביום ה]שבת ולא[...]

3 [א]ל יז איש מזרע אהרון .[... ואל ירחצו ואל]

4 [יכב]סו [בי]ום גדול וצום ביום [הכפורים ...]

5 [א]ת [ה]בהמה ילך אלפים אמה [...]

6 [המ]קדש שלושים רס אל ימ[וש ...]

7 [ב]היות בעצת היחד חמשה ע[שר אנשים ...]

8 [הנ]ביאים נכונה עצת היח[ד באמת ... ובחירי]

9 רצון וריח ניחוה לכפר על ה[א]רץ מ.[...]

10 וספה במשפט קצי עולה והמ[...]

11 בשבוע הראיש[ון נברא האדם וקודש לא היה לו עד]

12 אשר לא הובא אל גן עדן ועצם [מעצמיו לוקחה לאשה וקודש לא]

13 [ה]יה לה עד אשר לא הובאה אצ[לו בשבוע השני ...]

14 [כי] קדוש גן עדן וכול האב אשר בתוכו קודש [לכן אשה אשר ילדה זכר]

15 וטמאה שבעת ימים כימי נדת דותה תטמא ושל[שים ושלשת ימים תשב בדם]

16 טהרה ואם נקבה תלד וטמאה [שבעים כנדתה וששים יום וששת ימים]

17 [תש]ב בדם טוהרה בכול קודש [לא תגע ואל המקדש לא תבוא עד מלאת]

1. Text and translation is adapted from Baumgarten, DJD XXXV; Eshel, "Hermeneutical Approaches to Genesis in the Dead Sea Scrolls"; García Martínez and Tigchelaar, *The Dead Sea Scrolls Study Edition*.

1 [. . .] on the day of the[Sabbath . . .]

2 [. . . on the day of the] Sabbath and not [. . .]

3 [Let n]o man from the seed of Aaron sprinkle [. . . and they should not wash nor]

4 [bat]he [on] the great [d]ay and fast, on the Day [of Atonement . . .]

5 [wi]th [the] animals may walk two thousand cubits [. . .]

6 [the T]emple, thirty stadia. Do not rem[ove . . .]

7 [When] there will be in the council of the community fifte[en men . . .]

8 [the p]rophets, the council of the community will be established [in truth . . . those chosen by]

9 (His) will, and it shall be a sweet aroma to atone for the [l]and from(?) [. . .]

10 and the periods of iniquity will end in judgment and [. . .]

11 *vacat* In the firs[t] week [Adam was created, but there was nothing holy to him until]

12 he was brought to the Garden of Eden. And a bone [of his bones was taken for the woman, but nothing holy]

13 [w]as to her until she was brought to h[im in the second week . . .]

14 [for] the Garden of Eden is holy and every young shoot which is in the midst of it is holy. [Therefore, a woman who begets a male]

15 shall be impure seven days, as in the days of her menstruation shall she be impure, and th[irty-three days shall she remain in the blood]

16 of her purity. *vacat* And if she begets a female, she shall be impure [two weeks as in her menstruation, and sixty-six days]

17 [shall she rem]ain in the blood of her purity. [No] holy thing [shall she touch, and she shall not enter into the sanctuary until the completion of]

APPENDIX F

TEXT AND TRANSLATION OF COLUMNS V–VII OF JUBILEES (4Q Jub[a])

Column V

1 [ויאמר מלאך הפנים אל משה בדבר יהוה לאמר כתוב כל דב]רי הבריה כא[שר]
2 [ביום הששי כלה יהוה אלהים את כל מעשו וכל אשר ברא]וישבת בים [השביעי]
3 [ויקדש אתו לכל עולמים ויתן אתו לאות לכל]מעשו
4 [כי ביום הראשון ברא את השמ]ים העליונים ואת האר[ץ]
5 [ואת המים ואת כל הרוחות המשרתים לפניו מלאכי]הפנים ומלאכי הקו[דש]
6 ומ[לאכי רוחות האש ומלאכי הרוחות הנושבי]ם [ו]מלאכי רוחות ה[עננים]
7 לער[פל ולאלגביש ולכפור ולטל ולשלג ולברד ולק]רח ומלאכי הקולו[ת]
8 ולמלאכי הרוחות[הסערים ומלאכי הרוחות לקר ול]חום ולחרף ולקיץ[ולכל]
9 רוחות בריותו [אשר עשה בשמים ואשר עשה באר]ץ ובכל את התהו[מות]
10 מאפלה ושחר ו[אור וערב אשר הכין בד]עתו אז ראינו מעשיו ונ[ברכהו]
11 על כל [מ]עשיו ו[נהללה לפניו כי שבעה]מעשים גדולים ע[שה ביום הראשון]
12 וביו[ם השני עשה את הרקיע בתוו]ך ה[מי]ם [ויבדלו המים ביום הזה חצים]
13 עלו למע[לה לרקיע וחצים ירדו למטה לרקיע אשר בתווך על פני כל]
14 הארץ[ ]

1 [Then the angel of the presence said to Moses by the word of the Lord: "Write all the wo]rds of the creation, according to wh[ich]

2 [on the sixth day the Lord God completed all His works and everything that He created] and rested on the [seventh] day.

3 [He sanctified it for all ages and set it as a sign for all] His works. *vacat*

4 [*vacat* For on the first day He created] the upper [heave]ns and the ear[th]

5 [and the waters and all the spirits who serve before Him: the angels] of the presence and the angels of holi[ness]

6 and the a[ngels of the spirits of fire and the angels of the winds that blo]w [and] the angels of the spirits of the [clouds],

7 of dark[ness, ice, hoar-frost, dew, snow, hail, and fro]st, and the angels of sounds

8 and the angels of the [storm-]winds [and the angels of the spirits of cold and of] heat, of winter and of summer, [and of all]

9 the spirits of His creatures [which He made in the heavens and which He made on the ear]th, and in every (place); the dept[hs],

10 darkness and dawn [and light and evening which He prepared through] His [know]ledge. Then we saw His works and we [blessed Him]

11 concerning all His [wo]rks and [we offered praise before Him because] He ma[de seven] great works [on the first day.]

12 On the [second] da[y He made the firmament in the mid]st of the [wate]rs, [and the waters were divided on that day. Half of them]

13 went up abo[ve the firmament, and half of them went down beneath the firmament which is in the middle, above the surface of]

14 the earth. [. . .]

Column VI

1 [...]

2 [ואת האג]מים ואת כל ט[ל הארץ]

3 [וזרע מזריע בזרעו ואת כל הצמח ועץ עשה פרי ואת ה]יערים ואת גן ע[ד]ן[בעדן]

4 [לתענוג ולאכל את ארבעת המינים הגדולים האלה] עשה {עשה} ביום השל[ישי]

5 [וביום הרביעי עשה יהוה את הש]מש ואת הירח ואת הכוכבים [ויתן]

6 [אותם ברקיע השמים להאיר על כל הארץ ו]למשל ביום ובלילה ולהב[דיל בין]

7 [אור לחשך ויתן השמש לאות גד]ול [על הארץ] לימ[ים] ול[ש]בתות ול[חדשים]

8 [ולמועדים ולשנים ולשבועות השנים וליוב]לים ולכל תק[ופות השנים]

9 [ויבדיל בין האור ובין החשך ולמרפה למען ירפא כל ה]צמח וגדל בא[רץ את]

10 [שלושה המינים האלה עשה ביום הרביעי]

11 [וביום החמישי ברא את התנינים הגדו]לים בת[וך תהומ]ות המ[ים כי הם]

12 [מעשי ידיו הראשונים מבשר ואת כל השרץ ב]מים דגי[ם ואת]כל {ואת כ[ל} עוף]

13 [יעופף ואת כל מיניהם ויזרח השמש עליהם ל]מרפה וע[ל כל]אשר בא[רץ כל]

14 [הצמח מהארץ וכל עץ עשה פרי וכל בשר את]שלו[שה המיני]ם הגד[ולים האלה]

15 [עשה ביום החמישי]

1 [. . .]

2 [and the reser]voirs and all the de[w of the earth]

3 [and the seed which brings forth seed in its seed, and all that sprouts, and the tree that produces fruit, and the] forests, and the Garden of E[de]n [in Eden]

4 [for pleasure and for eating. These four great kinds] He made {He made} on the thi[rd] day.

5 [*vacat* On the fourth day the LORD made the s]un and the moon and the stars. [Then He placed]

6 [them in the firmament of the heavens to give light upon all the earth and] to rule over the day and the night, and to div[ide between]

7 [light and darkness. Then He placed the sun as a gr]eat [sign above the earth] for day[s], and for [sa]bbaths, and for [months],

8 [and for seasons, and for years, and for the weeks of years, and for jubi]lees, and for all cyc[les of the years.]

9 [And it separates between the light and the darkness and serves for healing in order that everything that] sprouts and grows in the ea[rth may be well.]

10 [These three kinds He made on the fourth day. *va*]*cat*

11 [On the fifth day He created] the gre[at sea creatures] in the mi[dst of the depth]s of the wa[ters, for these]

12 [were the first works of flesh by His hands, and everything that moves in the] waters, the fis[h and] all {and al[l} the birds]

13 [that fly, and all their kinds. And the sun shone upon them for] well-being and up[on everything] that was on the ea[rth, all]

14 [that sprouted from the earth and every tree that produces fruit and all flesh. These] thr[ee] gre[at kind]s

15 [He made on the fifth day.] *vacat*

Column VII

1 [וביו]ם הששי את כל חי[ת הארץ ואת כל הבהמה ואת כל הרמש על הארץ ואחרי כל אלה]

2 עשה את האדם זכר ונק[בה עשה אתם וימשילו בכל אשר על הארץ ובימים ובכל אשר יעופף]

3 ובחיה ובכל הרמש ה[רומש על הארץ ובבהמה ובכל הארץ ובכל אלה המשילו את ארבעה]

4 המנים האלה עשה ב[יום הששי ויהיו כלם עשרים ושנים מנים ויכל כל מעשו ביום הששי כל]

5 אשר בשמים ובארץ [ובימים ובתהומות ובאור ובחשך ובכל ויתן לנו אות גדול את יום]

6 השבת אשר שבת ב[ו]

7 עשוים ששת ימים [ ]

8 ונשבותה ביום הש[ביעי מכל מלאכה כי אנחנו כל מלאכי הפנים וכל מלאכי הקודש שני]

9 המינים האלה אמ[ר לנו לשבות שבת עמו בשמים ובארץ ויאמר לנו הנה אני מבדיל לי]

10 עם בתווך עממי ו[שבתו הם וקדשתי אתם לי לעם וברכתים והיו עמי והייתי לאלהיהם]

11 ובחר בזרע יעקוב ב[כל מאשר ראיתי וכתבתי אתו לי לבן בכור וקדשתי אתו לי]

12 לעולם ועד ואת היום ה[שביעי אגיד להם לשובתם בו מכל כאשר ברכם וקדשם לו עם סגולה]

13 מכל הגוים ולהיות יחד[עמנו שבתים ויעל את מצוותיו ריח ניחוח אשר ירצה לפניו]

14 כל הימים] שנים ועשרים ראשי אנשים]

15 מאדם עד אליו וש(נ)ים ועשרים מ[יני מעשה נעשו עד היום השביעי זה ברוך וקדש וזה ברוך]

16 וקדש וזה עם זה נעשו יחד לקדש[ולברכה וינתן לזה להיות כל הימים ברוכים וקדשים]

17 וזאת התעודה והתורה הראש[ונה]

1 [And on] the sixth [da]y {He made} all the anima[ls of the earth, and all the cattle, and everything that creeps upon the earth. After all these]

2 He made man, male and fem[ale He made them. Then He caused him to rule over everything that is upon the earth and in the seas and over everything that flies,]

3 and over the animals, and over every creeping thing that [creeps upon the earth, and over the cattle, and over all the earth. Over all these He caused him to rule.] These [four]

4 kinds He made on [the sixth day. And in all there were twenty-two kinds. And He finished all His works on the sixth day—all]

5 that is in the heavens, and on the earth, [and in the seas, and in the depths, and in the light, and in the darkness, and in every (place). He gave to us a great sign—the day]

6 of the Sabbath, which He rested on [it . . .]

7 they were made in six days. [ ]

8 and we keep the Sabbath on the se[venth] day [(refraining) from all work. For we, all the angels of the presence and all the angels of holiness—]

9 these [two] kinds—He sai[d to us to keep Sabbath with Him in heaven and on earth. Then He said to us, "Behold, I will separate to Me]

10 a people from among My nations. And [they will keep the Sabbath and I will sanctify them as My people and I will bless them. They will be My people and I will be their God."]

11 And He chose the descendants of Jacob from among [all those whom I saw. I have recorded them to me as the first-born son and I have sanctified them to me]

12 forever and ever. And the [seventh] day [I will teach to them in order that they may keep Sabbath on it from everything, according to which He blessed them and sanctified them for Himself as a special people]

13 from all the nations and to be [keeping Sabbath] together [with us. And He lifted up His commandments like a pleasant fragrance which is acceptable in His presence]

14 every day. *vac*[*at* There were twenty-two heads of men (patriarchs)]

15 from Adam until him and twenty-two k[inds of work were made until the seventh day. The one is blessed and holy and the other is blessed]

16 and holy. And this one with this one were made together for holiness [and for blessing. And it was given to this one to be for all days the blessed and holy ones.]

17 And this is the testimony and the fir[st] law [ ]

BIBLIOGRAPHY

Abegg Jr., Martin G. with James E. Bowley and Edward M. Cook in consultation with Emanuel Tov. *The Dead Sea Scrolls Concordance: The Non-Biblical Texts from Qumran*. Vol. 1, Leiden: E. J. Brill, 2003.

Abegg Jr., Martin, Peter W. Flint, and Eugene Ulrich. *The Dead Sea Scrolls Bible*. San Francisco: HarperSanFrancisco, 1999.

Alexander, Philip. "3 (Hebrew Apocalypse of) Enoch: A New Translation and Introduction." In *The Old Testament Pseudepigrapha*, edited by James H. Charlesworth, 223–302. New York, NY: Doubleday, 1983. Repr., Peabody, MA: Hendrickson, 2013.

———. "Rules." In vol. 2 of *Encyclopedia of the Dead Sea Scrolls*, edited by Lawrence Schiffman and James C. Vanderkam, 799–803. 2 vols. Oxford: Oxford University Press, 2000.

Alexander, Philip, and Geza Vermes. *Qumran Cave 4, XIX: 4Q Serekh Ha-Yahad and Two Related Texts*. Discoveries in the Judaean Desert XXVI. Oxford: Clarendon, 1998.

Allegro, J. M., with A. A. Anderson. *Qumran Cave 4, I (4Q158–4Q186)*. Discoveries in the Judaean Desert V. Oxford: Clarendon, 1968.

Arnold, Russell C. D. *The Social Role of Liturgy in the Religion of the Qumran Community*. Studies on the Texts of the Desert of Judah 60. Leiden: Brill, 2006.

Attridge, Harold W., John J. Collins, and Thomas H. Tobin, eds. *Of Scribes and Scrolls: Studies on the Hebrew Bible, Intertestamental Judaism, and Christian Origins*. College Theology Society Resources in Religion 5. Lanham, MD: University Press of America, 1990.

Baillet, Maurice. *Qumran Grotte 4, III (4Q482–4Q520)*. Discoveries in the Judaean Desert VII. Oxford: Clarendon, 1982.

———. "Un recueil liturgique de Qumran, Grotte 4: 'Les Paroles des Luminaires.'" *Revue Biblique* 68 (1961) 195–250, plates XXIV–XXVII.

Baillet, M., J. T. Milik, and Roland de Vaux. *Les 'Petites Grottes' de Qumran*. Discoveries in the Judaean Desert III. Oxford: Clarendon, 1962.

Bar-Ilan, Meir. "Writing in Ancient Israel and Early Judaism." In *Mikra: Text, Translation, Reading & Interpretation of the Hebrew Bible in Ancient Judaism & Early Christianity*, edited by Martin Jan Mulder, 21–38. Peabody, MA: Hendrickson, 2004.

Barr, James. Review of Josef M. Oesch, *Petucha und Setuma. Untersuchungen zu einer überlieferten Gliederung im hebräischen Text des Alten Testaments. Journal of Theological Studies* 32 (1981) 471–72.

Barthelemy, D. and J. T. Milik. *Qumran Cave 1*. Discoveries in the Judaean Desert I. Oxford: Clarendon, 1955.

Baumgarten, Joseph M. "The Calendar of the Book of Jubilees and the Bible" in *Studies in Qumran Law*. SJLA 24; Leiden: E. J. Brill, 1997.

———. "The Cave 4 Versions of the Qumran Penal Code." *Journal of Jewish Studies* 43 (1992) 268–76.

———. "Purification after Childbirth and the Sacred Garden in 4Q265 and Jubilees." In *New Qumran Texts and Studies: Proceedings of the First Meeting of the International Organization for Qumran Studies, Paris 1992*, edited by George J. Brooke and Florentino García Martínez, 3–10. Studies on the Texts of the Desert of Judah 15. Leiden: Brill, 1994.

———. *Qumran Cave 4, XIII: The Damascus Document (4Q266–273)*. Discoveries in the Judaean Desert XVIII. Oxford: Clarendon, 1996.

Baumgarten, J., et al. *Qumran Cave 4, XXV: Halakhic Texts*. Discoveries in the Judaean Desert XXXV. Oxford: Clarendon, 1999.

Benoit, P., J. T. Milik, and Roland de Vaux. *Les grottes de Murabbaat*. Discoveries in the Judaean Desert II (IIa). Oxford: Clarendon, 1961.

Bernstein, Moshe J. "Contours of Genesis Interpretation at Qumran: Contents, Context, and Nomenclature." In *Studies in Ancient Midrash*, edited by James L. Kugel, 57–85. Cambridge, MA: Harvard University Press, 2001.

———. "The Contribution of the Qumran Discoveries to the History of Early Biblical Interpretation." In *The Idea of Biblical Interpretation: Essays in Honor of James L. Kugel*, edited by Hindy Najman and Judith H. Newman, 215–38. Leiden: Brill, 2004.

———. "Interpretation of Scriptures." In vol. 1 of *Encyclopedia of the Dead Sea Scrolls*, edited by Lawrence Schiffman and James C. Vanderkam, 376–83. 2 vols. Oxford: Oxford University Press, 2000.

———. "Noah and the Flood at Qumran." In *The Provo International Conference on the Dead Sea Scrolls: New Texts, Reformulated Issues, and Technological Innovations*, edited by Donald W. Parry and Eugene C. Ulrich, 199–231. Leiden: Brill, 1999.

Bernstein, M., and G. Brooke with the assistance of J. Høgenhavn. *Qumran Cave 4, I: 4Q158–186*. Discoveries in the Judaean Desert V(a), Rev. ed. Oxford: Clarendon.

Bonani, Georges, Susan Ivy, Willy Wölfli, Magen Broshi, Israel Carmi, and John Strugnell. "Radiocarbon Dating of Fourteen Dead Sea Scrolls." *Radiocarbon* 34.3 (1992) 843–49.

Brooke, George J. "4QGenesis[d] Reconsidered." In *Textual Criticism and Dead Sea Scrolls Studies in Honor of Julio Trebolle Barrera*, edited by Andrés Piquer Otero and Pablo Torijano Morales, 51–70. Leiden: Brill, 2012.

———. "Biblical Interpretation in the Wisdom Texts from Qumran." In *The Wisdom Texts from Qumran and the Development of Sapiential Thought*, edited by Charlotte Hempel, Armin Lange, and Hermann Lichtenberger, 201–20. Leuven: Leuven University Press, 2002.

———. "Commentary on Genesis and Exodus (4Q422)." In *The Eerdmans Dictionary of Early Judaism*, edited by John J. Collins and Daniel C. Harlow, 663–64. Grand Rapids, MI: Eerdmans, 2010.

———. "From Bible to Midrash: Approaches to Biblical Interpretation in the Dead Sea Scrolls by Modern Interpreters." In *Northern Lights on the Dead Sea Scrolls: Proceedings of the Nordic Qumran Network 2003–2006*, edited by Anders Klostergaard Petersen, Torleif Elgvin, Cecilia Wassen, Hanne von Weissenberg, Mikael Winninge, and assistant editor Martin Ehrensvärd, 1–19. Studies on the Texts of the Desert of Judah, 80. Leiden: Brill, 2009.

———. "Genesis 1–11 in the Light of Some Aspects of the Transmission of Genesis in Late Second Temple Times." *Hebrew Bible and Ancient Israel* 1.4 (Dec. 2012) 465–82.

———. *Reading the Dead Sea Scrolls: Essays in Method*. Early Judaism and Its Literature 39. Atlanta, GA: Society of Biblical Literature, 2013.

———. "The Rewritten Law, Prophets and Psalms: Issues for Understanding the Text of the Bible." In *The Bible as Book: The Hebrew Bible and the Judaean Desert Discoveries*, edited by Edward D. Herbert and Emanuel Tov, 31–40. London: British Library and New Castle: Oak Knoll in association with Grand Haven: Scriptorium, 2002.

Brooke, G. J., J. Collins, P. Flint, J. Greenfield, E. Larson, C. Newsom, E. Puech, L. H. Schiffman, M. Stone, and J. Trebolle Barrera, in consultation with J. VanderKam. *Qumran Cave 4, XVII: Parabiblical Texts, Part 3*. Discoveries in the Judaean Desert XXII. Oxford: Clarendon, 1996.

Brooke, George J. and Florentino García Martínez, eds. *New Qumran Texts and Studies: Proceedings of the First Meeting of the International Organization for Qumran Studies, Paris 1992*. Studies on the Texts of the Desert of Judah 15. Leiden: Brill, 1994.

Broshi, M., E. Eshel, J. Fitzmyer, E. Larson, C. Newsom, L. Schiffman, M. Smith, M. Stone, J. Strugnell, and A. Yardeni, in consultation with J. C. VanderKam. *Qumran Cave 4, XIV: Parabiblical Texts, Part 2*. Discoveries in the Judaean Desert XIX. Oxford: Clarendon, 1995.

Brown, Francis., S. R. Driver, and Charles A. Briggs. *The Brown-Driver-Briggs Hebrew and English Lexicon*. Peabody, MA: Hendrickson, 2001.

Callaway, Phillip R. *The Dead Sea Scrolls for a New Millenium*. Eugene, OR: Cascade Books, 2011.

Cassuto, Umberto. *A Commentary on the Book of Genesis: Part One: From Adam to Noah*. Hebrew edition, 1944. Translated by Israel Abrahams. 1961. Repr., Skokie, IL: Varda, 2005.

Charles, R. H. *The Book of Jubilees or the Little Genesis*. London and New York: The MacMillan Co., 1917.

Charlesworth, James H., ed. *The Old Testament Pseudepigrapha*, 2 vols. New York, NY: Doubleday, 1985. Repr., Peabody, MA: Hendrickson, 2013.

Chazon, Esther G. "4QDibHam: Liturgy or Literature?" *Revue de Qumran* 15 (1991) 447–55.

———. "The Creation and Fall of Adam in the Dead Sea Scrolls." In *The Book of Genesis in Jewish and Oriental Christian Interpretation: A Collection of Essays*, edited by Judith Frishman and Lucas Van Rompay, 13–24. Traditio exegetica Graeca 5. Leuven: Peeters, 1997.

———. "Is *Divrei Ha-Me'orot* a Sectarian Prayer?" In *The Dead Sea Scrolls: Forty Years of Research*, edited by Devorah Dimant and Uriel Rappaport, 3–17. Studies on the Texts of the Desert of Judah 10. Leiden: Brill, 1992.

———. "Prayer and Identity in Varying Contexts: The Case of the *Words of the Luminaries*." *Journal for the Study of Judaism* 46 (2015) 484–511.

———. "Prayers from Qumran and Their Historical Implications." *Dead Sea Discoveries* 1.2 (1994) 265–84.

———. "Words of the Luminaries." In vol. 2 of *Encyclopedia of the Dead Sea Scrolls*, edited by Lawrence Schiffman and James C. Vanderkam, 989–90. 2 vols. Oxford: Oxford University Press, 2000.

———. "Words of the Luminaries (4Q504–506." In the *Eerdmans Dictionary of Early Judaism*, edited by John J. Collins and Daniel C. Harlow, 1349–50. Grand Rapids, MI: Eerdmans, 2010.

———. "תעודה ליטורגית מקומראן והשלכותיה: 'דברי המארות'." PhD diss., Hebrew University of Jerusalem, 1991.

Collins, C. John. *Genesis 1–4: A Linguistic, Literary, and Theological Commentary*. Phillipsburg, NJ: P & R, 2006.

Collins, John J. *Apocalypticism in the Dead Sea Scrolls*. New York, NY: Routledge, 1997.

———. "Before the Fall: The Earliest Interpretations of Adam and Eve." In *The Idea of Biblical Interpretation: Essays in Honor of James L. Kugel*, edited by Hindy Najman and Judith H. Newman, 293–308. Leiden: Brill, 2004.

———. *Beyond the Qumran Community: The Sectarian Movement of the Dead Sea Scrolls*. Grand Rapids, MI: Eerdmans, 2010.

———. *The Dead Sea Scrolls: A Biography*. Princeton, NJ: Princeton University Press, 2013.

———. "In the Likeness of the Holy Ones: The Creation of Humankind in a Wisdom Text from Qumran." In *The Provo International Conference on the Dead Sea Scrolls: Technological Innovations, New Texts, and Reformulated Issues*, edited by Donald W. Parry and Eugene Ulrich, 609–18. Leiden: Brill, 1999.

———. "Interpretations of the Creation of Humanity in the Dead Sea Scrolls." In *Biblical Interpretation at Qumran*, edited by Matthias Henze, 29–43. Studies in the Dead Sea Scrolls and Related Literature. Grand Rapids, MI: Eerdmans, 2005.

———. *Scriptures and Sectarianism: Essays on the Dead Sea Scrolls*. Grand Rapids, MI: Eerdmans, 2016.

———. "Torah as Narrative and Wisdom in the Dead Sea Scrolls." In *Reading the Bible in Ancient Traditions and Modern Editions: Studies in Memory of Peter W. Flint*, edited by Andrew B. Perrin, Kyung S. Baek, and Daniel K. Falk, 357–80. Early Judaism and Its Literature 47. Atlanta, GA: Society of Biblical Literature, 2017.

———. "Wisdom Reconsidered, in Light of the Scrolls." *Dead Sea Discoveries* 4.3 (1997) 265–81.

Collins, John J. and Daniel C. Harlow, eds. *The Eerdmans Dictionary of Early Judaism*. Grand Rapids, MI: Eerdmans, 2010.

Cook, Johann. "Genesis 1 in the Septuagint as an Example of the Problem: Text and Tradition." *Journal of Northwest Semitic Languages* 10 (1982) 25–36.

———. "Text and Tradition: A Methodological Problem." *Journal of Northwest Semitic Languages* 9 (1981) 3–11.

Cotton, H. M. and A. Yardeni. *Aramaic, Hebrew, and Greek Documentary Texts from Nahal Hever and Other Sites, with an Appendix Containing Alleged Qumran Texts*. Discoveries in the Judaean Desert XXVII. Oxford: Clarendon, 1997.

Crawford, Sidnie White. "Genesis in the Dead Sea Scrolls." In *The Book of Genesis: Composition, Reception, and Interpretation*, edited by Craig A. Evans, Joel N. Lohr, and David L. Petersen. Leiden: Brill, 2012.

———. "Interpreting the Pentateuch through Scribal Processes: The Evidence from the Qumran Manuscripts." In *Insights into Editing in the Hebrew Bible and the Ancient Near East*, edited by Reinhard Müller and Juha Pakkala, 59–80. Leuven: Peeters, 2017.

———. "Qumran Cave 4: Its Archaeology and its Manuscript Collection." In *Is There a Text in This Cave? Studies in the Textuality of the Dead Sea Scrolls in Honour of George J. Brooke*, edited by Ariel Feldman, Maria Cioată, and Charlotte Hempel, 105–19. Leiden: Brill, 2017.

———. *Rewriting Scripture in Second Temple Times*. Grand Rapids, MI: Eerdmans, 2008.

———. "A View from the Caves: Who Put the Scrolls in There?" *Biblical Archaeology Review* 37.5 (September/October, 2011) 30–39, 69.

Cross, Frank Moore. *The Ancient Library of Qumran and Modern Biblical Studies*. New York, 1958; 3rd ed. Sheffield, 1996.

———. "The Development of Jewish Scripts." In *The Bible and the Ancient Near East: Essays in Honor of William Foxwell Albright*, edited by G. E. Wright, 133–202. Garden City, NY: Doubleday, 1961; Anchor, reprint 1965.

———. "Paleography." In vol. 2 of *Encyclopedia of the Dead Sea Scrolls*, edited by Lawrence Schiffman and James C. VanderKam, 629–34. 2 vols. Oxford: Oxford University Press, 2000.

Cross, Frank M., D. W. Parry, and Eugene Ulrich. *Qumran Cave 4, XII: 1–2 Samuel*. Discoveries in the Judaean Desert XVII. Oxford: Clarendon, 2002.

Cross, Frank Moore and Shemaryahu Talmon, eds. *Qumran and the History of the Biblical Text*. Cambridge, MA: Harvard University Press, 1975.

Cryer, Frederick H. "Genesis in Qumran." In *Qumran Between the Old and New Testaments*, edited by Frederick H. Cryer and Thomas L. Thompson, 98–112. Sheffield: Sheffield Academic Press, 1998.

Cryer, Frederick H. and Thomas L. Thompson, eds. *Qumran Between the Old and New Testaments*. Sheffield: Sheffield Academic Press, 1998.

Davies, Philip R., George J. Brooke, and Phillip R. Callaway. *The Complete World of the Dead Sea Scrolls*. London and New York: Thames & Hudson, 2002.

Davila, James R. "4QGen-Exod[a]–4QGen[k]." In *Qumran Cave 4, VII: Genesis to Numbers*. Discoveries in the Judaean Desert XII. Oxford: Clarendon, 1994; reprint 1999.

———. "Book of Genesis." In vol. 1 of *Encyclopedia of the Dead Sea Scrolls*, edited by Lawrence Schiffman and James C. Vanderkam, 299–300. 2 vols. Oxford: Oxford University Press, 2000.

———. *Liturgical Works*. Eerdmans Commentaries on the Dead Sea Scrolls. Grand Rapids, MI: Eerdmans, 2000.

———. "New Qumran Readings for Genesis One." In *Of Scribes and Scrolls: Studies on the Hebrew Bible, Intertestamental Judaism, and Christian Origins*, edited by Harold W. Attridge, John J. Collins, and Thomas H. Tobin, 3–11. College Theology Society Resources in Religion, 5. Lanham, MD: University Press of America, 1990.

———. "Orthography." In vol. 2 of *Encyclopedia of the Dead Sea Scrolls*, edited by Lawrence Schiffman and James C. Vanderkam, 625–28. 2 vols. Oxford: Oxford University Press, 2000.

———. "Text-Type and Terminology: Genesis and Exodus as Test Cases." *Revue de Qumran* 16.1 (61) (1993) 3–37.

de Vaux, Roland. *Archaeology and the Dead Sea Scrolls*. The Schweich Lectures, 1959. Rev. ed. London: Oxford University Press, 1973.

de Vaux, Roland and J. T. Milik. *Qumran Grotte 4, II: I. Archeologie; II. Tefillin, Mezuzot et Targums (4Q128–4Q157)*. Discoveries in the Judaean Desert VI. Oxford: Clarendon, 1977.

Dimant, Devorah. *Qumran Cave 4, XXI: Parabiblical Texts, Part 4: Pseudo-Prophetic Texts*. Discoveries in the Judaean Desert XXX. Oxford: Clarendon, 2001.

Dimant, Devorah, ed. *Scripture and Interpretation: Qumran Texts that Rework the Bible*. Beihefte zur Zeitschrift für die alttestamentliche Wissenschaft 449. Berlin: De Gruyter, 2014.

Dimant, Devorah and Reinhard Kratz, eds. *The Dynamics of Language and Exegesis at Qumran*. Forschungen zum Alten Testament 2, Reihe 35. Tübingen: Mohr Siebeck, 2009.

Dimant, Devorah and Uriel Rappaport, eds. *The Dead Sea Scrolls: Forty Years of Research*. Studies on the Texts of the Desert of Judah 10. Leiden: Brill, 1992.

Eisenman, Robert and Michael Wise. *The Dead Sea Scrolls Uncovered*. New York: Barnes & Noble, 1994.

Elgvin, Torleif. "Admonition Texts from Qumran Cave 4." In *Methods of Investigation of the Dead Sea Scrolls and the Khirbet Qumran Site: Present Realities and Future Prospects*, edited by Michael O. Wise, Norman Golb, John J. Collins, and Dennis G. Pardee, 179–94. New York: New York Academy of Sciences, 1994.

———. "An Analysis of 4QInstruction." PhD diss., Hebrew University of Jerusalem, 1997.

———. "The Genesis Section of 4Q422 (4QParaGenExod)." *Dead Sea Discoveries* 1.2 (August, 1994) 180–96.

———. "The Reconstruction of Sapiential Work A." *Revue de Qumran* 16.4 (1995) 559–80.

———. "Wisdom and Apocalypticism in the Early Second Century BCE—The Evidence of 4QInstruction." In *The Dead Sea Scrolls Fifty Years After Their Discovery: Proceedings of the Jerusalem Congress, July 20–25, 1997*, edited by Lawrence H. Schiffman, Emanuel Tov, and James C. VanderKam, 226–47. Jerusalem: Israel Exploration Society, 2000.

Elgvin, T., et al. *Qumran Cave 4, XV: Sapiential Texts, Part 1*. Discoveries in the Judaean Desert XX. Oxford, Clarendon, 1997.

Enns, Peter. "Wisdom of Solomon." In vol. 3 of *Outside the Bible: Ancient Jewish Writings Related to Scripture*, edited by Louis H. Feldman, James L. Kugel, and Lawrence H. Schiffman, 2155–207. 3 vols. Philadelphia: Jewish Publication Society, 2013.

Eshel, Esther. "Hermeneutical Approaches to Genesis in the Dead Sea Scrolls." In *The Book of Genesis in Jewish and Oriental Christian Interpretation: A Collection of Essays*, edited by Judith Frishman and Lucas Van Rompay, 1–12. Traditio exegetica Graeca, 5. Leuven: Peeters, 1997.

Eshel, Esther and Hanan Eshel. "New Fragments from Qumran: 4QGen[f], 4QIsa[b], 4Q226, 8QGen, and XQpapEnoch." *Dead Sea Discoveries* 12.2 (2005) 134–57.

Evans, Craig A., Joel N. Lohr, and David L. Petersen, eds. *The Book of Genesis: Composition, Reception, and Interpretation*. Leiden: Brill, 2012.

Falk, Daniel. *Daily, Sabbath, and Festival Prayers in the Dead Sea Scrolls*. Studies on the Texts of the Desert of Judah 27. Leiden: Brill, 1998.

———. *The Parabiblical Texts: Strategies for Extending the Scriptures among the Dead Sea Scrolls*. Companion to the Qumran Scrolls, 8. Library of Second Temple Studies, 63. New York: T&T Clark, 2007.

———. "Words of the Luminaries." In vol. 2 of *Outside the Bible: Ancient Jewish Writings Related to Scripture*, edited by Louis H. Feldman, James L. Kugel, and Lawrence H. Schiffman, 1960–1984. 3 vols. Philadelphia: Jewish Publication Society, 2013.

Feldman, Ariel. "The Story of the Flood in 4Q422." In *The Dynamics of Exegesis and Language at Qumran*, edited by Devorah Dimant and Reinhard Kratz, 57–77. Forschungen zum Alten Testament 2, Reihe 35. Tübingen: Mohr Siebeck, 2009.

———. "פרשת המבול המקראית במגילות קומראן (1Q19, 4Q370, 4Q422, 4Q464 and 4Q577)" PhD diss., University of Haifa, 2007.

Feldman, Ariel, Maria Cioată, and Charlotte Hempel, eds. *Is There a Text in This Cave? Studies in the Textuality of the Dead Sea Scrolls in Honour of George J. Brooke*. Leiden: Brill, 2017.

Feldman, Louis H., James L. Kugel, and Lawrence H. Schiffman, eds. *Outside the Bible: Ancient Jewish Writings Related to Scripture*. 3 vols. Philadelphia: Jewish Publication Society, 2013.

Fields, Weston W. "Discovery and Purchase." In vol. 1 of *Encyclopedia of the Dead Sea Scrolls*, edited by Lawrence Schiffman and James C. Vanderkam, 208–212. 2 vols. Oxford: Oxford University Press, 2000.

———. *Unformed and Unfilled: A Critique of the Gap Theory*. Collinsville, IL: Burgener Enterprises, 1976; reprint 1994.

Fishbane, Michael. "Use, Authority and Interpretation of Mikra at Qumran." In *Mikra: Text, Translation, Reading & Interpretation of the Hebrew Bible in Ancient Judaism & Early Christianity*, edited by Martin Jan Mulder, 339–77. Peabody, MA: Hendrickson, 2004.

Fletcher-Louis, Crispin H. T. *All the Glory of Adam: Liturgical Anthropology in the Dead Sea Scrolls*. Leiden: Brill, 2002.

Flint, Peter W. *The Dead Sea Scrolls*. Core Biblical Studies. Nashville, TN: Abingdon, 2013.

Flint, Peter W. and Eugene Ulrich. *Qumran Cave 1, II: The Isaiah Scrolls*. Discoveries in the Judaean Desert XXXII. Oxford: Clarendon, 2010.

Frishman, Judith and Lucas Van Rompay, eds. *The Book of Genesis in Jewish and Oriental Christian Interpretation: A Collection of Essays*. Traditio exegetica Graeca 5. Leuven: Peeters, 1997.

Fröhlich, Ida. "'Narrative Exegesis' in the Dead Sea Scrolls." In *Biblical Perspectives: Early Use and Interpretation of the Bible in Light of the Dead Sea Scrolls. Proceedings of the First International Symposium of the Orion Center for the Study of the Dead Sea Scrolls and Associated Literature, 12–14 May 1996*, edited by Michael E. Stone and Esther G. Chazon, 81–99. Studies on the Texts of the Desert of Judah, 28. Leiden: Brill, 1998.

García Martínez, Florentino. "Creation in the Dead Sea Scrolls." In *The Creation of Heaven and Earth: Re-interpretations of Genesis I in the Context of Judaism, Ancient Philosophy, Christianity, and Modern Physics*, edited by George H. van Kooten, 49–70. Themes in Biblical Narrative 8. Leiden: Brill, 2005.

———. *The Dead Sea Scrolls Translated: The Qumran Texts in English*. Leiden: Brill; 2nd ed. Grand Rapids, MI: Eerdmans, 1996.

———. "The History of the Qumran Community in the Light of Recently Available Texts." In *Qumran Between the Old and New Testaments*, edited by Frederick H. Cryer and Thomas L. Thompson, 194–216. Sheffield: Sheffield Academic Press, 1998.

García Martínez, Florentino and Eibert J. C. Tigchelaar. *The Dead Sea Scrolls Study Edition*, 2 vols. Leiden: Brill, 1997, 1998.

García Martínez, F., Eibert J. C. Tigchelaar, and A. S. van der Woude. *Qumran Cave 11, II: 11Q2–18, 11Q20–31*. Discoveries in the Judaean Desert XXIII. Oxford: Clarendon, 1998.

Giere, Samuel D. "A New Glimpse of Day One: An Intertextual History of Genesis 1.1–5 in Hebrew and Greek Texts up to 200 CE." PhD diss., University of St. Andrews, 2006.

———. *A New Glimpse of Day One: Intertextuality, History of Interpretation, and Genesis 1.1–5*. Berlin: Walter de Gruyter, 2009.

Goff, Matthew. *4QInstruction*. Atlanta, GA: Society of Biblical Literature, 2013.

———. "Adam, the Angels and Eternal Life: Genesis 1–3 in the Wisdom of Solomon and 4QInstruction." In *Studies in the Book of Wisdom*, edited by Géza G. Xeravits and József Zsengellér, 1–21. Supplements to the Journal for the Study of Judaism 142. Leiden: Brill, 2010.

———. "Genesis 1–3 and Conceptions of Humankind in 4QInstruction, Philo and Paul." In *Early Christian Literature and Intertextuality: Volume 2: Exegetical Studies*, edited by Craig A. Evans and H. Daniel Zacharias, 114–25. Studies in Scripture in Early Judaism and Christianity 15. London and New York: T & T Clark, 2009.

———. "Instruction (4QInstruction)." In *The Eerdmans Dictionary of Early Judaism*, edited by John J. Collins and Daniel C. Harlow, 766–67. Grand Rapids, MI: Eerdmans, 2010.

———. "The Mystery of Creation in 4QInstruction." *Dead Sea Discoveries* 10.2 (2003) 163–86.

———. "Reading Wisdom at Qumran: 4QInstruction and the Hodayot." *Dead Sea Discoveries* 11.3 (2004) 263–88.

———. *The Worldly and Heavenly Wisdom of 4QInstruction*. Leiden: Brill, 2003.

Gropp, D.M. *Wadi Daliyeh II: The Samaria Papyri from Wadi Daliyeh*; James C. VanderKam and M. Brady, consulting editors. *Qumran Cave 4, XXVIII: Miscellanea, Part 2*. Discoveries in the Judaean Desert XXVIII. Oxford: Clarendon, 2001.

Grossman, Maxine L., ed. *Rediscovering the Dead Sea Scrolls: An Assessment of Old and New Approaches and Methods*. Grand Rapids, MI: Eerdmans, 2010.

Harkins, Angela K. "Thanksgiving Hymns (Hodayot)." In vol. 2 of *Outside the Bible: Ancient Jewish Writings Related to Scripture*, edited by Louis H. Feldman, James L. Kugel, and Lawrence H. Schiffman, 2018–94. 3 vols. Philadelphia: Jewish Publication Society, 2013.

Harrington, Daniel J. "Creation." In vol. 1 of *Encyclopedia of the Dead Sea Scrolls*, edited by Lawrence Schiffman and James C. Vanderkam, 155–57. 2 vols. Oxford: Oxford University Press, 2000.

———. "Sapiential Work." In vol. 2 of *Encyclopedia of the Dead Sea Scrolls*, edited by Lawrence Schiffman and James C. VanderKam, 825–26. Oxford: Oxford University Press, 2000.

———. "Two Early Jewish Approaches to Wisdom: Sirach and Qumran Sapiential Work A." In *The Wisdom Texts from Qumran and the Development of Sapiential Thought*, edited by Charlotte Hempel, Armin Lange, and Hermann Lichtenberger, 263–75. Leuven: Leuven University Press, 2002.

———. "Wisdom at Qumran." In *The Community of the Renewed Covenant: The Notre Dame Symposium on the Dead Sea Scrolls*, edited by Eugene Ulrich and James C. VanderKam, 137–53. IN: University of Notre Dame Press, 1994.

———. "Wisdom Texts." In vol. 2 of *Encyclopedia of the Dead Sea Scrolls*, edited by Lawrence Schiffman and James C. Vanderkam, 976–80. 2 vols. Oxford: Oxford University Press, 2000.

———. *Wisdom Texts from Qumran*. London: Routledge, 1996.

Hempel, Charlotte. "Cutting the Cord with the Familiar: What Makes *4Q265 Miscellaneous Rules* Tick?" In *Sibyls, Scriptures, and Scrolls: John Collins at Seventy*, edited by Joel Baden, Hindy Najman, and Eibert Tigchelaar, 509–16. Leiden: Brill, 2017.

———. *The Damascus Texts*. Sheffield: Sheffield Academic Press, 2000.

———. *The Qumran Rule Texts in Context*. Tübingen: Mohr Siebeck, 2013.

Hempel, Charlotte, Armin Lange, and Hermann Lichtenberger, eds. *The Wisdom Texts from Qumran and the Development of Sapiential Thought*. Leuven: Leuven University Press, 2002.

Hendel, Ronald S. "Assessing the Text-Critical Theories of the Hebrew Bible after Qumran." In *The Oxford Handbook of the Dead Sea Scrolls*, edited by Timothy H. Lim and John J. Collins, 281–302. Oxford: Oxford University Press, 2010.

———. *The Text of Genesis 1–11: Textual Studies and Critical Edition*. New York: Oxford University Press, 1998.

Henze, Matthias, ed. *Biblical Interpretation at Qumran*. Studies in the Dead Sea Scrolls and Related Literature. Grand Rapids, MI: Eerdmans, 2005.

Herbert, Edward D. and Emanuel Tov, eds. *The Bible as Book: The Hebrew Bible and the Judaean Desert Discoveries*. London: British Library and New Castle: Oak Knoll in association with Grand Haven: Scriptorium, 2002.

Hoffman, Yair and Graf Reventlow, eds. *Creation in Jewish and Christian Tradition*. JSOTSup 319. Sheffield: Sheffield Academic, 2002.

Jacobson, Howard. "Notes on 4Q303." *Dead Sea Discoveries* 6.1 (1999) 78–80.

Jastrow, Marcus. *Dictionary of the Targumim, the Talmud Babli and Yerushalmi, and the Midrashic Literature*. Peabody, MA: Hendrickson, 2006.

Jaubert, A. "Le Calendrier des Jubiles et de la Secte de Qumran. Ses Origines Bibliques." *Vetus Testamentum* 3 (1953) 250–64.

Jull, A. J. Timothy, Douglas J. Donahue, Magen Broshi, and Emanuel Tov. "Radiocarbon Dating of Scrolls and Linen Fragments from the Judean Desert." *Radiocarbon* 37.1 (1995) 11–19.

Kampen, John. *Wisdom Literature*. Eerdmans Commentaries on the Dead Sea Scrolls. Grand Rapids, MI: Eerdmans, 2011.

Kugel, James L. "Jubilees." In vol. 1 of *Outside the Bible: Ancient Jewish Writings Related to Scripture*, edited by Louis H. Feldman, James L. Kugel, and Lawrence H. Schiffman, 272–465. 3 vols. Philadelphia: Jewish Publication Society, 2013.

———. *Traditions of the Bible: A Guide to the Bible as It Was at the Start of the Common Era*. Cambridge, MA: Harvard University Press, 1998.

Kugler, Robert A. and Eileen M. Schuller, eds. *The Dead Sea Scrolls at Fifty: Proceedings of the 1997 Society of Biblical Literature Qumran Section Meetings*. Early Judaism and Its Literature, 15. Atlanta, GA: Society of Biblical Literature, 1999.

Kutsch, Ernst. "Der Kalender des Jubiläenbuches und das Neue Testament." *Vetus Testamentum* 11 (1961) 39–47.

Lange, Armin. *Handbuch der Textfunde vom Toten Meer: Band 1: Die Handschriften biblischer Bücher von Qumran und den anderen Fundorten*. Tübingen: Mohr Siebeck, 2009.

———. "Wisdom Literature from the Qumran Library." In vol. 3 of *Outside the Bible: Ancient Jewish Writings Related to Scripture*, edited by Louis H. Feldman, James L. Kugel, and Lawrence H. Schiffman, 2399–2443. 3 vols. Philadelphia: Jewish Publication Society, 2013.

Leith, M. J. W. *Wadi Daliyeh I: The Wadi Daliyeh Seal Impressions*. Discoveries in the Judaean Desert XXIV. Oxford: Clarendon, 1997.

Leupold, H. C. *Exposition of Genesis*, vol. 1. Grand Rapids, MI: Baker, 1950.

Levison, John R. *Portraits of Adam in Early Judaism: From Sirach to 2 Baruch*. Journal for the Study of the Pseudepigrapha, Supplement Series 1. Sheffield, 1988.

Lim, Timothy H. and John J. Collins, eds. *The Oxford Handbook of the Dead Sea Scrolls*. Oxford: Oxford University Press, 2010.

Luttikhuizen, Gerard P., ed. *The Creation of Man and Woman: Interpretations of the Biblical Narratives in Jewish and Christian Traditions*. Leiden: Brill, 2000.

———, ed. *Paradise Interpreted: Representations of Biblical Paradise in Judaism and Christianity*. Leiden: Brill, 1999.

Lyon, Jeremy D. *Qumran Interpretation of the Genesis Flood*. Eugene, OR: Pickwick, 2015.

Magness, Jodi. *The Archaeology of Qumran and the Dead Sea Scrolls*. Grand Rapids, MI: Eerdmans, 2002.

Martin, Malachi. *The Scribal Character of the Dead Sea Scrolls*. Bibliotheque du Museon, 44. Louvain: Publications Universitaires, 1958.

Martín-Contreras, Elvira and Lorena Miralles-Maciá, eds. *The Text of the Hebrew Bible: From the Rabbis to the Masoretes*. Göttingen: Vandenhoeck & Ruprecht, 2014.

Milik, J. T. *Ten Years of Discovery in the Wilderness of Judaea*. Translated by J. Strugnell. Studies in Biblical Theology 26. London: SCM Press, 1959.

Mulder, Martin Jan, ed. *Mikra: Text, Translation, Reading & Interpretation of the Hebrew Bible in Ancient Judaism & Early Christianity*. Peabody, MA: Hendrickson, 2004.

Müller, Reinhard and Juha Pakkala, eds. *Insights into Editing in the Hebrew Bible and the Ancient Near East*. Leuven: Peeters, 2017.

Najman, Hindy. *Seconding Sinai: The Development of Mosaic Discourse in Second Temple Judaism*. Leiden: Brill, 2003.

Naveh, Joseph. *Early History of the Alphabet*, 2nd rev. ed. Jerusalem, Israel: The Magnes Press, The Hebrew University, Jerusalem, 1987.

Nickelsburg, George W. E. *Jewish Literature between the Bible and the Mishnah: A Historical and Literary Introduction*. 2nd ed. Minneapolis, MN: Fortress, 2005.

Nitzan, Bilhah. "The Idea of Creation and Its Implications in Qumran Literature." In *Creation in Jewish and Christian Tradition*, edited by Yair Hoffman and Graf Reventlow, 250. Sheffield: Sheffield Academic, 2002.

———. "The Ideological and Literary Unity of 4QInstruction and Its Authorship." *Dead Sea Discoveries* 12.3 (2005) 257–79.

———. *Qumran Prayer and Religious Poetry*. Studies on the Texts of the Desert of Judah 12. Leiden: Brill, 1994.

Oegema, Gerbern S. "Creation." In *The Eerdmans Dictionary of Early Judaism*, edited by John J. Collins and Daniel C. Harlow, 496–500. Grand Rapids, MI: Eerdmans, 2010.

Oesch Josef M. *Petucha und Setuma. Untersuchungen zu einer überlieferten Gliederung im hebräischen Text des Alten Testaments*. Orbis Biblicus et Orientalis, 27. Göttingen: Vandenhoeck & Ruprecht, 1979.

Otero, Andrés Piquer and Pablo Torijano Morales, eds. *Textual Criticism and Dead Sea Scrolls Studies in Honor of Julio Trebolle Barrera*. Leiden: Brill, 2012.

Pagels, Elaine H. *Adam, Eve, and the Serpent*. New York: Random House, 1988.

Parry, Donald W. and Emanuel Tov, eds. *The Dead Sea Scrolls Reader*. 6 vols. Leiden: Brill, 2005.

Perrin, Andrew B., Kyung S. Baek, and Daniel K. Falk, eds. *Reading the Bible in Ancient Traditions and Modern Editions: Studies in Memory of Peter W. Flint*. Early Judaism and Its Literature 47. Atlanta, GA: Society of Biblical Literature, 2017.

Peters, Dorothy M. *Noah Traditions in the Dead Sea Scrolls: Conversations and Controversies of Antiquity*. Early Judaism and Its Literature 26. Atlanta, GA: Society of Biblical Literature, 2008.

Pfann, Stephen J. "Scripts and Scribal Practice." In *The Eerdmans Dictionary of Early Judaism*, edited by John J. Collins and Daniel C. Harlow, 1204–07. Grand Rapids, MI: Eerdmans, 2010.

Pfann, Stephen J., James C. Vanderkam, and M. Brady, consulting editors. *Cryptic Texts; Miscellenea, Part 1: Qumran Cave 4, XXVI*. Discoveries in the Judaean Desert XXXVI. Oxford: Clarendon, 2000.

Puech, Émile. "Hodayot." In vol. 1 of *Encyclopedia of the Dead Sea Scrolls*, edited by Lawrence Schiffman and James C. Vanderkam, 365–69. 2 vols. Oxford: Oxford University Press, 2000.

———. *Qumran Cave 4, XVIII: Textes hebreux (4Q521–4Q528, 4Q576–4Q579)*. Discoveries in the Judaean Desert XXV. Oxford: Clarendon, 1998.

———. *Qumran Cave 4, XXII: Textes arameens, premiere partie: 4Q529–549*. Discoveries in the Judaean Desert XXXI. Oxford: Clarendon, 2001.

———. *Qumran Cave 4, XXVII: Textes arameens, deuxieme partie: 4Q550–575, 580–582*. Discoveries in the Judaean Desert XXXVII. Oxford: Clarendon, 2009.

———. Review of Maurice Baillet, *Qumran Grotte 4, III (4Q482–4Q520)*. *Revue Biblique* 95 (1988) 404–11.

Qimron, Elisha. *The Hebrew of the Dead Sea Scrolls*. Harvard Semitic Series 29. Harvard Semitic Museum Publications, 1986; repr., Winona Lake, IN: Eisenbrauns, 2008.

Qimron, E. and J. Strugnell. *Qumran Cave 4, V: Miqsat Ma'ase ha-Torah*. Discoveries in the Judaean Desert X. Oxford: Clarendon, 1994.

Rey, Jean-Sébastien. "In the Garden of Good and Evil: Reimagining a Tradition (Sir 17:1–14, 4Q303, 4QInstruction, 1QS 4:25–26, and 1QSa 1:10–11)." In *Is There a Text in This Cave? Studies in the Textuality of the Dead Sea Scrolls in Honour of George J. Brooke*, edited by Ariel Feldman, Maria Cioată, and Charlotte Hempel, 473–92. Leiden: Brill, 2017.

Reymond, Eric D. *Qumran Hebrew: An Overview of Orthography, Phonology, and Morphology*. Atlanta, GA: Society of Biblical Literature, 2014.

Ringgren, Helmer. *The Faith of Qumran: Theology of the Dead Sea Scrolls*. Expanded ed. New York: Crossroad, 1995.

Roitman, Adolfo D., Lawrence H. Schiffman, and Shani L. Tzoref, eds. *The Dead Sea Scrolls and Contemporary Culture: Proceedings of the International Conference held at the Israel Museum, Jerusalem (July 6–8, 2008)*. Studies on the Texts of the Desert of Judah, 93. Leiden: Brill, 2011.

Sailhamer, John H. *The Pentateuch as Narrative: A Biblical-Theological Commentary*. Grand Rapids, MI: Zondervan, 1992.

Sanders, J. A. *The Psalms Scroll of Qumran Cave 11 (11QPs^a)*. Discoveries in the Judaean Desert IV. Oxford: Clarendon, 1965.

Scanlin, Harold. *The Dead Sea Scrolls & Modern Translations of the Old Testament.* Wheaton, IL: Tyndale House, 1993.

Schiffman, Lawrence H. "The Dead Sea Scrolls and the Early History of Jewish Liturgy." In *The Synagogue in Late Antiquity*, edited by Lee I. Levine, 33–48. New York: Jewish Theological Seminary, 1987.

———. *Reclaiming the Dead Sea Scrolls: Their True Meaning for Judaism and Christianity.* New Haven and London: Yale University Press, 2009.

———. "Serekh-Damascus (4Q265)." In vol. 2 of *Encyclopedia of the Dead Sea Scrolls*, edited by Lawrence Schiffman and James C. Vanderkam, 868–69. 2 vols. Oxford: Oxford University Press, 2000.

———, ed. *Archaeology and History in the Dead Sea Scrolls.* Sheffield: JSOT, 1990.

Schiffman, Lawrence H. and James C. VanderKam, eds. *Encyclopedia of the Dead Sea Scrolls.* 2 Vols. Oxford: Oxford University Press, 2000.

Schuller, Eileen. "Hodayot (1QH and Related Texts)." In *The Eerdmans Dictionary of Early Judaism*, edited by John J. Collins and Daniel C. Harlow, 747–49. Grand Rapids, MI: Eerdmans, 2010.

Segal, Michael. "Book of Jubilees." In *The Eerdmans Dictionary of Early Judaism*, edited by John J. Collins and Daniel C. Harlow, 843–46. Grand Rapids, MI: Eerdmans, 2010.

———. *The Book of Jubilees: Rewritten Bible, Redaction, Ideology and Theology.* Leiden: Brill, 2007.

———. "The Literary Relationship between the Genesis Apocryphon and Jubilees: The Chronology of Abram and Sarai's Descent to Egypt." *Aramaic Studies* 8.1–2 (2010) 71–88.

Shanks, Hershel, ed. *Understanding the Dead Sea Scrolls.* New York, NY: Random House, 1992.

Siegel, Jonathan Paul. "The Scribes of Qumran: Studies in the Early History of Jewish Scribal Customs, with Special Reference to the Qumran Biblical Scrolls and to the Tannaitic Traditions of the Massekheth Soferim." PhD diss., Brandeis University, 1971; Ann Arbor, MI: University Microfilms, 1972.

Skehan, Patrick W., Eugene Ulrich, and Judith E. Sanderson. *Qumran Cave 4, IV: Palaeo-Hebrew and Greek Biblical Manuscripts.* Discoveries in the Judaean Desert IX. Oxford: Clarendon, 1992.

Stegemann, Hartmut. *The Library of Qumran: On the Essenes, Qumran, John the Baptist, and Jesus.* Grand Rapids, MI: Eerdmans, 1998.

Stern, Sacha. "Qumran Calendars and Sectarianism." In *The Oxford Handbook of the Dead Sea Scrolls*, edited by Timothy H. Lim and John J. Collins, 232–53. Oxford: Oxford University Press, 2010.

Stone, Michael E. *A History of the Literature of Adam and Eve.* Early Judaism and Its Literature 3. Atlanta, GA: Society of Biblical Literature, 1992.

Strack, H. L. and Günter Stemberger. *Introduction to the Talmud and Midrash.* Translated and edited by Markus Bockmuehl. Minneapolis, MN: Fortress, 1996.

Strugnell, J., D. J. Harrington, and T. Elgvin. *Qumran Cave 4, XXIV: Sapiential Texts, Part 2, 4QInstruction: 4Q415 ff.* Discoveries in the Judaean Desert XXXIV. Oxford: Clarendon, 1999.

Stuckenbruck, Loren. "4QInstruction and the Possible Influence of Early Enochic Traditions: An Evaluation." In *The Wisdom Texts from Qumran and the Development of Sapiential Thought*, edited by Charlotte Hempel, Armin Lange, and Hermann Lichtenberger, 245–61. Leuven: Leuven University Press, 2002.

Talmon, Shemaryahu. "The Textual Study of the Bible—A New Outlook." In *Qumran and the History of the Biblical Text*, edited by Frank Moore Cross and Shemaryahu Talmon, 321–400. Cambridge, MA: Harvard University Press, 1975.

Talmon, S., J. Ben-Dov, and U. Glessmer. *Qumran Cave 4, XVI: Calendrical Texts*. Discoveries in the Judaean Desert XXI. Oxford: Clarendon, 2001.

Tigchelaar, Eibert. "Eden and Paradise: The Garden Motif in Some Early Jewish Texts." In *Paradise Interpreted: Representations of Biblical Paradise in Judaism and Christianity*, edited by Gerard P. Luttikhuizen, 37–57. Leiden: Brill, 1999.

———. *To Increase Learning for the Understanding Ones: Reading and Reconstructing the Fragmentary Early Jewish Sapiential Text 4QInstruction*. Studies on the Texts of the Desert of Judah 44. Leiden: Brill, 2001.

———. "Towards a Reconstruction of the Beginning of 4QInstruction (4Q416 Fragment 1 and Parallels)." In *The Wisdom Texts from Qumran and the Development of Sapiential Thought*, edited by Charlotte Hempel, Armin Lange, and Hermann Lichtenberger, 99–126. Leuven: Leuven University Press, 2002.

Tov, Emanuel. "Copying of a Biblical Scroll." *The Journal of Religious History* 26.2 (June 2002) 189–209.

———. "The Exodus Section of 4Q422." *Dead Sea Discoveries* 1.2 (August, 1994) 197–209.

———. "A Modern Textual Outlook Based on the Qumran Scrolls." *Hebrew Union College Annual* 53 (1982) 11–27.

———. "The Myth of the Stabilization of the Text of Hebrew Scripture." In *The Text of the Hebrew Bible: From the Rabbis to the Masoretes*, edited by Elvira Martín-Contreras and Lorena Miralles-Maciá, 37–45. Göttingen: Vandenhoeck & Ruprecht, 2014.

———. "The Origins, Development, and Characteristics of the Ancient Translations of the Hebrew Scriptures." In *Reading the Bible in Ancient Traditions and Modern Editions: Studies in Memory of Peter W. Flint*, edited by Andrew B. Perrin, Kyung S. Baek, and Daniel K. Falk, 35–64. Early Judaism and Its Literature 47. Atlanta, GA: Society of Biblical Literature, 2017.

———. "Scribal Practices." In vol. 2 of *Encyclopedia of the Dead Sea Scrolls*, edited by Lawrence Schiffman and James C. Vanderkam, 827–30. 2 vols. Oxford: Oxford University Press, 2000.

———. *Scribal Practices and Approaches Reflected in the Texts Found in the Judean Desert*. Leiden: Brill, 2004.

———. *Textual Criticism of the Hebrew Bible*, 2nd rev. ed. Minneapolis, MN: Fortress, 2001.

———. "The Writing of Early Scrolls and the Literary Analysis of Hebrew Scripture." *Dead Sea Discoveries* 13.3 (2006) 339–47.

———, editor. *The Texts from the Judaean Desert: Indices and an Introduction to the* Discoveries in the Judaean Desert *Series*. Discoveries in the Judaean Desert XXXIX. Oxford: Clarendon, 2002.

Tov, Emanuel with collaboration of R. A. Kraft. *The Greek Minor Prophets Scroll from Nahal Hever (8HevXIIgr)*. Discoveries in the Judaean Desert VIII. Oxford: Clarendon, 1990; reprint with corrections, 1995.

Trever, John C. *The Dead Sea Scrolls: A Personal Account*. Rev. ed. Grand Rapids, MI: Eerdmans, 1977.

———. *The Untold Story of Qumran*. Westwood, NJ: Fleming H. Revell, 1965.

Ulrich, Eugene, ed. *The Biblical Qumran Scrolls: Transcriptions and Textual Variants.* Leiden, Boston: Brill, 2010.

———. *The Dead Sea Scrolls and the Origins of the Bible.* Studies in the Dead Sea Scrolls and Related Literature. Grand Rapids, MI: Eerdmans, 1999.

———. "The Scrolls and the Study of the Hebrew Bible." In *The Dead Sea Scrolls at Fifty: Proceedings of the 1997 Society of Biblical Literature Qumran Section Meetings*, edited by Robert A. Kugler and Eileen M. Schuller, 31–41. Early Judaism and Its Literature, 15. Atlanta, GA: Society of Biblical Literature, 1999.

———. "Variant Editions of Biblical Books Revealed by the Qumran Scrolls." In *Reading the Bible in Ancient Traditions and Modern Editions: Studies in Memory of Peter W. Flint*, edited by Andrew B. Perrin, Kyung S. Baek, and Daniel K. Falk, 13–34. Early Judaism and Its Literature 47. Atlanta, GA: Society of Biblical Literature, 2017.

Ulrich, Eugene, Frank Moore Cross, James R. Davila, et al. *Qumran Cave 4, VII: Genesis to Numbers.* Discoveries in the Judaean Desert XII. Oxford: Clarendon, 1994; reprint 1999.

Ulrich, Eugene, Frank Moore Cross, Sidnie White Crawford, Julie Ann Duncan, Patrick W. Skehan, Emanuel Tov, and Julio Trebolle Barrera. *Qumran Cave 4, IX: Deuteronomy, Joshua, Judges, Kings.* Discoveries in the Judaean Desert XIV. Oxford: Clarendon, 1995.

Ulrich, Eugene, Frank Moore Cross, Russell E. Fuller, Judith E. Sanderson, Patrick W. Skehan, and Emanuel Tov. *Qumran Cave 4, X: The Prophets.* Discoveries in the Judaean Desert XV. Oxford: Clarendon, 1997.

Ulrich, Eugene, et al. *Qumran Cave 4, XI: Psalms to Chronicles.* Discoveries in the Judaean Desert XVI. Oxford: Clarendon, 2000.

VanderKam, James C. "Book of Jubilees." In vol. 1 of *Encyclopedia of the Dead Sea Scrolls*, edited by Lawrence Schiffman and James C. Vanderkam, 434–38. 2 vols. Oxford: Oxford University Press, 2000.

———. *The Book of Jubilees.* Guides to Apocrypha and Pseudepigrapha. Sheffield: Sheffield Academic Press, 2001.

———. *The Book of Jubilees: A Critical Text.* CSCO 510; Scriptores Aethiopici 87. Louvain: Peeters, 1989.

———. *The Book of Jubilees* (Translation). CSCO 511; Scriptores Aethiopici 88. Louvain: Peeters, 1989.

———. *Calendars in the Dead Sea Scrolls: Measuring Time.* London/New York: Routledge, 1998.

———. "Calendrical Texts and the Origins of the Dead Sea Scroll Community." In *Methods of Investigation of the Dead Sea Scrolls and the Khirbet Qumran Site: Present Realities and Future Prospects*, edited by Michael O. Wise, Norman Golb, John J. Collins, and Dennis G. Pardee, 371–88. New York: New York Academy of Sciences, 1994.

———. *The Dead Sea Scrolls and the Bible.* Grand Rapids, MI: Eerdmans, 2012.

———. *The Dead Sea Scrolls Today.* 2nd ed. Grand Rapids, MI: Eerdmans, 2010.

———. "Some Thoughts on the Relationship between the Book of Jubilees and the Genesis Apocryphon." In *Is There a Text in This Cave? Studies in the Textuality of the Dead Sea Scrolls in Honour of George J. Brooke*, edited by Ariel Feldman, Maria Cioată, and Charlotte Hempel, 371–84. Leiden: Brill, 2017.

———, consulting editor. *Qumran Cave 4, VIII: Parabiblical Texts, Part 1.* Discoveries in the Judaean Desert XIII. Oxford: Clarendon, 1994.

VanderKam, James C., and J. T. Milik. "The First Jubilees Manuscript from Qumran Cave 4: A Preliminary Publication." *Journal of Biblical Literature* 110.2 (1991) 243–70.

VanderKam, James C. and M. Brady, consulting editors. *Qumran Cave 4, VI: Poetical and Liturgical Texts, Part 1*. Discoveries in the Judaean Desert XI. Oxford: Clarendon, 1998.

———, consulting editors. *Qumran Cave 4, XX: Poetical and Liturgical Texts, Part 2*. Discoveries in the Judaean Desert XXIX. Oxford: Clarendon, 1999.

———, consulting editors. *Miscellaneous Texts from the Judaean Desert*. Discoveries in the Judaean Desert XXXVIII. Oxford: Clarendon, 2000.

———, consulting editors. *Qumran Cave 4, XXIII: Unidentified Fragments*. Discoveries in the Judaean Desert XXXIII. Oxford: Clarendon, 2001.

VanderKam, James C. and Peter Flint. *The Meaning of the Dead Sea Scrolls: Their Significance for Understanding the Bible, Judaism, Jesus, and Christianity*. New York, NY: HarperSanFrancisco, 2002.

van der Kooij, Arie. "The Textual Criticism of the Hebrew Bible before and after the Qumran Discoveries." In T*he Bible as Book: The Hebrew Bible and the Judaean Desert Discoveries*, edited by Edward D. Herbert and Emanuel Tov, 167–77. London: British Library and New Castle: Oak Knoll in association with Grand Haven: Scriptorium, 2002.

Vermes, Geza. *The Complete Dead Sea Scrolls in English*. Revised edition. London and New York: Penguin, 2004.

———. "Genesis 1–3 in Post-Biblical Hebrew and Aramaic Literature before the Mishnah." *Journal of Jewish Studies* 43.2 (1992) 221–25.

———. *The Story of the Scrolls: The Miraculous Discovery and True Significance of the Dead Sea Scrolls*. London and New York: Penguin, 2010.

Wacholder, B. Z. and Martin Abegg Jr. *A Preliminary Edition of the Unpublished Dead Sea Scrolls: The Hebrew and Aramaic Texts from Cave Four II*. Washington, DC: Biblical Archaeology Society, 1992.

Waltke, Bruce K. *Genesis: A Commentary*. Grand Rapids, MI: Zondervan, 2001.

Weinfeld, Moshe. "Prayer and Liturgical Practice in the Qumran Sect." In *The Dead Sea Scrolls: Forty Years of Research*, edited by Devorah Dimant and Uriel Rappaport, 241–58. Studies on the Texts of the Desert of Judah 10. Leiden: Brill, 1992.

Wevers, John W. *Notes on the Greek Text of Genesis*. Septuagint and Cognate Studies 35. Atlanta, GA: Scholars, 1993.

Wintermute, O. S. "Jubilees." In vol. 2 of *The Old Testament Pseudepigrapha*, edited by James H. Charlesworth, 35–142. 2 vols. New York, NY: Doubleday, 1985. Repr., Peabody, MA: Hendrickson, 2013.

Wise, Michael, Martin Abegg Jr., and Edward Cook. *The Dead Sea Scrolls: A New Translation*. San Francisco: HarperSanFrancisco, 1996.

Wise, Michael O., Norman Golb, John J. Collins, and Dennis G. Pardee, eds. *Methods of Investigation of the Dead Sea Scrolls and the Khirbet Qumran Site: Present Realities and Future Prospects*. New York, NY: New York Academy of Sciences, 1994.

Wold, Benjamin. "Genesis 2–3 in Early Christian Tradition and 4QInstruction." *Dead Sea Discoveries* 23 (2016) 329–46.

———. "The Universality of Creation in 4QInstruction." *Revue de Qumran* 26 (2013) 211–26.

———. *Women, Men and Angels: The Qumran Wisdom Document "Musar leMevin" and Its Allusions to Genesis Creation Traditions*. Tübingen: Mohr Siebeck, 2005.

Wright III, Benjamin G. "Wisdom of Ben Sira." In vol. 3 of *Outside the Bible: Ancient Jewish Writings Related to Scripture*, edited by Louis H. Feldman, James L. Kugel, and Lawrence H. Schiffman, 2208–352. 3 vols. Philadelphia: Jewish Publication Society, 2013.

Würthwein, Ernst. *The Text of the Old Testament*. 2nd ed. Grand Rapids, MI: Eerdmans, 1995.

Yeivin, Israel. *Introduction to the Tiberian Masorah*. Translated and edited by E. J. Revell. Masoretic Studies, 5. Atlanta, GA: Society of Biblical Literature, 1980.

Young, Edward J. *Studies in Genesis One*. Grand Rapids, MI: Baker, 1964. Repr., Phillipsburg, NJ: P & R.

Zahn, Molly M. "Rewritten Scripture." In *The Oxford Handbook of the Dead Sea Scrolls*, edited by Timothy H. Lim and John J. Collins, 323–50. Oxford: Oxford University Press, 2010.

Zias, Joseph. "Palestine Archaeological Museum." In vol. 2 of *Encyclopedia of the Dead Sea Scrolls*, edited by Lawrence Schiffman and James C. Vanderkam, 634–35. 2 vols. Oxford: Oxford University Press, 2000.

Zingerman, Yevgeniy Y. "3 Baruch." In vol. 2 of *Outside the Bible: Ancient Jewish Writings Related to Scripture*, edited by Louis H. Feldman, James L. Kugel, and Lawrence H. Schiffman, 1586–1603. 3 vols. Philadelphia: Jewish Publication Society, 2013.

Zuckerman, Bruce. "The Dynamics of Change in the Computer Imaging of the Dead Sea Scrolls and Other Ancient Inscriptions." In *Rediscovering the Dead Sea Scrolls: An Assessment of Old and New Approaches and Methods*, edited by Maxine L. Grossman, 69–88. Grand Rapids, MI: Eerdmans, 2010.

Zuckerman, Bruce, Asher Levy, and Marilyn Lundberg. "A Methodology for the Digital Reconstruction of Dead Sea Scroll Fragmentary Remains." In *Dead Sea Scrolls Fragments in the Museum Collection*, edited by Emanuel Tov, Kipp Davis, and Robert Duke, 36–58. Publications of the Museum of the Bible, 1. Leiden: Brill, 2016.

ANCIENT DOCUMENT INDEX

HEBREW BIBLE/OLD TESTAMENT

Genesis

Genesis (continued)

Exodus

NEW TESTAMENT

APOCRYPHA AND PSEUDEPIGRAPHA

4Q166 (Hosea Pesher – 4QpHos[a])

4Q204 (4QEnoch[c])

4Q209 (4QAstronomical Enoch[b])

4Q216 (4QJubilees[a])

4Q219 (4QJubilees[d])

4Q252 (Commentary on Genesis)

4Q259 (4QS[e] – 4QCommunity Rule[e])

4Q261 (4QS[g] – 4QCommunity Rule[g])

4Q265 (Miscellaneous Rules)

RABBINIC LITERATURE

TARGUM NEOFITI 85n45